Cloud Storage
Forensics

Cloud Storage
Forensics

Darren Quick

Ben Martini

Kim-Kwang Raymond Choo

Brett Shavers, Technical Editor

ELSEVIER

AMSTERDAM • BOSTON • HEIDELBERG • LONDON
NEW YORK • OXFORD • PARIS • SAN DIEGO
SAN FRANCISCO • SINGAPORE • SYDNEY • TOKYO
Syngress is an imprint of Elsevier

Acquiring Editor: *Chris Katsaropoulos*
Editorial Project Manager: *Benjamin Rearick*
Project Manager: *Punithavathy Govindaradjane*
Designer: *Mark Rogers*

Syngress is an imprint of Elsevier
225 Wyman Street, Waltham, MA 02451, USA

Library of Congress Cataloging-in-Publication Data
Quick, Darren.
Cloud storage forensics/Darren Quick, Ben Martini, Kim-Kwang Raymond Choo.
pages cm
ISBN 978-0-12-419970-5
1. Computer crimes–Investigation. 2. Forensic sciences–Data processing. 3. Cloud computing. 4. Information
storage and retrieval systems. I. Martini, Ben, 1990- II. Choo, Kim-Kwang Raymond. III. Title.
HV8079.C65Q53 2014
363.250285′46782--dc23
                    2013037978

British Library Cataloguing-in-Publication Data
A catalogue record for this book is available from the British Library

For information on all Syngress publications,
visit our werbsite at *store.elsevier.com/Syngress*

ISBN: 978-0-12-419970-5

Printed and bound in the United States of America
14 15 16 17 18   10 9 8 7 6 5 4 3 2 1

This book is dedicated to our families for their tireless support and understanding throughout all the time we spent on this research.

Contents

Acknowledgments

We would like to acknowledge the support provided by the University of South Australia and South Australia Police, and in particular the first author's supervisor, Detective Senior Sergeant Barry Blundell. The second author is supported by funding from the University of South Australia and the Defence Systems Innovation Centre (DSIC).

We are also grateful to Chris Katsaropoulos, Senior Acquisitions Editor, and Ben Rearick, Editorial Project Manager at Syngress, and the technical reviewer for their support in this project. It is not easy to keep on schedule, but they were relentless ... in a good way.

The views and opinions expressed in this book are those of the authors alone and not the organizations with whom the authors have been associated or supported. This book was hosted, and some parts written, using cloud storage.

Darren Quick
Ben Martini
Kim-Kwang Raymond Choo

About the Authors

Darren Quick is an Electronic Evidence Specialist with the South Australia Police and a PhD Scholar at the Information Assurance Research Group, Advanced Computing Research Centre at the University of South Australia. He has undertaken over 550 forensic investigations involving thousands of digital evidence items including computers, hard drives, mobile telephones, servers, and portable storage devices. He holds a master of science degree in Cyber Security and Forensic Computing, and has undertaken formal training in a range of forensic software and analysis techniques. In 2012, Darren was awarded membership of the Golden Key International Honour Society. Darren has coauthored a number of publications in relation to digital forensic analysis and cloud storage, and is a member of the Board of Referees for Digital Investigation—The International Journal of Digital Forensics and Incident Response. He still has his first computer, a VIC20, in the original box.

Ben Martini is the Digital Forensics Research Administrator, a Course Coordinator, and a PhD Scholar at the Information Assurance Research Group, Advanced Computing Research Centre at the University of South Australia. His PhD research focus is in the field of Digital Forensics looking at the implications of cloud computing. He has a broad range of research interests in the information technology sector with a focus on computer security and digital forensics issues. Ben has worked actively in the South Australian IT industry in sectors including government departments, education, and electronics across various organizations and continues to deliver occasional invited presentations to industry organizations in his area of expertise. He holds a master's degree in Business Information Systems and a bachelor degree in Information Technology (Networking and Security). He is supported by scholarships from both the University of South Australia and the Defence Systems Innovation Centre.

Dr Kim-Kwang Raymond Choo is a Fulbright Scholar and Senior Lecturer at the University of South Australia. He has (co)authored a number of publications in the areas of anti-money laundering, cyber and information security, and digital forensics including a book published in Springer's *Advances in Information Security* book series and six Australian Government Australian Institute of Criminology refereed monographs. He has been an invited speaker for a number of events (e.g., 2011 UNODC-ITU Asia-Pacific Regional Workshop on Fighting Cybercrime and 2011 KANZ Broadband Summit 2011) and delivered Keynote/Plenary Speeches at ECPAT Taiwan 2008 Conference on Criminal Problems and Intervention Strategy, 2010 International Conference on Applied Linguistics and 2011 Economic Crime Asia Conference, and 2014 International Conference on Applied Linguistics & Language Teaching, and Invited Lecture at the Bangladesh Institute of International and Strategic Studies. He was one of over 20 international (and one of two Australian) experts consulted by the research team preparing McAfee's commissioned report entitled "Virtual Criminology Report 2009: Virtually Here: The Age of Cyber Warfare"; and his opinions on cyber crime and cyber security are regularly published in the media. In 2009, he was named one of 10 Emerging Leaders in the Innovation category of The Weekend Australian Magazine/Microsoft's Next 100 series. He is also the recipient of several awards including the 2010 Australian Capital Territory (ACT) Pearcey Award for "Taking a risk and making a difference in the development of the Australian ICT industry," 2008 Australia Day Achievement Medallion in recognition of his dedication and contribution to the Australian Institute of Criminology, and through it to the public service of the nation, British Computer Society's Wilkes Award for the best paper published in the 2007 volume of The Computer Journal, and the Best Student Paper Award by the 2005 Australasian Conference on Information Security and Privacy.

Forewords

Cloud computing is widely regarded as the next transformational wave of information and communications technology (ICT) for business, governments, and individual consumers. The elastic supply of ICT storage and computing capabilities at low cost is likely to open up numerous game changing opportunities. Apart from reducing operational costs, cloud computing is driving business innovation with radical new business models and step change improvements in the effectiveness of ICT for all users.

The Australian Government has recognized the potential of this new technology through its Cloud Computing Strategic Direction Paper of April 2011. Today, Australian Government agencies can choose to use cloud computing services where they provide value for money and adequate security.

New technology advancements such as cloud computing can create disruptive outcomes and new risks. Cloud computing not only aggregates computing power, but it also amasses information. Users, providers, and government policy makers are quite rightly concerned about privacy and security risks. Will the benefits of cloud computing outweigh the risks for governments, industry, and society?

This book is concerned with the risks associated with the criminal exploitation of cloud computing.

Due to the virtual, dynamic, and borderless nature of cloud computing services, government and law enforcement investigations into malicious cyber activities will require cooperation between government agencies from multiple countries.

Government and law enforcement investigators face difficulty in accessing the physical hardware to locate evidential data. The data may also be spread across multiple data centers in different countries. To reduce the risk of digital (forensic) evidence being called into question in judicial proceedings, it is important to have a rigorous methodology and set of procedures for conducting digital forensic investigations and examinations.

This book presents the first published framework on cloud forensics. The framework is used to examine three popular public and one private cloud storage services. The reported findings will contribute to a better understanding of the types of artifacts that are likely to remain for digital forensics practitioners. It is an essential companion for digital forensic practitioners and researchers who wish to understand cloud (storage) forensics and how to collect digital evidence from cloud storage services.

The book's publication is timely as it provides new insights in managing risk in cloud computing and addresses the growing challenge associated with cyber security.

Dr. Alexander Zelinsky
Chief Defence Scientist
Defence Science and Technology Organisation (DSTO) Canberra, Australiax

In just a few short years, forensic computing has gone from a new field of forensic opportunity to an area with complex technical challenges that are constantly evolving. With constant change comes enormous technical challenge for forensic computing practitioners to keep up with those intent on using electronic devices to aid them in their criminal activities or help them avoid detection.

Previously, access to computing devices was easy and access to information held on the devices was relatively straightforward. With the proliferation of smart mobile devices and the data sharing and storage opportunities, the challenges around accessing and securing data for forensic examination is considerable.

With the advent and now ubiquitous access to *"cloud storage"* combined with the shear volume of data that is recorded, stored, and shared, research such as this is critical in guiding practitioners in how best to secure and examine off-site data. While cloud storage and cloud computing offer real benefits to the legitimate computer or smart device user, it also creates enormous opportunity for those with intent to commit any sort of criminal offending, whether it be child exploitation or financial crime, to stay one step ahead of investigators.

The challenge is to assess whether cloud storage may have been used, identify key indicators that confirm cloud use, determine where the cloud storage service actually is, and attempt to secure the data for forensic examination. Through a number of case studies, the authors have demonstrated that it is possible to lay robust frameworks to enable practitioners to identify, locate, and secure key evidence from cloud based services.

This book draws on the authors' considerable operational and research experiences and will become a key reference manual enabling practitioners in forensic computing to keep up with cloud storage developments in this rapidly evolving area.

Mike Whitaker
Senior Sergeant
Chair, Electronic Evidence Specialist Advisory Group (EESAG)
Senior Managers of Australian and New Zealand
Forensic Laboratories (SMANZFL), Australia

Introduction

INFORMATION IN THIS CHAPTER[1]

- Introduction to cloud computing
- Cybercrime and cloud computing

INTRODUCTION

It is not clear when the term cloud computing was first coined. For example, Bartholomew (2009), Bogatin (2006), and several others suggested that "cloud computing" terminology was, perhaps, first coined by Google™ Chief Executive Eric Schmidt in 2006. Kaufman (2009) suggests that cloud computing terminology "originates from the telecommunications world of the 1990s, when providers began using virtual private network (VPN) services for data communication." Desisto, Plummer, and Smith (2008) state that "[t]he first SaaS [Software as a Service] offerings were delivered in the late 1990s...[a]lthough these offerings weren't called cloud computing." In this paper, we adopt the definition introduced by the National Institute of Standards and Technology (NIST): "Cloud computing is a model for enabling ubiquitous, convenient, on-demand network access to a shared pool of configurable computing resources (e.g., networks, servers, storage, applications, and services) that can be rapidly provisioned and released with minimal management effort or service provider interaction" (Mell & Grance, 2011).

In recent years, there has been a marked increase in the adoption of cloud computing. Gartner's 2011 Hype Cycle for Cloud Computing report, for example, referred to cloud computing as the "most hyped concept in IT" (Smith, 2011: 3). "Cloud computing" has been a trending search on Google since 2009 with continued interest (Google, 2013). Another Gartner report suggested that cloud computing could be a US$149 billion market by 2014 and by 2016 could have 100% penetration in Forbes list of the Global 2000 companies (McGee, 2011). It can be reasonably assumed that many of those top 2000 companies will provide some

---

[1]Material in this chapter has been adapted from Hooper, Martini and Choo (2013) and other publications of the authors.

level of online access via cloud computing to both their internal users and their customers.

The availability of cloud storage services is becoming a popular option for consumers to store data that is accessible via a range of devices, such as personal computers, tablets, and mobile phones. There are a range of cloud storage hosting providers, and many offer free cloud storage services, such as Dropbox™, Microsoft® SkyDrive®2, and Google Drive™. Due to the large number of these services available, many commentators have used the phrase Storage as a Service (StaaS) to describe this type of service (Kovar, 2009; Meky & Ali, 2011; Waters, 2011; Wipperfeld 2009). This is an addition to the traditional cloud computing architectures documented by Mell and Grance (2011) of Software as a Service (SaaS), Platform as a Service (PaaS) and Infrastructure as a Service (IaaS). Consumers have adopted the cloud storage paradigm in huge numbers with Gartner forecasting massive growth in the area stating that users will be storing a third of their data in the cloud by 2016 (Gartner, 2012). However, many enterprises have remained cautious in moving their data into the public cloud storage environment due to issues such as data sovereignty and security, and complying with regulatory obligations. For example, enterprises who fail to comply with data protection legislation may lead to administrative, civil, and criminal sanctions.

A number of open and closed source cloud software products have been developed and/or are in development to address the needs of the enterprises and even individuals who want to leverage the features of cloud computing while continuing to store data on-site or otherwise under the control of the data custodian. Storing data on-site and/or having the data centers physically in the jurisdiction are increasingly seen as ways to reduce some of the location risks that cloud (storage) service clients currently face. For example, it was suggested at one of the hearings of the Australian Government Parliamentary Joint Committee on Intelligence and Security that "the default position should be that governments, agencies and departments ought to keep their information onshore but use cloud for providers, because there are great cost savings to government by using cloud, using digital storage and accessing the digital economy, being a model user of things like the NBN, data cente[r]s and cloud computing. We think there is a real leadership role for government, but it needs to be done within something of a risk minimi[z]ation strategy, which means that you keep the data onshore and you do not look to send it offshore to a jurisdiction that you do not know about" (Australian Government Parliamentary Joint Committee on Intelligence and Security, 2012: 16). More recently in 2013, the Australian Government has also released the National Cloud Computing Strategy (Australian Government Department of Broadband, 2013) and the policy and risk management guidelines for the storage and processing of Australian Government information in

---

[2]It has been reported in the media that "Microsoft confirms it will change SkyDrive name after trademark suit" (see Ludwig, 2013; British Sky Broadcasting Group Plc & Ors v Microsoft Corporation Microsoft & Anor [2013] EWHC 1826 (Ch) (28 June 2013)).

outsourced or offshore information and communications technologies (ICTs) arrangements (Australian Government Attorney-General's Department, 2013).

Cybercrime and the cloud

ICTs, such as personal computers, laptops, smartphones and tablets, are fundamental to modern society and open the door to increased productivity, faster communication capabilities, and immeasurable convenience. However, it also changes the way criminals conduct their activities, and vulnerabilities in ICT infrastructure are fertile grounds for criminal exploitation. Few today would challenge the assertion that the era of globalization has been accompanied by an increase in the sophistication and volume of malicious cyber activities. Cyberspace can be used as an extension to facilitate and enhance traditional forms of crime as well as to create new forms of crime. In this chapter, the use of ICT as a tool for the commission of a crime or as the object of a crime (Choo, Smith, & McCusker, 2007) will be referred to as "cybercrime" for the purposes of linguistic simplicity. The term is, for example, referred to in Australia's *Cybercrime Act 2001* (Cth) as well as the Council of Europe Convention on Cybercrime with different meanings. Commonly, it is understood by reference to the types of conduct to which it applies; these include offences under Part 10.7 of the *Criminal Code Act 1995* (Cth) and conduct such as online fraud, cyber-bullying and using the Internet to view or store child exploitation material or for the purposes of child grooming.

While the advent of ICT has allowed for the emergence of new types of criminal behavior such as the use of malware (malicious software such as Trojan horses, viruses, and worms), there is a growing consensus that existing laws in relation to areas such as theft, forgery, and malicious damage to property are generally capable of suitable modification so as to adequately handle many of the situations envisaged by more specific laws directly targeting such behavior (Brenner, 2001). Indeed, it is possible to argue that cybercrime is best thought of as "the exploitation of a new technology to commit an old crime in new ways and...to engage in a limited variety of new types of criminal activity" (Brenner, 2001: np).

Nevertheless, there is no doubt that that use of malware for the facilitation of crimes such as Internet banking and credit card fraud, identity theft, and money laundering has increased markedly in recent years (Choo, 2011; FireEye, 2013; Tendulkar, 2013). The same is true of the use of the Internet by pedophiles in connection with online child exploitation activities such as online child grooming and dissemination of child abuse and exploitative material (Choo, 2009a, b).

A 2012 report by the Australian Crime Commission found that in the last five years, Australians have lost over AUD 113 million to serious organized crime investment fraud. That is, the use of deceptive mechanisms including cold calling, fake web sites, and false recovery services ("phishing") to convince individuals to part with their money or personal information on bogus investment opportunities (ACC, 2012). Furthermore, in 2011, a report prepared by Norton-Symantec

(2011) showed that cybercrime cost the Australian economy just over US$4.5 billion in 2010. US$1.8 billion of this sum was directly or indirectly misappropriated while the remaining sum was accounted for by resultant increases in productivity costs associated with fixing the problems raised by cybercrime (Caldwell, 2011). The same report identified a cost of US$32 billion to the US economy and US $25 billion in direct losses to China. It showed that 69% of surveyed adults who used online services have been victims of cybercrime (Norton-Symantec, 2011).

The vast majority of reports on patterns and trends in cybercrime disseminated (and in turn cited) are from the commercial sector and do not include details such as the research methodology or provide access to the raw data (see Gray, 2011). Guinchard (2011: 75–78) explained that the "diversity of methods used to collect information on cyber incidents can produce widely different results ... [and] this facilitates extrapolations about the scale of the problem and the cost of cyber crimes." For example, there have been assertions that cybercrime has "[s]urpassed Illegal Drug Trafficking as a Criminal Moneymaker" (Symantec, 2009) and a more recent report by Detica (2012: 2) commissioned by the UK cabinet office estimated "the cost of cyber crime to the UK to be £27 billion per annum." However, such figures have been criticized in both the media (see Gray, 2011) and by academics (see Anderson et al., 2012; Florencio & Herley, 2011). The currency of cybercrime as a term among members of the community means that it may be imprecisely applied to a wide range of criminal behavior with the consequence that the scope of the problem is apt for overstatement; although this is not to suggest that the problem is not widespread.

Despite the size and gravity of the problem however, individuals to a certain extent, and business in most cases, do not report many instances of cybercrime when they are affected. In 2009, on average only 8% of Australian businesses (surveyed in the Australian Business Assessment of Computer User Security—see Richards, 2009) who had been the victim of cybercrime reported it to the police. In many cases, this was because the crime was not considered serious enough (Richards, 2009).

Cloud computing (like other networked cyber infrastructure) is subject to attacks by cyber criminals, who may be able to hijack and use resources for criminal purposes, thus adding to the challenge of growing volumes of digital evidence in cases under investigation. Cloud computing services can also be used as a launching pad for new attacks, or to store and distribute criminal data (e.g., child abuse materials and terrorism-related materials) by cyber criminals, organized crime groups, and politically motivated actors to avoid the scrutiny of law enforcement and national security agencies (Choo, 2010).

Use of cloud computing by criminals (or their victims) means that data of interest may be virtualized, geographically distributed, and ephemeral, presenting technical and jurisdictional challenges for identification and seizure by law enforcement and national security agencies. These issues can impede digital forensic investigators and potentially prevent law enforcement and national security agencies from acquiring digital evidence and forensically analyzing digital content in a timely fashion.

Challenges faced by law enforcement and government agencies

Security and privacy issues associated with cloud services are generally better documented and understood than digital forensic issues. By physically displacing the storage from the user, cloud storage solutions introduce numerous challenges for digital forensic and eDiscovery practitioners. A 2012 report by the European Network and Information Security Agency (ENISA) explained that "[m]ulti-tenant outsourced services usually cannot give access to raw log data as it contains records of multiple users and thus would compromise the privacy of other customers" (ENISA, 2012: 45) Therefore, features synonymous with cloud (storage) services such as multi-tenancy, data security, file encryption, and communications encryption also need to be addressed as part of a digital forensics investigation, as suggested by various other researchers (Chung et al., 2012).

A key component of cloud computing is its "multi-tenancy" capability, which is referred to as a "shared pool of resources" in the NIST definition (Mell & Grance, 2011). This refers to the ability of cloud services to support use of the same resources or applications by multiple users. In an IaaS model, server virtualization allows several virtual machines to run their own operating system within a single physical machine/server, which helps to facilitate multi-tenancy. It also facilities the cost-effective provisioning of scalable resources for the use of cloud computing customers. Multi-tenancy generally occurs as part of both compute operations (active processing of computing requests using processing, memory, and network resources), via virtual machines, and storage operations where data will be stored on shared disks. Under certain circumstances, individual files from individual customers may be distributed across multiple disks and storage systems across multiple jurisdictions if a cloud service provider (CSP) has facilities in more than one country. This is a particularly important point for the preservation and collection of electronic evidence.

The servers located in the cloud will commonly be owned by a company or entity (the CSP) that will enter into a contract (service level agreement, SLA) with the client. The SLA sets out the obligations of the parties and may allow for contingencies in the event of a digital forensic investigation. These matters include a definition of the applicable jurisdiction and laws that apply to the CSP and the client. The SLA may also touch on data seizure procedures and how this would affect the integrity of the user's data, privacy and service delivery, or continuity of the users' data. Finally, the SLA can deal with issues such as intellectual property rights in relation to data stored on the cloud. Some agreements provide that the CSP obtains an interest in such material. This makes the area rather multidisciplinary in nature and raises issues in terms of data protection and the CSP's obligation to safeguard the intellectual property rights of its clients (Overby, 2012).

In addition to these environmental characteristics, cloud technology is commonly understood as existing in a number of different deployment models ranging from open access public clouds and community clouds to private clouds which service a specific organization. There is also the potential for hybrid clouds which combine one or more of the above models. In many cases, the cloud deployment model changes the methodology for collection and preservation of electronic evidence. For example, the public cloud model may result in data of potential evidential value being stored outside of the physical jurisdiction of the LEA which complicates traditional methods of preservation and collection. The hybrid cloud model may result in some data being physically stored in a public cloud and with other data stored in a private cloud which may also complicate identification of electronic evidence.

A CSP may offer any one of a number of services to clients, allowing them to interact with the cloud environment in a variety of ways. These include the following widely accepted (cloud service model) descriptions:

- Cloud IaaS: This provides clients with access to storage space, bandwidth, and other fundamental computing services. It effectively expands the computing capability of the customer, allowing them to run their own software and applications using the cloud infrastructure.
- Cloud PaaS: This allows the customer to gain access to the computer platform or operating systems of the cloud instances (e.g., Windows and Linux) and an underlying database so that they can create or acquire applications.
- Cloud SaaS: This allows clients of the CSP to utilize software and applications running on the cloud infrastructure. The applications are accessed via remote computers and mobile devices using the appropriate cloud interface software. The consumer's device acts like a portal to the software and data stored in the cloud.

These deployment (e.g., public cloud, private cloud, hybrid cloud, and community cloud) and service models will vary the type and amount of electronic evidence that can be collected on the client, server, and network layers. Common across all the deployment and service models is the collection of log data; i.e., information on how the primary/content data has been used or accessed is often collected as part of the standard operations of the cloud computing environment.

Many conventional forensic tools have focused upon having physical access to the media that stores the data of potential interest. However, in a cloud computing environment, it is often not possible or feasible to access the physical media which stores a customer's data. This is due to a number of features intrinsic to cloud computing. For example, in many instances, cloud data will be stored overseas (and out of the jurisdiction) from the investigating LEA. Even if the data is stored within jurisdiction, data distribution technologies may split a user's data across a number (potentially thousands) of storage devices within the cloud computing environment. LEAs would need to rely upon the cloud technology and the CSP to gain access to the data that is stored by a customer, and this can introduce issues with chain-of-custody best practices.

Before this data is exported for use by the LEA, the data must be "preserved" (to ensure that the potential evidence is not modified)—a function which many cloud computing environments do not currently support. Consequently, this could result in accidental modification of data as it is exported from the cloud computing environment for LEA use or intentional destruction of data by the suspect. Preservation requests should also include backup data (tapes, disks, offsite storage, etc.) to allow the practitioner to recover evidence that may have been deleted or modified before preservation of the live data occurred.

Once the LEA has secured access to the cloud computing data, the format of the data is still not guaranteed and most of the prevalent digital forensic analysis tools have not yet been updated to decode the major cloud computing data export formats (Iorga, 2012). While many IaaS data exports will likely mimic the data format that is currently supported as virtual machines, SaaS instances are more likely to use proprietary data formats and as such are unlikely to be supported by current tools.

Summary

The advent of cloud computing poses a number of significant issues for cybercrime investigations. With private individuals, companies, and groups placing an ever-increasing volume of data into cloud systems, LEAs are increasingly finding that the data in question can become either inaccessible or at least very difficult to access (Harrington, 2011). The process of data distribution leads to a situation where information may be disseminated across a huge number of physical machines, some of which may be outside of the investigating body's national or even international jurisdiction (Vincent & Hart, 2011). As part of the operations of a cloud computing environment, a provider may store a customer's data across multiple servers (that may result in "transborder data-flow"), challenging the ability of LEAs to enforce seizure warrants and rendering access to the data difficult without infringing on the privacy of innocent individuals or breaching confidentiality laws. Furthermore, the global nature of data storage in clouds means that in some cases, the legislative frameworks of various jurisdictions apply to different packets of information. This requires increased communication and cooperation between various LEAs.

The private sector may be involved in the investigation of cybercrime offences by LEAs in three capacities: as an Internet service provider ("ISP"), a telecommunications service provider ("TSP") (some firms may provide both services simultaneously, e.g., Telstra), and as a CSP. Companies who act as an ISP/TSP facilitate the passage of information from personal computers or other electronic devices to the cloud and vice versa. As data passes across these firms' networks or infrastructure, the interception and access regime set out above in a country (e.g., Australia) would apply to require them to maintain the capacity to give LEAs access to this data as mandated by the relevant legislation.

Thus, ISP/TSPs serve an intermediary function insofar as we are concerned with cloud computing and its consequences for law enforcement investigations.

The more complicated problem is: what laws apply to the interaction between LEAs and CSPs. It becomes significantly more complicated if the investigation involves ISP/TSPs who have networks which span multiple jurisdictions, or where the CSP is located in a jurisdiction other than that in which the investigation is taking place. As explained earlier, the practice of data distribution makes this latter situation commonplace. These transborder data-flows highlight the need for international cooperation when investigating cybercrime generally, and crimes which make use of cloud technology more specifically.

Structure of book and contributions to knowledge

Academic publications in the area of cloud forensics remain somewhat elusive. Many of the published papers in the area have provided a sound grounding for the research required in cloud forensics by highlighting the issues for digital forensic practitioners (Birk & Wegener, 2011; Martini & Choo, 2012). Papers with a specific technical focus often focus on server forensic analysis providing recommendations for issues such as logging and remote extraction of data (see Marty, 2011). In recent months (at the time of writing), a small number of papers discussing the forensic collection of cloud storage products have appeared, and their focus is on the client side digital forensic process assumedly due to the difficulties in obtaining access to a cloud providers data center to conduct server analysis (see Chung et al., 2012, and Chapters 3–5).

The small quantity of existing research demonstrates that research in the area of cloud StaaS forensics is still in its infancy and there are a number of gaps in the existing research which need to be addressed. While addressing all of the research needs in this area is beyond the scope of a single book, this book seeks to address a number of gaps.

We now present a brief outline of the structure of this book and the main contributions.

Chapter 2. In this chapter, we present our cloud (storage) forensic framework. Material presented in this chapter has appeared in Martini & Choo (2012); Quick & Choo (2013a, b, c). The framework is applied in the next four chapters discussing the research of cloud storage providers to provide a guiding framework to step the process through, as would be the case in a digital forensic investigation, and validate the framework in a variety of circumstances.

Chapter 3. In this chapter, we use Microsoft SkyDrive as a case study and identify the types of terrestrial artifacts that are likely to remain on a client's machine, and where the access point(s) for digital forensic practitioners are, which will allow them to undertake steps to secure evidence in a timely fashion. Material presented in this chapter has appeared in Quick and Choo (2013a).

Chapter 4. In this chapter, we use Dropbox as a case study to determine the data remnants on a client's machine when a user undertakes a variety of methods to store, upload, and access data in the cloud. By determining the data remnants on client devices, we contribute to a better understanding of the types of terrestrial artifacts that are likely to remain for digital forensics practitioners and investigators. Material presented in this chapter has appeared in Quick & Choo (2013b).

Chapter 5. In this chapter, we use Google Drive as a case study to determine the data remnants on a client's machine when a user undertakes a variety of methods to store, upload, and access data in the cloud. Similar to the previous two chapters, this chapter contributes to a better understanding of the types of terrestrial artifacts that are likely to remain for digital forensics practitioners and investigators. Material presented in this chapter has appeared in Quick & Choo (2013c).

Chapter 6. In this chapter, we use a widely used open source cloud StaaS application—ownCloud—as a case study and document a series of digital forensic experiments with the aim of providing forensic researchers and practitioners with an in-depth understanding of the artifacts available to forensics researchers and practitioners when conducting analysis on cloud StaaS environments on both the client and server. Material presented in this chapter has appeared in Martini and Choo (2013).

Chapter 7. In this chapter, we present the process that forensic practitioners can use to collect data from cloud storage services when legal authority exists to access an account. Material presented in this chapter has appeared in Quick and Choo (2013d).

Chapter 8. In this chapter, a summary of the book and a discussion of open problems and possible research directions are presented.

References

Anderson, R., Barton, C., Böhme, R., Clayton, R., van Eeten, M., Levi, M., et al. (2012). *Measuring the cost of cybercrime* (25—26 June). *Proceedings of the 11th workshop on Economics of Information Security (WEIS 2012)* Berlin, Germany: Berlin Brandenburg Academy of Sciences, 25—26 June.

Australian Crime Commission (ACC) (2012). *Serious and organised investment fraud in Australia* Canberra, ACT: Australian Crime Commission.

Australian Government Attorney-General's Department (2013). *Australian Government Policy and Risk management guidelines for the storage and processing of Australian Government information in outsourced or offshore ICT arrangements* Barton, ACT: Australian Government Attorney-General's Department.

Australian Government Parliamentary Joint Committee on Intelligence and Security. (2012). Proof Committee Hansard (Public) Wednesday, 5 September 2012. <http://parlinfo.aph.gov.au/parlInfo/download/committees/commjnt/c84503ae-f74f-4e82-a5a4-d4a788d87f9d/toc_pdf/Parliamentary%20Joint%20Committee%20on%20Intelligence%20and%20Security_2012_09_05_1343.pdf;fileType = application%2Fpdf#search = %22committees/commjnt/c84503ae-f74f-4e82-a5a4-d4a788d87f9d/0000%22>.

Bartholomew, D. (2009). Cloud rains opportunities for software developers. *Dice* 29 May 2009.

Birk, D., & Wegener, C. (2011). Technical issues of forensic investigations in cloud computing environments. In: *Proceedings of 6th international workshop on systematic approaches to digital forensic engineering (IEEE/SADFE 2011)* (pp. 1—10). Oakland, CA, USA.

Bogatin, D. (2006). Google CEO's new paradigm: 'Cloud computing and advertising go hand-inhand'. *Zdnet*, 2006. 23 April. <http://www.zdnet.com/blog/micro-markets/google-ceos-new-paradigm-cloud-computing-and-advertising-go-hand-in-hand/369>.

Brenner, S. (2001). Cybercrime investigation and prosecution: The role of penal and procedural law. *Murdoch University Electronic Journal of Law*, 8(2) <http://www.murdoch.edu.au/elaw/issues/v8n2/brenner82.html>

Caldwell, A. (2011). Cybercrime cost Australia over $4.5 billion last year. *ABC Radio National*, 8 September, http://www.abc.net.au/am/content/2011/s3312727.htm

Choo, K.-K. R. (2009a). *Online child grooming: A literature review on the misuse of social networking sites for grooming children for sexual offences*. Research and public policy No 103, Canberra, ACT: Australian Institute of Criminology.

Choo, K. -K. R. (2009b). Responding to online child sexual grooming: An industry perspective. *Trends & Issues in Crime and Criminal Justice, 379*, 1–6.

Choo, K. -K. R. (2010). Cloud computing: Challenges and future directions. *Trends & Issues in Crime and Criminal Justice, 400*, 1–6.

Choo, K. -K. R. (2011). The cyber threat landscape: Challenges and future research directions. *Computers & Security, 30*(8), 719–731.

Choo, K.-K. R., Smith, R., & McCusker, R. (2007). *Future directions in technology-enabled crime: 2007-09*. Research and public policy series No 78, Canberra, ACT: Australian Institute of Criminology.

Chung, H., Park, J., Lee, S., & Kang, C. (2012). Digital forensic investigation of cloud storage services. *Digital Investigation, 9*(2), 81–95.

Desisto, R. P., Plummer, D. C., & Smith, D. M. (2008). *Tutorial for understanding the relationship between cloud computing and SaaS* Stamford, CT: Gartner.

Detica (2012). *The cost of cyber crime: A Detica report in partnership with the Office of Cyber Security and Information Assurance in the cabinet office* Surrey, UK: Detica.

European Network and Information Security Agency (ENISA) (2012). *Procure secure: A guide to monitoring of security service levels in cloud contracts* Heraklion, Greece: European Network and Information Security Agency.

FireEye (2013). *The advanced cyber attack landscape* Milpitas, CA: FireEye, Inc.

Florencio, D., & Herley, C. (2011). *Sex, lies and cybercrime* (14–15 June). *Proceedings of the Tenth Workshop on Economics of Information Security (WEIS 2011)* USA: George Mason University, 14–15 June.

Gartner. (2012). Gartner says that consumers will store more than a third of their digital content in the cloud by 2016. <http://www.gartner.com/it/page.jsp?id = 2060215>.

Google. (2013). *Google trends: Cloud computing.* <http://www.google.com/trends/explore#q = cloud + computing&geo = AU>.

Gray, P. (2011). Exposing Norton's cybercrime scare campaign. *The Age*, 21 September, <http://www.theage.com.au/it-pro/security-it/exposing-nortons-cybercrime-scare-campaign-20110921-1kkip.html>.

Guinchard, A. (2011). Between hype and understatement: Reassessing cyber risks as a security strategy. *Journal of Strategic Security, IV*(2), 75–96.

Harrington, S. (2011). Collaborating with a digital forensics expert: Ultimate tag-team or disastrous duo?. *William Mitchell Law Review, 38*(1), 354–393.

Kaufman, L. M. (2009). Data security in the world of cloud computing. *IEEE Security & Privacy, July/August*, 61–64.

Kovar, J. (2009). Storage-As-A-Service poised for big boost. *CRN, 1291*, 14–18.

Ludwig, S. (2013). Microsoft confirms it will change SkyDrive name after trademark suit. *Venturebeat.com*, 31 July, http://venturebeat.com/2013/07/31/microsoft-changing-skyd-rive-name/#f7TzSaVh4WmxQh6Z.99

Iorga, M. (2012). *Challenging security requirements for US government cloud computing adoption.* <http://www.nist.gov/customcf/get_pdf.cfm?pub_id = 912695>.

Martini, B., & Choo, K. -K. R. (2012). An integrated conceptual digital forensic framework for cloud computing. *Digital Investigation, 9*(2), 71−80.

Martini, B., & Choo, K. -K. R. (2013). Cloud storage forensics: ownCloud as a Case Study. *Digital Investigation,* In press. Available from http://dx.doi.org/10.1016/j.diin.2013.08.005.

Marty, R. (2011). Cloud application logging for forensics. In: *Proceedings of 2011 ACM symposium on applied computing,* Taichung, Taiwan, pp. 178−184.

McGee, K. (2011). The 2011 Gartner scenario: Current states and future directions of the IT industry. Gartner.

Meky, M., & Ali, A. (2011). A novel and secure data sharing model with full owner control in the cloud environment. *International Journal of Computer Science and Information Security, 9*(6), 12−17.

Mell, P., & Grance, T. (2011). *The NIST definition of cloud computing: Recommendations of the National Institute.* NIST Special Publication, 800−415.

Norton-Symantec (2011). *Cybercrime report: The human impact.* Mountain View, CA: Symantec Corporation.

Overby, S. (2012). Keeping secrets in the cloud: how to protect your intellectual property in the cloud. *CIO Magazine,* 6 February, <http://www.cio.com/article/699494/How_to_Protect_Your_Intellectual_Property_in_the_Cloud>

Quick, D., & Choo, K. -K. R. (2013a). Digital droplets: Microsoft SkyDrive forensic data remnants. *Future Generation Computer Systems, 29*(6), 1378−1394.

Quick, D., & Choo, K. -K. R. (2013b). Dropbox analysis: Data remnants on user machines. *Digital Investigation, 10*(1), 3−18.

Quick, D., & Choo, K. -K. R. (2013c). Google drive: Forensic analysis of data remnants. *Journal of Network and Computer Applications,* In press.

Quick, D., & Choo, K. -K. R. (2013d). Forensic collection of cloud storage data: Does the act of collection result in changes to the data or its metadata? *Digital Investigation, 10*(3), 266−277.

Richards, K. (2009). *The Australian business assessment of computer user security: A national survey.* Research and public policy series No 102, Canberra, ACT: Australian Institute of Criminology.

Smith, D. M. (2011). Hype cycle for cloud computing, 2011. G00214915, Gartner.

Symantec (2009). Cyber crime has surpassed illegal drug trafficking as a criminal money-maker; 1 in 5 will become a Victim. *Press Release,* 10 September, <http://www.symantec.com/about/news/release/article.jsp?prid = 20090910_01>.

Tendulkar, R. (2013). *Cyber-crime, securities markets and systemic risk: Joint Staff Working Paper of the IOSCO Research Department and World Federation of Exchanges.* <http://www.iosco.org/research/pdf/swp/Cyber-Crime-Securities-Markets-and-Systemic-Risk.pdf>.

Vincent, M., & Hart, N. (2011). Law in the cloud. *Law Society Journal, 49*(5), 50−51.

Waters, J. (2011). Cloud-based data storage. *The Education Digest, 76*(8), 28−34.

Wipperfeld, M. (2009). How to choose a storage as a service provider. *eWeek,* 18 February

Cloud Storage Forensic Framework

INFORMATION IN THIS CHAPTER

- Cloud (storage) forensic framework
- Evidence source identification and preservation
- Collection of evidence from cloud storage services
- Examination and analysis of collected data

INTRODUCTION

Over the years, a number of digital forensics models/frameworks have been proposed (see Slay et al., 2009, for an overview of digital forensics models). However, these existing models/frameworks may not be fit-for-purpose in the cloud environment (Birk, 2011). There is a need for a cloud forensic framework to guide investigations, which is flexible enough to be able to work with future providers offering new services. Any proposed framework needs to be generic enough to apply to a range of circumstances and services, but be able to step an investigation through a formalized process to ensure information sources are identified and preserved. There are generally accepted standards, rules, and procedures that digital forensic practitioners follow (ACPO, 2006; NIJ, 2004, 2008). McKemmish (1999: 1) identifies and specifies four stages of a digital forensic investigation: "identification of digital evidence, preservation of digital evidence, analysis of digital evidence, and presentation of digital evidence." When investigating cloud services, a framework should allow for the discovery of new information, such that a practitioner can move through different stages and may return to previous steps as new data storage is discovered. Hence, the digital forensic process should not be viewed as a rigid process of steps undertaken in order, but as a flexible process with the ability to return to previous steps during analysis (Martini & Choo, 2012; Quick & Choo, 2013a, b).

Cloud (storage) forensic framework

The practice of intelligence analysis concerns itself with data analysis and has been refined over the years. As outlined by Ratcliffe (2003), the intelligence process is a continuous cycle of tasking, collection, collation, analysis, dissemination, and feedback. While the definition of digital forensic by McKemmish (1999) lends itself to form a model consisting of the following steps; identify, preserve, analyze, and present; when investigating cloud services there will be a cycle of identification and preservation which may branch off from the examination and analysis of evidence already seized. For example, a practitioner should not stop the examination and analysis of already seized evidence to wait for identified data stored in the cloud to be preserved and provided for investigation. The practitioner should continue analyzing the evidence at hand, and when the cloud data is collected, should include that for examination and analysis. It is possible that examination of the cloud data may identify further cloud stored data which needs to be preserved, collected, examined, and analyzed. Hence the digital forensic process should be viewed as iterative, akin to the intelligence analysis process, rather than a linear process where the investigation follows from one step to the next. Furthermore, there are some additional phases which can be adapted from the intelligence cycle, namely, tasking and feedback. The framework (Figure 2.1) is based on the intelligence analysis cycle and the frameworks of McKemmish (1999) and the National Institute of Standards and Technology (Kent, Chevalier, Grance, & Dang, 2006), and comprises the following phases:

1. Commence (scope)
2. Preparation
3. Evidence source identification and preservation
4. Collection
5. Examination and analysis
6. Presentation
7. Complete

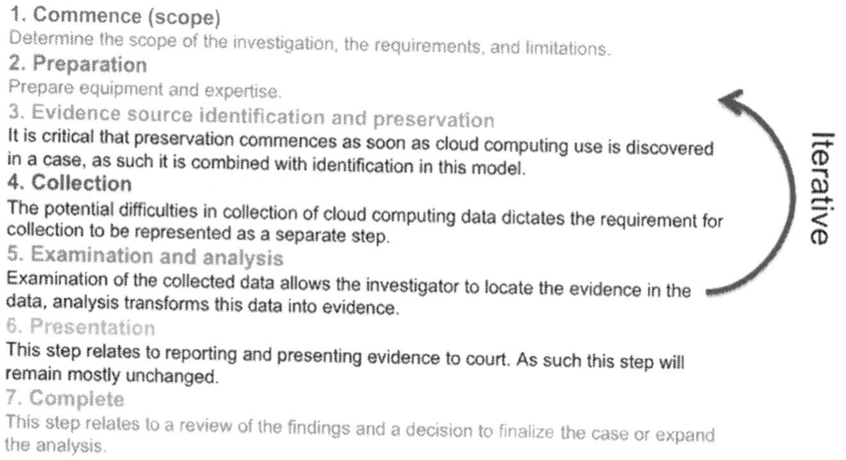

1. Commence (scope)
Determine the scope of the investigation, the requirements, and limitations.
2. Preparation
Prepare equipment and expertise.
3. Evidence source identification and preservation
It is critical that preservation commences as soon as cloud computing use is discovered in a case, as such it is combined with identification in this model.
4. Collection
The potential difficulties in collection of cloud computing data dictates the requirement for collection to be represented as a separate step.
5. Examination and analysis
Examination of the collected data allows the investigator to locate the evidence in the data, analysis transforms this data into evidence.
6. Presentation
This step relates to reporting and presenting evidence to court. As such this step will remain mostly unchanged.
7. Complete
This step relates to a review of the findings and a decision to finalize the case or expand the analysis.

Iterative

FIGURE 2.1

Cloud (storage) forensic framework.

Commence (Scope)

At the beginning of an investigation, it is important to outline the scope, nature, and background of the analysis. Taylor, Haggerty, Gresty, and Lamb (2011: 8) state that "[i]t is important that the purpose of a computer forensic investigation is clearly defined so that the full scope of the investigatory process can be decided." Investigators and forensic practitioners need to understand the "what, where, when, who, why, and how" of an investigation and to determine the boundaries of an investigation. This should all be documented, as practitioners and investigators will refer to this during the entire process. The scope would include the persons involved, any data or evidence already seized, keyword terms, any urgent time frames, and other relevant information. The initial scope may be quite generic, and as the investigation proceeds, will be refined to focus on issues as they arise.

Preparation

Once the scope is determined, the next step of any investigation, criminal or civil, is to understand the requirements and ensure that the correct equipment and information is available. Preparation can include training and equipment acquisition. There is a need for a practitioner to have the correct skills, as per ACPO Principle 2 (ACPO, 2006) "competency," and this can be addressed by undertaking the appropriate training prior to undertaking an examination. Advances in information and communications technologies (ICTs), such as the cloud computing environment, will require ongoing training and research in digital forensics, and this will include for general ICT professionals. The latter is becoming more actively involved in the investigation and prosecution of cybercrime. For example, ICT professionals may be called upon to help facilitate compliance with legal obligations, develop, and operate secure computer and cloud computing systems to ensure the privacy of protected information is not compromised. Training would equip ICT professionals with a working knowledge of key legal challenges and issues they are likely to encounter in the course of professional activities.

Preparation can also include research and development, undertaken to gain an understanding of a particular issue or aspect of an investigation. For example, if the scope of an investigation relates to a particular cloud storage service, a practitioner can conduct research using virtual computers or available equipment to gain an understanding prior to an investigation commencing. This can also occur during an investigation if cloud storage becomes an aspect of an investigation. Inferences can be outlined and tested in a controlled environment to determine outcomes, which can then be applied to an investigation to answer particular questions, or gain an understanding of the presence of data or information, and form hypotheses.

Preparation also includes other aspects of an investigation, such as timely response, time frame, personnel, duties, and locations of interest. An investigation plan can outline the various issues that need to be considered and addressed. The investigation scope would be outlined to the relevant people, and the appropriate equipment organized and available. Additional expertise can be sought to ensure the process can flow in a timely manner, or a practitioner can undertake research to ensure they have the requisite knowledge to undertake an examination. Furthermore, general forensic issues which include note-taking, logging, auditing, documentation, the integrity of evidence and methods, chain of custody, and other issues can be outlined and addressed (Haggerty & Taylor, 2006; Peisert, Bishop, & Marzullo, 2008).

Evidence source identification and preservation

The next stage of the framework (and in a typical forensic investigation) is to identify and preserve the relevant potential evidence sources. The timely preservation of potential evidence in the volatile cloud computing environment is critical, and hence the combination of identification and preservation into a single phase. Evidence source identification is likely to commence with traditional devices that have been subject to forensic analysis (e.g., personal computers (PCs) and mobile devices). It is during the forensic examination of these devices that pointers to cloud storage services will be detected. Once the potential cloud storage services sources are identified, the identification phase concerns itself with locating the cloud storage service (both electronically and physically) to determine the providers of the cloud storage service. Law enforcement agencies (LEAs) have existing processes for locating providers based upon domain or IP address, and this information is being sourced from the configuration on the physical devices examined.

Once provided with the relevant user identification data (e.g., username, and dates and times of access), the cloud storage service provider would be expected to assist according to relevant legal process to identify and preserve the identified data, and ultimately enable the investigator and practitioner access to the data. In the case of a desktop computer, preservation may be as simple as powering off the device, or capturing a logical forensic image of the PC and client device while the device is logged in (including potential volatile evidence) from the console. Forensic preservation in the cloud environment is almost certainly a more complicated process. Large cloud computing instances tend to be very volatile environments where scalability and rapid provision and release of services can result in deleted data being made irrecoverable very quickly. The online nature of cloud services also affords suspects the opportunity to login and securely delete data in real time, while the forensic practitioner is requesting preservation and collection of the data. This can be a time-consuming process for an investigator and practitioner potentially involving legislative processes such as mutual legal assistance requests with other jurisdictions.

While the legislative processes are followed, cloud storage providers could assist LEAs by activating a preservation method (such as a litigation hold) within their cloud environment for the particular user specified. This would make the users access to their cloud instance read only and institute other preservation techniques depending on the cloud environment (e.g., taking a copy of the current stored data state and using hashing techniques to show the data has not been modified). Depending on the case, it may be more appropriate that a preservation method takes a forensic copy of the data currently associated with the account and continues to permit access by the user while preserving any further data uploaded by the user. This would allow for the collection of additional evidence (e.g., IP addresses, data uploaded from the users' devices) without alerting the user to their activities (which could potentially cause them to destroy other noncloud hosted data).

If no such automated system is available, liaison with the service provider's legal contact may be the first step to preserve data. An investigator may need to assist the service provider with advice on how to preserve the data. This could include providing advice on using forensic software, such as AccessData FTK® Imager, to create a logical container of the identified files. Write-protection may not be possible (although some products claim to provide live forensic capabilities for cloud environments, little published academic research exists to verify these claims), and hence the person preserving the data will need to make notes (at the time) of the steps they undertook to preserve the data, including the reasons for the steps they are undertaking. Notes are crucial as legal examination may not occur for many years, and relying on memory may result in intricate details being forgotten. ICT professionals employed by the service provider may be responsible for preserving the identified data, and hence there is a need for training in forensic response and preservation methods. Consultation with the ACPO guidelines (2006), NIJ publications (2004, 2008), and Standards[1] such as HB 171-2003 (SAI, 2003) are also recommended for those tasked with preserving data.

Collection

Traditional PC-based storage systems have been generally straightforward to forensically collect for a forensic practitioner. A common practice for collecting evidence from a PC would involve removing the hard disk drive, attaching the drive to a forensic bridge/write blocker and using forensic software on a host PC to collect a physical bit-stream image of the disk. Collection in the cloud storage environment is complicated, however, by two major factors: location and technology. Therefore, collection is represented as a separate phase in our framework. The physical location of data in the cloud environment is commonly a different proposition from the

---

[1]A recent review of several ICT standards by Butler and Choo (2013: np) suggested that "in their current form, they should not be solely relied upon by IT practitioners with no digital forensics background to prepare for and respond to cyber security incidents that can provide admissible digital forensic data."

PC-based storage described above, which is likely generally located within or around the PC itself. With the exception of private clouds in an enterprise environment, cloud data is generally stored with the cloud provider which may or may not be within the jurisdiction of the LEA. If the cloud provider's storage is outside of the jurisdiction, the LEA may need to rely upon a "Mutual Legal Assistance Request" or similar agreement to seek assistance from an LEA in the cloud service provider's jurisdiction or where possible from the cloud provider themselves. If the cloud service provider's data is stored within the LEA's jurisdiction, technology can still introduce significant issues with the traditional collection models employed on PCs. To increase redundancy and efficiency, cloud service providers often operate storage systems that stripe and replicate single files across a number of physical storage devices. In this environment, the seizure and collection of a single physical device resulting in the collection of all evidence relating to a suspect is highly improbable. In many cases, including the striping and replication example, the LEA will need to rely upon built-in file access methods for collection of evidence. This could be executed by the cloud provider on behalf of the LEA or by the LEA directly, perhaps from the user interface to the cloud environment using credentials sourced from the client devices or directly from the suspect.

In some cases, a formal collection plan should be used to provide high-level guidance to the process. The compilation of a collection plan will ensure that all the relevant data and information relating to the investigation is identified and preserved. A collection plan can outline and address personnel requirements, anticipated locations, time frames, contingencies, documentation to be used such as evidence logs and chain of custody for each evidence item, equipment required, and ensure any legal permissions or orders are obtained, such as court warrants. The collection plan also details the process to undertake when confronted with running (live) computer systems, the secure storage of seized data, maintaining a chain of evidence, and a log of access.

Examination and analysis

Initial examination of the collected data is an important next step to determine the type of the collected evidence and locate any other cloud services which may be linked to the device/service being examined. If data is collected in an abstract method, the examination phase is used to reconstruct the data for use with traditional forensic analysis tools.

Analysis of the forensic data is undertaken to locate information and test hypotheses in relation to the investigation parameters. This can draw on a range of different processes, using various software and hardware to address and answer questions in relation to the scope of the investigation (Willassen, 2008). During the examination, there may be discovery of other sources of data, and in which case, the practitioner will commence an iterative process (i.e., the "preparation" phase for the newly identified data). Analysis would continue with the already collected data, and the new data would be examined and analyzed when available.

At any phase of the framework, a range of people can undertake different steps, including having multiple forensic practitioners. Practitioners with specific expertise can be brought in to undertake analysis of specific aspects, drawn together by a manager of an investigation.

Presentation

This next phase of the framework is to explain the information in a manner which is understandable to investigators, judiciary (including juries), and other decision makers. For the findings of the analysis to be meaningful, they must be reported in a legally acceptable manner. The information must be explained in a thorough manner to ensure false conclusions are not reached, but still be understood. This communication can be verbal or written, and should include information about the analysis process, the systems used, and any limitations (McKemmish, 1999; Yeager, 2006).

A spreadsheet timeline of events can be created using data and information from the various sources, which can assist to explain the course of events. Merging the information from the hard disk drive, network captures, memory, and the cloud storage account into one timeline may also be of assistance during the analysis process to gain an understanding of the sequence of events (examples are in the Case Study sections of Chapters 3 and 4).

Complete

This phase begins with the gathering of information from those involved in the investigation, relating to the validity of the analysis and reported findings. The digital forensic model of Baryamureeba and Tushabe (2006) includes the final step of "review." Review of the findings is an important consideration to ensure that:

- The questions of an investigator have been answered.
- The process undertaken was correct for the circumstances.
- All avenues for further analysis are identified.
- The processes and practices for future investigations can be recommended.

Prior to the completion of an investigation, a decision needs to be made whether further analysis is required, based on the feedback from the investigator or legal counsel. If further enquires are required, another iterative process will begin at the "preparation" phase. If there are no further avenues for investigation, the case can be completed, data archived, and backed-up as required. As prosecution or legal processes can continue for many years, or data may be required sometime in the future, archiving must be done in a manner so that information can be accessed at a later date, and not destroyed.

Framework summary

This chapter outlined our framework, which serves to expand upon the process used for traditional digital forensic analysis with the inclusion of the initial phases of commence (scope) and preparation. Emphasis is placed upon the need for prompt identification and preservation of cloud computing data once cloud computing use is suspected in an investigation. Due to the complications of cloud computing data collection, we introduce collection as a separate phase. The importance of the final phase of complete is also discussed. The framework is iterative, and a practitioner can start one or more iterative processes, while the overall investigation progresses.

Our framework is applied in the next four chapters discussing the research of cloud storage providers to (a) provide a guiding framework to step the process through, as would be the case in a digital forensic investigation, and (b) validate the framework in a variety of circumstances. We follow the process of a common digital forensic examination, enabling forensic practitioners to apply the framework to real-world investigations and to research the data remnants using a real-world process of analysis.

References

ACPO (2006). Good Practice Guidelines for Computer Based Evidence v4.0, from <www.7safe.com/electronic_evidence>.

Baryamureeba, V., & Tushabe, F. (2006). The enhanced digital investigation process model. Asian Journal of Information Technology, 5(7), 790−794.

Birk, D. (2011). *Technical Challenges of Forensic Investigations in Cloud Computing Environments*. Paper presented at the Workshop on Cryptography and Security in Clouds, IBM Forum Switzerland, Zurich.

Butler, A., & Choo, K. K. R. (2013). IT standards and guides do not adequately prepare IT practitioners to appear as expert witnesses: An Australian perspective. *Security Journal*, In press.

Haggerty, J., & Taylor, M. (2006). Managing corporate computer forensics. *Computer Fraud and Security, 2006*(6), 14−16. doi: citeulike-article-id:6856200

Kent, K., Chevalier, S., Grance, T., & Dang, H. (2006). *Guide to Integrating Forensic Techniques into Incident Response*. SP800-86, Gaithersburg: U.S. Department of Commerce.

Martini, B., & Choo, K. K. R. (2012). An integrated conceptual digital forensic framework for cloud computing. *Digital Investigation, 9*(2), 71−80.

McKemmish, R. (1999). What is forensic computing? *Trends and Issues in Crime and Criminal Justice, Australian Institute of Criminology, 118*, 1−6.

NIJ. (2004). *Forensic examination of digital evidence: A guide for law enforcement*, from <http://nij.gov/nij/pubs-sum/199408.htm>.

NIJ. (2008). *Electronic crime scene investigation: A guide for first responders* (2nd ed.), from <http://www.nij.gov/pubs-sum/219941.htm>.

Peisert, S., Bishop, M., & Marzullo, K. (2008). Computer forensics in forensis. *ACM SIGOPS Operating Systems Review, 42*(3), 112−122.

Quick, D., & Choo, K. K. R. (2013a). Digital droplets: Microsoft SkyDrive forensic data remnants. *Future Generation Computer Systems, 29*(6), 1378−1394.

Quick, D., & Choo, K. K. R. (2013b). Dropbox analysis: Data remnants on user machines. *Digital Investigation, 10*(1), 3−18.

Ratcliffe, J. (2003). Intelligence-led policing. *Trends and Issues in Crime and Criminal Justice, 248,* 1−6.

SAI (2003). *HB 171-2003 Guidelines for the management of IT evidence* Sydney, Australia: Standards Australia.

Slay, J., Lin, Y., Turnbull, B., Beckett, J., & Lin, P. (2009). Towards a formalization of digital forensics. *Advances in Digital Forensics V IFIP AICT, 2009,* 37−47.

Taylor, M., Haggerty, J., Gresty, D., & Lamb, D. (2011). Forensic investigation of cloud computing systems. *Network Security, 2011*(3), 4−10.

Willassen, S. (2008). *Using simplified event calculus in digital investigation.* Paper presented at the SAC '08: Proceedings of the 2008 ACM symposium on Applied computing, Fortaleza, Ceara, Brazil.

Yeager, R. (2006). *Criminal computer forensics management.* Paper presented at the InfoSecCD '06: Proceedings of the third annual conference on Information security curriculum development, Kennesaw, Georgia.

Microsoft SkyDrive Cloud Storage Forensic Analysis

3

INFORMATION IN THIS CHAPTER

- Microsoft SkyDrive forensic analysis
- Evidence source identification and preservation
- Collection of evidence from cloud storage services
- Examination and analysis of collected data

INTRODUCTION

The focus of this chapter is to discover the remnants left on client devices, a computer running the Windows 7 operating system, and an Apple iPhone 3G, after a user accesses Microsoft SkyDrive, and to examine the benefits of using the framework from Chapter 2 when undertaking forensic analysis of a cloud computing environment (see Quick & Choo, 2013a).

Using SkyDrive as a case study, we attempt to answer:

1. What data remains on a computer hard drive after a SkyDrive user has used client software or accessed cloud storage via a browser, and the location within the Windows 7 operating system of data remnants?
2. What data can be seen in network traffic, and what data remains in memory?
3. What data remains on an Apple iPhone running iOS version 4.2.1 after a user has used the Safari browser to access SkyDrive cloud storage, and what data remains when the SkyDrive iOS Application is installed and used to access SkyDrive cloud storage?

By determining the data remnants, we aim to provide a better understanding of the types of artifacts that are likely to remain, and the access point(s) for digital forensics practitioners to assist in the "identification" stage of an investigation.

In the following discussion, we will outline the use of the cloud (storage) forensic framework in conjunction with the preparation and analysis of SkyDrive access using Windows 7. Following this, we discuss the analysis of SkyDrive access using an iPhone 3G running iOS version 4.2.1, and then a hypothetical case study is used to explore the relevance of the research. The last section outlines the research findings and potential future research opportunities.

SkyDrive forensics: Windows 7 PC

The framework from Chapter 2 is used to guide the research process. This is undertaken with Microsoft SkyDrive cloud storage to validate the framework to ensure that it is forensically sound and is flexible enough to work with different cloud storage services. There will most certainly be variation in the way criminal investigation is carried out for each type of cloud service, hence we demonstrate using the framework with a cloud storage provider.

In the framework (Figure 2.1), the processes can be cyclic and iterative as it is common that during an investigation, a forensic practitioner may need to return to a previous step. For example, during the analysis phase, a practitioner may uncover information relating to data stored with a particular cloud storage provider. The practitioner may return to a previous step, such as "prepare" or "evidence source identification and preservation" and undertake enquiries to locate, identify, and collect the newly identified data using available legal processes. At the same time, the forensic analysis of other data already collected would continue. Once the (new) data has been acquired from the identified provider, the practitioner will preserve the collected data by creating a forensic copy and include the new data under the scope of the investigation for analysis. We now demonstrate how the framework can be used in the forensic analysis of client devices relating to SkyDrive use.

Commence (Scope)

The focus of this research is to determine what data remnants or digital "droplets" remain after a user has uploaded, accessed, or downloaded data from SkyDrive using either the SkyDrive client software or a browser. Popular browsers include Microsoft Internet Explorer, Mozilla Firefox, Google Chrome, and Apple Safari (W3Counter, 2012). These four browsers will be examined as part of this research to determine any differences in the ability to retrieve data remnants. The scope of this research is to determine the remnants such as a username, password, filenames, dates and times, or the presence of client software to indicate which cloud service, if any, had been used on a Windows 7 PC.[1] We also assumed criminals

---

[1]At the time of conducting this research Windows 8 was in beta release and not widely used. A future research opportunity is to undertake the same experiments on a Windows 8 system and compare the results to determine if the same remnants are available.

would use anti-forensic tools such as Eraser or CCleaner to remove evidence of using SkyDrive, and hence simulate such a scenario in our research. Memory analysis is increasingly becoming a source of evidence which should be captured and examined when possible (ACPO, 2006; NIJ, 2008). Network data capture is another potential source of information which will form part of the scope to determine what data is present within the network traffic from a host PC.

Preparation

To gather the data required to answer the research questions in relation to the use of SkyDrive, a variety of virtual machines (VMs) were created. It was decided to examine a variety of circumstances of a user accessing SkyDrive and also to examine any differences when using different browsers. Multiple scenarios were explored, each making use of SkyDrive with the following browsers: Internet Explorer (IE), Mozilla Firefox (FF), Google Chrome (GC), and Apple Safari (AS). Ultimately there were 36 VMs created which replicate different circumstance of usage. A benefit of using virtual machines (VMs) is the ease of capturing memory, by copying the "VMEM" files as VM was running. It was also easy to capture network traffic by running Wireshark on the host PC and monitoring and capturing network traffic on the VM interface. Attempting this using physical hardware would have been difficult, and the time and equipment required undertaking this would have reduced the scope of the research.

The Enron dataset is useful for testing purposes and consists of a large set of email messages made public by the US Federal Energy Regulatory Commission during legal proceedings (Klimt & Yang, 2004). For this research, the UC Berkeley Enron Email subset data file was used as the sample data and was downloaded from the project web site on the February 9, 2012 (http://bailando .sims.berkeley.edu/enron_email.html). Hash values (MD5) were calculated for these files, and key terms were identified to enable searching and location of the data and files in subsequent analysis.

Virtualized PCs were created using VMware Player 4.0.1. For each scenario, a base image was created, and Windows 7 Home Basic was installed on a 20 GB virtual hard drive with 1 GB RAM. The Base-VMs were used as control media to determine the files created when user activity was undertaken in each scenario. The different actions undertaken were as follows:

1. The first step was to install the browser software to separate Base-VMs for each browser: Mozilla Firefox 13.0, Internet Explorer 9.0.8112.16421IC, Google Chrome 19.0.1084.56m, and Apple Safari 5.1.7 for Windows 7.
2. Next was to make a copy of the Base-VM for each browser. These four VMs were labeled IE, FF, GC, or AS Upload-VM, and were used to access the SkyDrive web site and download and install the client software ("SkyDriveSetup.exe" version 2012 16.4.3347.0416 Beta and 16.4.4111.0525). A SkyDrive account was created for this research, and

sign-in undertaken using the client software. The Enron sample files were uploaded to the SkyDrive account using the client software.

3. Additional copies of the Base-VM for each browser were made, labeled Access-VM. These were used to access the SkyDrive web site (https:// skydrive.live.com) using each installed browser. The sign-in option was used to log in to the user account created in step 2. Each of the stored files was opened within the browser but not deliberately downloaded.

4. Copies were made of the four Base-VMs, labeled Download-VM. Each installed browser was used to access the SkyDrive web site. The sign-in option was used to log in to the user account created in step 2. All of the files in the SkyDrive cloud storage account were downloaded to the VM hard drive as a ZIP file. The contents of the ZIP file were extracted to the Desktop and then each file was opened and closed.

5. Copies were made of the four Download-VMs, labeled Eraser-VM. Eraser v6.09.2343 or v6.0.10.2620 was installed and used to erase each of the Enron data files and the ZIP files.

6. Copies were made of the four Eraser-VMs, labeled CCleaner-VM. CCleaner v3.18.1707 or v3.19.1721 was installed and run across the VM hard drives to remove the browsing history and file references.

7. Copies were made of the Four CCleaner-VMs, labeled DBAN-VM. Darik's Boot and Nuke (DBAN) version 2.2.6 Beta was used to boot each DBAN-VM. DBAN was run with the option to erase the entire 20 GB hard drive with the "US DoD level 3" setting. This is an overwrite of "all locations three (3) times (first time with a character, second time with its complement, and the third time with a random character)" (USDoD, 1995).

Whilst preparing each VM, Wireshark 1.6.5 was run on the Host computer to capture network traffic from the VM network interface. Memory capture was facilitated by copying the Virtual Memory (VMEM) files created by VMWare. The VMEM files were copied while the VM was running, just prior to shutdown. The network capture files were saved at various points while the VMs were running, and also after shutdown.

Evidence source identification and preservation

In the context of this research, files were identified that would contain the information needed to conduct the analysis: the virtual hard drives (VMDK files) in each VM folder, each memory instance (VMEM files), and each saved network capture file (PCAP). These were identified for each of the VMs.

Collection

To observe the principles of digital forensic acquisition and analysis (ACPO, 2006; NIJ, 2008), a forensic copy was made of each virtual hard drive (VMDK file) using AccessData FTK Imager CLI 2.9.0 in the Encase Evidence format (E01). In regard to the each memory file (VMEM) and network capture (PCAP) file, a forensic copy was made using Encase version 6.19.4, in the Logical Evidence format (L01), and the X-Ways Evidence File Container format (ctr). Hash values (MD5) were used to ensure the forensic integrity of the data.

Examination and analysis

For this research, each of the forensic copies of the VM hard drives, memory, and network captures were examined using a range of forensic analysis tools, including X-Ways Forensic version 16.5, Guidance Software EnCase version 6.19.4, AccessData FTK version 1.81.6 and version 4.01, Network Miner 1.0, Wireshark 1.6.5, Magnet Forensics (formerly JADSoftware) Internet Evidence Finder 5.52, and RegRipper version 20080909. Many of these tools are widely used for digital forensic analysis by law enforcement agencies and the private sector. In addition, Encase 6.5 and FTK Imager 2.5.3.14 have been tested by the Office of Law Enforcement Standards of the National Institute of Standards and Technology (NIST, 2012).

Control—Base-VMs

Analysis of the four control Base-VM hard drive images confirmed there was no data originally present relating to the Enron sample test data and SkyDrive client software files. References were located for the term "skydrive" in temporary Internet files such as "welcome[1].htm" and "ie[1].htm;" and in system files such as "$MFT," "$UsnJrnl.$J," "$LogFile," and "AgRobust.db." References were also located in unallocated clusters. This should be borne in mind, as this indicates the presence of the keyword term "skydrive" does not necessarily indicate that SkyDrive has been used. This highlights that the context of a search result needs to be analyzed to determine the reason for a keyword match, rather than drawing a conclusion at face value of the presence of data.

SkyDrive client software

Analysis of the four Upload-VMs located the SkyDriveSetup.exe file that was downloaded from the Microsoft SkyDrive web site. When run, the SkyDrive software was installed into the Users "C:\Users\[username]\AppData\Local \Microsoft\" directory in a folder called "SkyDrive." SkyDrive synchronized files and folders were observed at the default SkyDrive folder location ("C: \Users\[username]\SkyDrive\"), and the following folders were created: "Documents," "Pictures" and "Public." Unlike Dropbox™ (which was used as the case study in our first experiment), SkyDrive had no sample files, and the folders were empty when first installed. Information regarding the setup file for the client software is listed in Table 3.1. When a new release of the SkyDrive Windows client software is released, the hash values of the standard files should be recalculated. In comparing the files across two different client software

Table 3.1 SkyDrive Setup Information (Using X-Ways 16.5)

Name	SkyDriveSetup.exe	SkyDriveSetup.exe
Path	\Users\cloud\AppData\Local\Microsoft\SkyDrive**16.4.3347.0416**	\Users\cloud\AppData\Local\Microsoft\SkyDrive**16.4.4111.0525**
Size	4.7 MB	4.9 MB
Created	27/05/2012 17:07	10/06/2012 11:43
Int. creation	16/04/2012 9:18	25/05/2012 16:39
Hash	C95FBC79481F3B705ADF289B94DAACDB	6961F3AEC7F861C65091B8FB35086561
Metadata	signed: true CA: Microsoft Timestamping PCA Signing date: 16/04/2012 19:02:46	signed: true CA: Microsoft Timestamping PCA Signing date: 26/05/2012 02:25:52

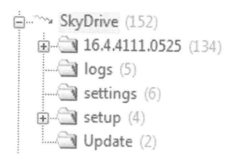

FIGURE 3.1

Folder List of the AppData\local\SkyDrive Folder (X-Ways 16.5).

releases, hash matches were observed for the following files: "CollectSkyDriveLogs.bat," msvcp.dll, sqmapi.dll, and msvcr.dll. All other installed files had different hash values in the subsequent release.

Approximately 152 files were created when the installation software was run. The observed folder structure is listed in Figure 3.1, and version number is displayed as a folder. Within this folder was the executable file. The Logs folder is of particular interest as there is a SyncDiagnostics.log file which has a list of the files synchronized, sizes, dates, and times — an example is listed in Table 3.2. The information in this file is particularly important as it displays the history of files associated with a SkyDrive account.

Details for the SkyDrive executable are listed in Table 3.3, including the MD5 hash value, which can be used to quickly locate the presence of SkyDrive client software; even in the instance it has been renamed. As the software is updated, a forensic practitioner will need to calculate new hash values. This can be done by installing the software to a clean PC and calculate hash values for the installed files.

Table 3.2 Example of SyncDiagnostices.log File Contents

```
Sync Diagnostics v1

UtcNow: 2012-06-10T03:31:52.0000000Z

Cloud Metadata:
 - folder    FDXXXXXX89F707D0!106 'C:\Users\[username]\SkyDrive\Dataset', creationTime=1338104478,
             modTime=1338104478
 - file      FDXXXXXX89F707D0!107 'C:\Users\[username]\SkyDrive\Dataset\3111.txt', size=2734,
             creationTime=1338104500, modTime=1100097650
 - file      FDXXXXXX89F707D0!109 'C:\Users\[username]\SkyDrive\Dataset\Enron3111.docx', size=14072,
             creationTime=1338104500, modTime=1328766856
 - file      FDXXXXXX89F707D0!110 'C:\Users\[username]\SkyDrive\Dataset\Enron3111.jpg', size=315868,
             creationTime=1338104500, modTime=1328766794
 - file      FDXXXXXX89F707D0!111 'C:\Users\[username]\SkyDrive\Dataset\Enron3111.rtf', size=34215,
             creationTime=1338104500, modTime=1330133578
 - file      FDXXXXXX89F707D0!108 'C:\Users\[username]\SkyDrive\Dataset\enron_with_categories.tar.gz',
             size=4523350, creationTime=1338104500, modTime=1308027150
 - folder    FDXXXXXX89F707D0!104 'C:\Users\[username]\SkyDrive\Documents', creationTime=1335323578,
             modTime=1335323578
 - folder    FDXXXXXX89F707D0!102 'C:\Users\[username]\SkyDrive\Pictures', creationTime=1335323577,
             modTime=1335323577
 - folder    FDXXXXXX89F707D0!103 'C:\Users\[username]\SkyDrive\Public', creationTime=1335323577,
             modTime=1335323577

Cloud Total: 4 folders, 6 files, 5607286 bytes

File System:
Scanning 'C:\Users\[username]\SkyDrive'
```

(Continued)

Table 3.2 (Continued)

```
Sync Diagnostics v1

  - file     'C:\Users\[username]\SkyDrive\.lock' ignored, size = 0, creationTime = 1339299083,
             modTime = 1339299083

  - folder   'C:\Users\[username]\SkyDrive\Dataset'
  - folder   'C:\Users\[username]\SkyDrive\Documents'
  - folder   'C:\Users\[username]\SkyDrive\Pictures'
  - folder   'C:\Users\[username]\SkyDrive\Public'

    Folder   'C:\Users\[username]\SkyDrive' Total: 4 folders, 1 files

Scanning 'C:\Users\[username]\SkyDrive\Dataset'

  - file     'C:\Users\[username]\SkyDrive\Dataset\3111.txt', size = 2734, creationTime = 1339299089,
             modTime = 1100097650

  - file     'C:\Users\[username]\SkyDrive\Dataset\Enron3111.docx', size = 14072, creationTime = 1339299107,
             modTime = 1328766856

  - file     'C:\Users\[username]\SkyDrive\Dataset\Enron3111.jpg', size = 315868, creationTime = 1339299108,
             modTime = 1328766794

  - file     'C:\Users\[username]\SkyDrive\Dataset\Enron3111.rtf', size = 34215, creationTime = 1339299109,
             modTime = 1330133578

  - file     'C:\Users\[username]\SkyDrive\Dataset\enron_with_categories.tar.gz', size = 4523350,
             creationTime = 1339299090, modTime = 1308027150

    Folder   'C:\Users\[username]\SkyDrive\Dataset' Total: 0 folders, 5 files
FileSystem Total: 4 folders, 6 files, 0 symLinks, 5607286 bytes

----------------------------------------------------------------------

DAT Total: 4 folders, 6 full files, 0 stub files, 5607286 bytes, quotaState = 1
```

Table 3.3 SkyDrive Executable Information (Using X-Ways 16.5)

Name	SkyDrive.exe	SkyDrive.exe
Path	\Users\cloud\AppData\Local\Microsoft\ SkyDrive	\Users\cloud\AppData\Local\Microsoft\ SkyDrive
Size	290 KB (296,672)	290 KB (296,672)
Created	27/05/2012 17:07:59	09/06/2012 12:46:34
Int. creation	16/04/2012 09:18:43	25/05/2012 16:40:09
Hash	D943C6ADF16045E7FE00233FF9C15376	4F7C80E5A420E47B584055EB1AC61562
Metadata	signed true CA Microsoft Timestamping PCA Signing date 16/04/2012 18:50:38	signed true CA Microsoft Timestamping PCA Signing date 26/05/2012 02:12:21

Table 3.4 OwnerID INI File Contents

nickname =
installID = 1
installName = WIN-TH8PP2HRCSG
maxNumRequests = 10
originatorID = a083ec80-17ac-4537-89c9-c723a05a2c64
library = 1 4 FDXXXXXX89F707D0!101 1339211794 "SkyDrive" Me personal "C:\Users\
[username]\SkyDrive"

Analysis of the SyncDiagnostics.log file located a range of information of interest. There is file system and metadata information contained within the log file. The SkyDrive OwnerID is listed for each file, and the associated file or folder number. The filename and path is listed, and the creation and modified time information appears to be in Unix Numeric Value time format, which can be decoded using conversion software such as Digital Detective's DCode v4.02a; e.g., creationTime = 1338104500 is converted to "Sun, 27 May 2012 17:11:40 +0930," which is the creation time for the Enron jpg file. The file size is listed, as are file and folder totals.

Located in the "settings" folder is a data file with the name matching the Owner ID number of the SkyDrive account, which also lists the file and folder names of the files and folders synchronized with the SkyDrive account, such as SkyDrive\settings\FDXXXXXX89F707D0.dat. Also located in the settings folder is an INI file with the Owner ID as the name, FDXXXXXX89F707D0.ini. Contained within this file are the computer name, OwnerID, and SkyDrive sync folder information, as listed in Table 3.4.

Also in the settings folder is a file named `ApplicationSettings.xml`, within which there is a reference to a web site with the name "EnableDogFood"; `http://g.live.com/8SESkyDrive/EnableDogfood`. Browsing to this URL connects to a web site which requires a login. The term "EnableDogFood" is also located in the `SkyDrive.Resources.dll` file. A search was conducted of the Base-VM and other VMs created for this research, and determined that "EnableDogFood" is not located anywhere else within a standard Microsoft Windows 7 installation, and hence could be used to determine if SkyDrive software has been installed on a PC.

Another file of interest is in the `\Users\[username]\AppData\Local\ Microsoft\SkyDrive\ 16.4.4111.0525\` folder, called "`CollectSkyDriveLogs. bat`." Examining the code in this file indicates it will package the SkyDrive log files into a CAB file with the date and time of preparation. The CAB file will be placed on the User's Desktop by default. The hash value of the.bat file remained the same across two different client software releases, and is `40A379C64F2A1B473D8A5F8B760FC7C8`.

Located at the root of the hard drive was a temporary folder for SkyDrive, which had a sub-folder named with the Base Machine SID and the Users Windows ID number, for example:

```
C:\SkyDriveTemp\S-1-5-21-4040090636-1120983347-324155541-1000
```

The SkyDrive username was located in cookie file `\Users\[username]\ AppData\Roaming\Microsoft\ Windows\Cookies\cloud@login.live[1].txt`, in `$MFT` and also `$LogFile`. However, in the Internet Explorer Upload-VM, the username was in `\Users\[username]\AppData\Roaming\ Microsoft\Windows \Cookies\WGYG41GV.txt` and the `$MFT`.

When installed, the SkyDrive client software runs automatically when the Windows operating system starts and logs in to the user account without prompting for a password. This can be of assistance in an investigation, as a forensic copy of a seized computer hard drive can be used with any software that allows the forensic copy of a hard drive to be run within a virtual environment (e.g., Virtual Forensic Computing (VFC) or LiveView will scan the image of a hard drive and prepare the requisite files to run an operating system on a hard drive within VMWare Player). If the forensic copy of the hard drive contains the SkyDrive client software with a user account and password already stored, the PC when started will automatically sign in to the SkyDrive account and provide a practitioner access to the files stored within the SkyDrive user account. Care would also need to be taken when connecting a forensic image to the Internet. Legal authority would be required to ensure a practitioner has the appropriate authority within their jurisdiction to examine the data stored within the cloud storage account, which could potentially be stored overseas or in another jurisdiction. In Australia, Section 3L of the *Crimes Act 1914* (Cth) has a provision for the executing officer of a warrant or a constable assisting to access data which includes data not held at the premises, i.e., accessible from a computer or data storage device.

For this research, we also attempted to copy all the files contained within the installed SkyDrive folders to another PC; however, this did not allow access to the SkyDrive account without knowing the username and password (the process of copying the software files from a PC previously worked with Dropbox client software (also see McClain, 2011; Chung, Park, Lee, & Kang, 2012).

SkyDrive account when accessed via a browser

It was observed that the SkyDrive web account (accessed via `https://skydrive.live.com`) retains a record of computers used to access and synchronize with an account. The information is shown when using a browser to access the SkyDrive account and is available on the left of the displayed page with the heading, "Computers." When selecting a computer name, there is an attempt to connect to the selected computer. When unable to connect, a message is displayed. There is also the ability to unlink a linked computer. The username is displayed at the top right of the browser, and the OwnerID number can be observed in the URL, e.g., `https://skydrive.live.com/?cid=XXXXXXXXXXXXXXXX#`

When selecting a file in a SkyDrive account using a browser, there is an option to display the metadata within the file by clicking on an "Information" link on the right hand of the page. Folder information is also displayed under Information and includes the time and date, and a folder was added and modified. Version history is displayed for files when viewing the file, and previous versions can be viewed or downloaded.

When downloading folders from SkyDrive via the browser, the folder and files are packed into an uncompressed ZIP file. When done from the browser choosing the root SkyDrive folder, the ZIP is named "skydrive" with the date, e.g., "`skydrive-2012-06-09.zip`." When a download is undertaken from a folder, the ZIP is named with the folders name but not the date, e.g., "`Dataset.zip`." As these are uncompressed ZIP files, the contents would be located when conducting a data carve across a hard drive when ignoring sector or cluster boundaries, including deleted files.

Keyword search terms

Keyword search terms were determined from the filenames observed and the text from within the Enron data files. These included the following:

- the username and password of the SkyDrive account created for this research
- "www.skydrive.com," and "https://skydrive.live.com"
- "skydrive"
- "skydrivesetup.exe"
- "dataset.zip", "3111.txt," and "enron3111"
- "Enron Wholesale Services"

- "enabledogfood"
- SkyDrive OwnerID

Directory listings

Analysis was conducted using X-Ways Forensic 16.5 and Encase 6.19.4 to view the filenames stored within the VMs, determined from the directory listing ($MFT[2] files). Analysis of the directory and file listings of the four control Base-VM hard drives revealed no references to the Enron sample data filenames or SkyDrive client software filenames. It was concluded that references to SkyDrive and the Enron sample files were not present in the control media directory listings prior to installing the software or accessing the files. However, references were located for deleted SkyDrive icon files in the Internet Explorer Base-VM. This highlights that while there were no references to the SkyDrive software or sample data, it is possible to locate references to filenames with SkyDrive in the name. The presence of the search term does not indicate the use of SkyDrive, as in this instance it was related to the installation and update of Internet Explorer, and not any use of the client software or intentional browsing to the SkyDrive web site. The reason for the presence of a search term or filename needs to be determined prior to a conclusion to be reached.

Not surprisingly, there were references to the SkyDrive client software in the Upload-VMs, which correlated to the VMs where the client software was used. There were no references to the client software in the other VMs. There were references to the filenames for the Enron sample files in all the other VMs (excluding the Base-VMs) and when the files were downloaded via the browser from the root folder. In the Upload-VMs, there was a substantial amount of filenames seen, including on the User's Desktop, in the Downloads folder, and in the SkyDrive folder, "`C:\User\[username]\SkyDrive`."

When a browser was used to access a SkyDrive account, there were fewer filename references for the Enron files (in comparison with when the client software was used to access cloud storage). However, with a browser being used to access the SkyDrive account stored files, there were sufficient file name references remaining on the hard drives to identify the filenames that were accessed, such as the Enron sample data filenames. In the circumstances when the files were downloaded and opened from the SkyDrive cloud storage, there were additional filename references observed on the hard drive, including link files. This indicates when a user accesses SkyDrive, there will potentially be references in the $MFT directory listing to indicate this and also to potentially determine the filenames associated with SkyDrive use by searching for SkyDrive filename entries in the $MFT.

---

[2]*"The NTFS file system contains at its core, a file called the master file table (MFT). There is at least one entry in the MFT for every file on an NTFS volume, including the MFT itself"* (Microsoft, 2008).

Table 3.5 SkyDrive.EXE Prefetch (X-Ways 16.5)

***Prefetch ***

SKYDRIVE.EXE-76AB3CF5

Run Count: 1

Last Run: : 10/06/2012 11:43:09

000 32 200   \DEVICE\HARDDISKVOLUME1\WINDOWS\SYSTEM32\NTDLL.DLL

234 66 200   \DEVICE\HARDDISKVOLUME1\USERS\CLOUD\APPDATA\LOCAL\
             MICROSOFT\SKYDRIVE\16.4.4111.0525\SKYDRIVECLIENT.DLL

Link file references remained after Eraser and CCleaner had been used to remove the files and to "clean" the hard drive. Using CCleaner with all options selected remove the link files (however sufficient information remained in other locations such as prefetch files, relating to SkyDrive and the Enron sample files, will be discussed in the next section). The use of Darik's Boot and Nuke (DBAN) completely erased the hard drives, and there was no data to analyze in these VMs.

Prefetch files

Analysis of the VM hard drives identified that prefetch[3] files stored information relating to the filenames of the SkyDrive executable and Enron test data filenames. This was located in all the VM hard drives except the control Base-VM hard drives. It was observed that even after running CCleaner, there was enough information in prefetch files, such as `notepad.exe.pf`, `wordpad.exe.pf`, `explorer.exe.pf`, and `dllhost.exe.pf`, to indicate the presence and path of the Enron sample data files. Also located were `skydrive.exe.pf`, `skydriveconfig. exe.pf`, and `skydrivesetup.exe.pf` prefetch files when the client software was installed. Information located within the prefetch files included the number of times run and last run time and date (Table 3.5).

Analysis was conducted using X-Ways Forensic 16.5 (which parses information out of Windows Prefetch files). For example, an extract from the `c:\windows \prefetch\wordpad.exe.pf` prefetch file from the Internet Explorer CCleaner-VM displays the Run Count, Last run time, and the path of the files opened, including an entry for the Enron3111.docx file used as a sample, highlighted in bold (output from the Preview window in X-Ways 16.5) (Table 3.6).

An example from the `Notepad.exe.pf` prefetch file from the Google Chrome Upload-VM displays the path which includes the SkyDrive default storage location (highlighted in bold in Table 3.7).

---

[3]"Windows keeps track of the way a computer starts and which programs are commonly opened. Windows saves this information as a number of small files in the prefetch folder" (Microsoft, 2012b).

Table 3.6 Wordpad.EXE Prefetch (X-Ways 16.5)

*** Prefetch ***

WORDPAD.EXE-1BCC3DB7

Run Count: 2

Last Run: : 27/05/2012 18:08:07

E11 42 1   \DEVICE\HARDDISKVOLUME1\USERS\[username]\DESKTOP\DATASET\
　　　　　　ENRON3111.DOCX

Table 3.7 Notepad.EXE Prefetch (X-Ways 16.5)

*** Prefetch ***

NOTEPAD.EXE-EB1B961A

Run Count: 1

Last Run: : 10/06/2012 11:45:23

38C 3D 2   \DEVICE\HARDDISKVOLUME1**USERS\[username]\SKYDRIVE**\DATASET\
　　　　　　3111.TXT

Link files

Analysis of link files[4] was undertaken using X-Ways 16.5, which parses the information within link files and displays this in a Preview pane. There were no SkyDrive associated link files found within the four control Base-VMs or the Access-VMs. Link files relating to SkyDrive and the Enron sample data files were observed for all Upload-VM, Download-VM, Eraser-VM, and CCleaner-VM hard drives. When CCleaner was used with all options selected, there were no logical link files containing SkyDrive or the Enron sample data filenames (however, the information from the deleted link files was still present and recoverable from the hard drives).

The link files observed are related to the filenames and folder names for the SkyDrive executable, such as (Table 3.8):

*   \Users\[username\Links\SkyDrive.lnk
*   \Users\[username]\AppData\Roaming\Microsoft\Windows\Recent\SkyDrive.lnk
*   \Users\[username]\AppData\Roaming\Microsoft\Windows\Start Menu\Programs\ Microsoft SkyDrive.lnk

Link files relating to the Enron test data were also located. These were located in the "Windows\Recent" and "Windows\Start" folders in the Users "AppData" directory, such as (Table 3.9):

---

[4]A link file is a shortcut to a file or program (Microsoft, 2012a).

Table 3.8 \Users\[username\Links\SkyDrive.lnk Link File Contents (X-Ways 16.5)

Link target information	
Target Attributes	RX (Directory)
Target File Size	0
Show Window	SW_NORMAL
Target Created	10/06/2012 11:43:10
Last Written	10/06/2012 11:43:10
Last Accessed	10/06/2012 11:43:10
ID List	{59031A47-3F72-44A7-89C5-5595FE6B30EE}\SkyDrive\
	M = 09/06/2012 14:13:12
	C = 09/06/2012 14:13:12
	A = 09/06/2012 14:13:12\
Volume Type	Fixed
Volume Serial	0xB862D483
Volume Name	
Local Path	C:\Users\cloud\SkyDrive
Relative Path	..\SkyDrive
Owner	S-1-5-21-4040090636-1120983347-324155541-1000
Host Name	win-th8pp2hrcsg
Volume ID	{88A2C812-7A91-4C6F-9F2F-E281768EB2AF}
Object ID	{5E953154-B2A1-11E1-92E2-000C294B0311}
MAC Address	00 0C 29 4B 03 11
Timestamp	10/06/2012 11:39:54, Seq: 4834

There were no SkyDrive or Enron link files within the four Access-VM hard drives, indicating that if files were not downloaded from SkyDrive to the computer and opened, link files were not created.

Thumbcache files

Analysis of the thumbnail pictures stored within the thumbcache[5] files within the four control Base-VMs determined that there were no Enron sample picture thumbnails present prior to installing or accessing SkyDrive. Thumbnails for the Enron sample picture were located in the Upload-VM, Download-VM, and Eraser-VMs; however, none were found in the Access-VMs or the CCleaner VMs. This indicates that the thumbnail cache is a source for possible data relating to SkyDrive use, but results may not be definitive. It is possible for SkyDrive to be used in certain circumstances without leaving thumbnails, e.g., accessing files

---

[5]"Windows 7 creates small thumbnail images of graphic files. There are files named Thumbcache_32.db, Thumbcache_96.db, Thumbcache_256.db & Thumbcache_1024.db which correspond to the thumbnails stored for that specific user account and size" (Mueller, 2010).

Table 3.9 \Users\[username\AppData\Roaming\Microsoft\Windows\Recent\ Enron3111.lnk Link File Contents (X-Ways 16.5)

Link target information

Target Attributes	A
Target File Size	14072
Show Window	SW_NORMAL
Target Created	10/06/2012 11:44:35
Last Written	09/02/2012 15:24:16
Last Accessed	10/06/2012 11:44:35
ID List	{59031A47-3F72-44A7-89C5-5595FE6B30EE}\SkyDrive\ \Dataset\ C = 10/06/2012 02:13:58 M = 10/06/2012 02:14:38 Enron3111.docx C = 10/06/2012 02:14:36 M = 09/02/2012 05:54:16 A = 10/06/2012 Size = 14072
Volume Type	Fixed
Volume Serial	0xB862D483
Volume Name	
Local Path	C:\Users\cloud\SkyDrive\Dataset\Enron3111.docx
Relative Path	..\..\..\..\..\SkyDrive\Dataset\Enron3111.docx
Working Directory	C:\Users\cloud\SkyDrive\Dataset
Known Folder Tracking	false
PROPERTYSTORAGE	{46588AE2-4CBC-4338-BBFC-139326986DCE}
Size	0
Host Name	win-th8pp2hrcsg
Volume ID	{88A2C812-7A91-4C6F-9F2F-E281768EB2AF}
Object ID	{5E953157-B2A1-11E1-92E2-000C294B0311}
MAC Address	00 0C 29 4B 03 11
Timestamp	10/06/2012 11:39:54, Seq: 4834

using a browser but not downloading the files to a computer. Hence analysis of other data is necessary before forming a conclusion that SkyDrive was not used, such as Internet browser history or a keyword search. An example output for thumbcache information is included in Table 3.10.

Event log files

Event log files can be good sources of information relating to system, software, and other events recorded by Windows operating systems. In this research, there were no records relating to SkyDrive or the Enron sample files within the event log files in any of the VMs created for this research. Our research into other cloud service client software suggested that event log files can contain information of interest, and hence, event log files should not be precluded when conducting

Table 3.10 Thumbcache Information for Enron jpg File (X-Ways 16.5)

Name	3DE592C2E9065148
Description	existing file
Type	jpg
Type status	newly identified
Type descr.	JPEG
Category	Pictures
Evidence object	Safari 5 erase, Partition 1
Path	\Users\[user]\AppData\Local\Microsoft\Windows\Explorer\ thumbcache_256.db
Size	11.7 KB (11,932)
Modified	10/06/2012 13:24:38
Int. ID	57845
Int. parent	55325
Report table	thumbcache carved
Comment	file:C:/Users/[user]/Desktop/skydrive-2012-06-09/Dataset/Enron3111. jpg

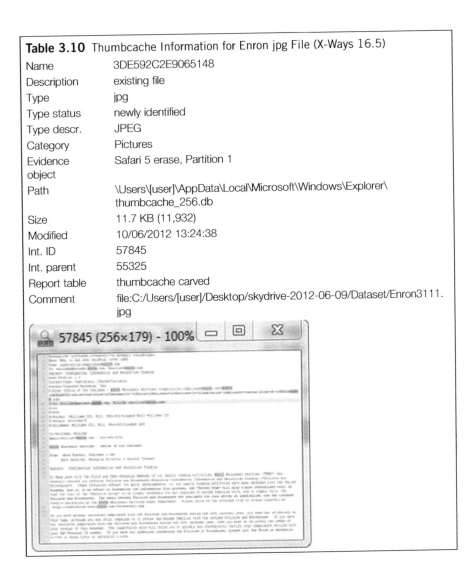

analysis and are one of the primary items an examiner can review to gain an understanding of the system and events.

Registry files

Windows Registry files were parsed using RegRipper version 20080909 and parsed and analyzed with X-Ways Forensic 16.5. Analysis revealed there were no references to SkyDrive or the Enron sample files in the four control Base-VM hard drives. There were no references to the SkyDrive username or password within the registry files in any of the VMs. When the SkyDrive client software was used, there were references found in the Upload-VMs for all browsers in NTUser.dat, UsrClass.dat, SOFTWARE, and SYSTEM Registry files. This information was located using keyword searches for the term "skydrive" across the Registry files and also the parsed text from the Registry files (output from RegRipper and the X-Ways HTML reports). Specific keys were created when the client software was installed, such as SkyDrive.SyncFileInformationProvider in UsrClass.dat and Software\Microsoft\SkyDrive in NTUSER.dat files.

When a browser was used to access SkyDrive accounts, there were references to the filenames of the files in the Download-VM registry files for all browsers. When Internet Explorer was used for accessing but not downloading the files (IE Access-VM), there were also references, but not for the other browsers' Access-VMs. There were references to SkyDrive URLs, SkyDrive software files and folders, and the Enron test files located in the browser VMs. For example, the "RecentDocs" key in the NTUSER.dat registry file provided a list of SkyDrive and Enron-related files and folders, and a sample RegRipper output is listed as follows:

```
------------------------------------------------------------
RecentDocs - recentdocs
**All values printed in MRUList\MRUListEx order.
Software\Microsoft\Windows\CurrentVersion\Explorer\RecentDocs
LastWrite Time Sat Jun 9 03:42:27 2012 (UTC)
  3 = Dataset
  6 = Enron3111.rtf
  5 = Enron3111.jpg
  4 = Enron3111.docx
  2 = 3111.txt
  1 = Downloads
  0 = skydrive-2012-06-08.zip
------------------------------------------------------------
```

Deleted information regarding SkyDrive was located within the NTUSER.dat registry files after CCleaner was run, such as the previously observed filenames and URL references. References were also found within the UsrClass.dat registry files when the SkyDrive client software was used, such as the download of the file "skydrive-2012-xx-xx.zip."

$Recycle.Bin

Files that were deleted were easily located in the $Recycle.Bin folder in a folder with the SID of the user. The information files (beginning with $I) included the data relating to the original file and when it was deleted, the following example relating to the SkyDrive folder was extracted from the ZIP file (Table 3.11).

Also located in the Recycle.Bin were the file contents files (beginning with $R), which contained the original file or folder contents. In the scope of this

Table 3.11 $Recycle.Bin $I information for Deleted SkyDrive Folder (X-Ways 16.5)

Size: 5.3 MB

Moved to recycle bin: 23/07/2012 13:15:23

C:\Users\cloud\Desktop\skydrive-2012-06-08

research, this included the unzipped contents of the ZIP file downloaded from SkyDrive account using the Firefox browser.

Data carve

Data carving is the process of searching through allocated or unallocated data to locate files based on known headers and footers, such as 0xFFD8 and 0xFFD9 for a jpg file. This was undertaken using X-Ways 16.5 File Header Signature Search across all VMs created for this research. Thumbnail icons and large size pictures were carved from all VMs, except the Base-VMs.

Browser analysis

Internet browsing information was analyzed using Magnet Forensics (formerly JADsoftware) Internet Evidence Finder (IEF) v5.52 Standard Edition, X-Ways Forensic 16.5 64-bit, and SQLite Database Browser v1.3. It was confirmed there were no references to SkyDrive or Enron sample data in the Internet history of the four control Base-VMs. The SkyDrive account username could be determined when Mozilla Firefox and Google Chrome were used to access the account using the browser, but the username was not located when Internet Explorer or Safari was used. The username was stored in Firefox in the "formhistory.sqlite" database and in Chrome in the Autofill "Web Data" file. If the username and password were stored by the user when using IE version 9, the details were able to be retrieved by using Nirsoft IE PassView v1.26.

SkyDrive web site URLs (skydrive.live.com or login.live.com) were located in a range of areas, such as Cookie files, web history, FavIcons, in the FileSlack of other files, unallocated space, and Pagefile.sys. This occurred for all browsers. The previously mentioned term "enabledogfood" found in the SkyDrive client software was not located in the extracted Internet history.

Filenames for files downloaded were located in the web history for all browsers (except for the Base-VMs). Data was located in browser history files, such as index.dat files and downloads.sqlite. When using the Google Chrome browser to access SkyDrive, references were located in a range of browser system files, such as Top Sites, History, Shortcuts, Preferences, History Provider Cache, FavIcons, Current Tabs, and Current Sessions. When using the SkyDrive client software, references to the Enron sample data filenames and file paths was located in the Internet Explorer History even when other browsers were used, such as Mozilla Firefox, Google Chrome, and Apple Safari.

Using CCleaner with standard options did not remove the references previously located in relation to SkyDrive use. Using all options on CCleaner removed all references in the Internet Explorer VMs, but information remained in the other browsers, Firefox, Chrome, and Safari to identify SkyDrive usage, which included filenames and times and dates of access. Interestingly, this included filename and path history stored in Internet Explorer index.dat, but not web browsing history.

IEF 5.5 introduced the ability to report information relating to cloud storage, including SkyDrive. Using this option, data was located in the Upload-VM files. This data included filenames and folder names, the owner name, and the owner ID number. Information was also located in the Internet Explorer and Safari Access-VMs. It appears information is read from the "AppData\local\Microsoft \SkyDrive\setting\[OwnerID].dat" file. Information was recovered from the Internet Explorer Access, Download, Eraser, and CCleaner-VMs, and also from the Safari Access-VM. Information was also recovered from Unallocated space, Pagefile.sys, and fileslack. No additional information was located in the Google Chrome or Firefox VMs (apart from when the client software was used, as previously mentioned). Running IEF 5.52 over the captured RAM files resulted in files and folder names relating to SkyDrive when the client software was used for all browsers (Upload-VMs), and the Internet Explorer Access-VM and Download-VMs highlight the potential information available from RAM captures. No information was reported when IEF was run over the Wireshark network PCAP capture files.

Metadata

Using X-Ways 16.5, it is possible to extract metadata from files, such as the EXIF data from jpg files or information from documents. This can then be used to conduct analysis. It was possible to determine the picture files which related to the Enron test data by searching on the metadata contents. It was also possible to locate the rtf document files based on the author information stored within the file.

Network analysis

Analysis of the network traffic capture files was undertaken using Network Miner v1.0, Wireshark Portable 1.6.5, and X-Ways 16.5. The network traffic uses Port 80 (HTTP) and 443 (HTTPS) only. When accessing SkyDrive accounts using the client software or a browser, it appears that login sessions are first established with Microsoft Live using IP numbers registered to Microsoft, such as in the range 64.4.0.0–64.4.63.255 and 65.52.0.0–65.55.255.255 (login.live.com, skydrive.live.com). When accessing files or data in an account, IPs in the range 70.37.0.0–70.37.181.255 were observed. See Table 3.12 for a list of IP number ranges observed in the captured network traffic and the registered owner for the range. Security certificates appeared to be approved using VeriSign/Thawte services, in the 199.7.48.0–199.7.63.255 range. The URL ocsp.verisign.net was

Table 3.12 IP Addresses Observed in Network Traffic

Registered Owner	IP Start	IP Finish	URLs Observed in Network Traffic
MS Hotmail	64.4.0.0	64.4.63.255	skydrive.live.com msnmessenger
Microsoft	65.52.0.0	65.55.255.255	www.skydrive.com, login .live.com skydrivesync.policies.live .net
Microsoft global online services	70.37.0.0	70.37.191.255	s1-word-view, S1-word-edit S1-excel.vo, S1-powerpoint.vo S1-onenote.vo
Microsoft Singapore	111.221.16.0	111.221.31.255	word-view.officeapps.live .com
Microsoft	131.253.12.0	131.253.18.255	us.c01.cb3.glbdns. microsoft.com
Microsoft-global-net	207.46.0.0	207.46.255.255	sn2.storage.msn.com
Microsoft internet data center	213.199.160.0	213.199.191.255	ncsi.glbdns.microsoft .com
Akamai Technologies	118.214.0.0	118.215.255.255	e2044.c.akamaiedge.net
Akamai Technologies	122.252.32.0	122.252.63.255	secure.shared.live.com .edgekey.net
Akamai Technologies	173.222.0.0	173.223.255.255	e4344.g.akamaiedge.net
Verisign Global Registry	199.7.48.0	199.7.63.255	ocsp.verisign.net

also observed in the network traffic; OCSP is the Online Certificate Status Protocol used by VeriSign/Thawte.

When the SkyDrive Windows client software was downloaded, the URL name made reference to Microsoft Disservice, and the following path was observed in the network traffic: `/~live.SkyDrive.UpdateBinary/~16.4.2/~/~/~/ship/ skydrivesetup.exe`. The same URL names were observed when using either the SkyDrive client software or accessing via a browser. Previous analysis of Dropbox network traffic determined that Dropbox uses different URLs when using a browser compared to when using the client software.

Network Miner 1.0 was used to rebuild files from the captured packets. These included SkyDrive certificate files, such as "`skydrive.live.com.cer`." The contents of the Enron sample data files were not seen in the network traffic, suggesting the data was encrypted. Analysis of the files downloaded from SkyDrive revealed the download was contained in an uncompressed ZIP, so if this was not encrypted it would be possible to recover the contents of files from the network traffic. Of note was the presence of the filenames and some information in cleartext (not encrypted) for the Enron files. Information extracted from the Firefox Upload-VM is included in Table 3.13. The filename (enron3111.docx) and SkyDrive OwnerID are highlighted. The details of the file are easily discerned from the text, including the file size, created and modified times (in UTC), and the parent resource (folder) information is also listed. These highlight that relevant information may be present in network traffic, even if the traffic is expected to be encrypted and unreadable, and should be a major consideration when determining whether to capture this information if possible.

No username or password information was observed in the cleartext network traffic. The term "skydrive" was observed in all network traffic, including the control Base-VMs. However, the web site URLs "www.skydrive.com" and "https://skydrive.live.com" were not observed in the Base-VM network traffic. The web site URLs were observed in all Access-VMs and Download-VMs, and also in the Google Chrome Upload-VM and Eraser-VM network traffic. SkyDrive icon pictures were recovered from Upload-VMs, associated with the setup.exe files.

System Volume Information

When either Eraser or CCleaner was used, information was still located in various System Volume Information files (also known as Restore Points or Volume Shadow Copies). The information included the username for the SkyDrive account, the URLs for the SkyDrive web sites (https://skydrive.live.com or www.skydrive.com), the filenames and full text of the Enron files located, and the SkyDrive OwnerID. When limited information was located in during analysis, such as filenames only, the System Volume Information files contained a wider range of information, such as file contents or deleted URLs. System Volume Information was highlighted as an important source of information when anti-forensic methods had been used; in this research, Eraser and CCleaner.

Memory (RAM) analysis

Analysis of the memory captures (VMEM files) was undertaken using X-Ways 16.5, Encase 6.19.4, and AccessData FTK 4.01. The term "skydrive" was located in all the memory captures, including the control Base-VM memory files. However, the URL's ("www.skydrive.com" and "https://skydrive.live.com") were not located in the control Base-VM memory files, but were located in all other memory capture files. The SkyDrive account username was located in all Upload-VMs, and in the Firefox, Google Chrome, and Internet Explorer Access and Download-VMs. The SkyDrive username was located in memory capture files near the text; "skydrive" or "live.com" in the format of; "&login=[username] &passwd=[password]'." The text "&login" and "&passwd" can be used to search and locate potential usernames for SkyDrive accounts (also Hotmail and

Table 3.13 Unencrypted Data Observed in Network Traffic

```
<DataSize>4523350</DataSize>
<PreAuthURL>http://goq98w.sn2.livefilestore.com/y1pw2VKKDHtrZiyuS7ZvapeK2AyYN3fm0GacPjiYau9shgm5pZCJqbdvrgf9g4Fz7aqHXZn
78DSeA_mq66md4GY6AjLCmK6rP_N</PreAuthURL>
    <PreAuthURLPartner>http://internal.sn2.pvt-livefilestore.com/y1pw2VKKDHtrZiyuS7ZvapeK2AyYN3fm0GacPjiYau9shgm5pZC
Jqbdvrgf9g4Fz7aqHXZn78DSeA_mq66md4GY6AjLCmK6rP_N</PreAuthURLPartner>
        <SHA1Hash>M + 82OolIrVWYrjPOlj9KCMN6LBsk = </SHA1Hash>
        <StreamDataStatus>None</StreamDataStatus>
        <Genie>False</Genie>
        <StreamVersion>1</StreamVersion>
        <DocumentStreamType>Binary</DocumentStreamType>
    </DocumentStream>
    <DocumentStreams>
    <FileAttributes>0</FileAttributes>
    </Document>
    <Document>
        <ItemType>Document</ItemType>
        <ResourceID>FDXXXXX89F707D0!109</ResourceID>
        <Size>14072</Size>
        <ETag>FDXXXXX89F707D0!109.0</ETag>
        <DateCreated>2012-05-27T07:43:57.41Z</DateCreated>
        <DateModified>2012-05-27T07:43:57.41Z</DateModified>
        <DateCreatedOnClient>2012-05-27T07:41:40Z</DateCreatedOnClient>
        <DateModifiedOnClient>2012-02-09T05:54:16Z</DateModifiedOnClient>
        <RelationshipName>Enron3111.docx</RelationshipName>
        <ParentResourceID>FDXXXXX89F707D0!106</ParentResourceID>
        <skydrivesync.xschema.wlx.live.com>
        <CreationTime>2012-05-27T07:41:40Z</CreationTime>
        <LastModifiedTime>2012-02-09T05:54:16Z</LastModifiedTime>
```

Windows Live accounts). The password was also located in freetext in the Upload-VM memory files for Firefox, Internet Explorer, and Safari browsers.

The username was also located in the Eraser-VM memory captures, in the Firefox and Google Chrome CCleaner-VM memory captures, and also in the Google Chrome memory capture file when CCleaner was used with all options. However, when the Safari browser was used, the username was only recovered in the Upload-VM memory capture, near the text; "&login." Also located in the memory files was the SkyDrive Owner ID, near the text "?cid=" or "?id=," such as https://skydrive.live.com/?cid=FD79E4BB87F9XXXX&id=FD79E4BB87F9XXXX.

The full text of the Enron data files was recovered in the Upload-VM, Access-VM, and Download-VM memory captures. In addition, the text was located in the Google Chrome and Internet Explorer Erase-VM memory files. No text was located in the control Base-VM memory files. Observed within memory captures were Enron filename references in all VM memory files, except the control Base-VM memory files. The previously mentioned term, "enabledogfood" was located in the Upload-VM memory files, associated with the web site "http://g.live .com/8SESkyDrive/EnableDogFood."

Data carving was undertaken across the memory capture files and resulted in the recovery of thumbnail pictures, partial and full picture files of the Enron sample pictures, and SkyDrive logos from the memory captures for all VM memory files except the Base-VM memory files.

Analysis of Pagefile.sys files was also undertaken. The username was only located in the Safari Access-VM pagefile.sys file. The web site URLs (www. skydrive.com and https://skydrive.live.com) were located in the Google Chrome, Internet Explorer, and Safari browser pagefile.sys files, but not in the Firefox browser pagefile.sys. The filenames for the Enron test files were located in browser Upload, Access, and Download-VM pagefile.sys files when Firefox, Chrome, and Internet Explorer were used, but not when Safari was used to download files. Filenames were also located after Eraser and CCleaner were used, again highlighting pagefile.sys as an area for examination if anti-forensic methods are suspected of being used.

The full text of the Enron email was found in the pagefile.sys file when Firefox and Google Chrome browsers were used, but not when Internet Explorer or Safari were used. The SkyDrive OwnerID was located when Firefox, Internet Explorer, and Safari were used, but not when Google Chrome was used.

Eraser, CCleaner, and DBAN

As discussed, many remnants indicating the use of SkyDrive and the presence of the Enron sample files were located after Eraser and CCleaner were used. This indicated that Eraser or CCleaner did not necessarily remove all data remnants in relation to the use of SkyDrive or completely remove the information relating to the previous presence of the Enron sample files. The use of a full erasing tool, in this case DBAN, was found to remove all traces, but this also erased the operating system and user files. The operating system and user files would need to be reinstalled, which could be a lengthy process and may dissuade the average user from undertaking this process to remove evidence of SkyDrive usage.

Presentation

Analysis findings

In our case study, a variety of data remnants were located when a user used SkyDrive to store or access data. The focus (or scope) was to determine what data remnants were left to identify if SkyDrive had been used on a Windows 7 PC. Conducting a search for the term "skydrive" was shown to be inconclusive to demonstrate use, as it was shown that the term is present even when SkyDrive has not been accessed, as outlined in the analysis of the control Base-VMs. The SkyDrive username was able to be discerned from a variety of locations, such as cookie files, memory captures (searching for "&login="), in pagefile.sys, from SQLite database files, and IEF output.

Surprisingly, the **password** for the SkyDrive account was able to be located **unencrypted** in the memory captures from the Upload-VMs. Passwords are commonly used in a variety of locations, and when conducting analysis to determine a password to view encrypted files, one practice is to build an index of data to use with password analysis tools such as AccessData Password Recovery Toolkit, Passware, or Elcomsoft password analysis tools. With the actual password in cleartext, this would vastly speed up the process of password discovery. Hence, memory capture and analysis should be a key consideration when determining the possible sources of data in step 3 of the framework (evidence source identification and preservation—see Figure 2.1) for indexing purposes. However, if the password is not located in memory or if memory capture is not possible, it is still possible to access a SkyDrive account using the forensic image of a hard drive where the SkyDrive client software has been used to access an account. This can be achieved by running the hard drive forensic image as a VM. When the VM starts up, it will automatically synchronize with the SkyDrive cloud service and update files in the local SkyDrive folder. Appropriate legal authority would be required to ensure that the account and information can be accessed and used for analysis.

Analysis to determine the method of access, whether the client software was used, a browser used to upload, access, or download, or a combination of both, is possible. When the client software was downloaded, there was a SkyDriveSetup. exe file downloaded to the local hard drive. Hash values for the client software can be calculated and searched across forensic image files, memory, and network captures. In addition, registry entries may indicate the use of the setup software or the client software, as will link files. Prefetch files were observed for the client software and also include the number of times run and associated dates and times. The file "CollectLogFiles.bat" appears to have a consistent hash value across SkyDrive client software releases and the hash value for this file can be used to conduct searches. Also, searching for the term "enabledogfood" may determine if the client software has been installed on a PC. A folder was observed with the client software version as the folder name in the AppData\local\ folder.

When a browser was used to access SkyDrive, there were many references in the output from IEF, but when access was undertaken with no downloading there were no references to the filenames in the IEF output. When bulk files were downloaded using the web account from the root folder, an uncompressed ZIP file was observed with the name "skydrive" and the date.

Filenames, dates, and times were observed in the "SyncDiagnostics.log" file and the ".dat" file with the OwnerID as the filename. Filenames were also observed in the Registry "RecentDocs" keys, $MFT entries, and Prefetch files such as DLLHost.pf, Wordpad.pf, and Notepad.pf. Link files and the IEF output also listed the filenames. The contents of the files were also recovered from temporary Internet files, thumbcache, memory captures, pagefile.sys, system volume restore points, and unallocated space. Eraser and CCleaner were not effective in removing all data remnants, and information was able to be determined from these VMs relating to the SkyDrive accounts, filenames, dates and times, and file contents (Table 3.14).

Complete

In summary, it has been demonstrated that it is possible to determine the username, password, method of access, filenames, contents, and dates and times of access when SkyDrive is used to store, access, or download data from cloud storage. Memory captures and network files were an important source of information, especially locating the username and password in memory files when the client software was set up and used.

Once forensic analysis has determined, a SkyDrive account has potential evidence of relevance to an investigation, and the practitioner can communicate this to relevant persons to enable them to respond to secure evidence in a timely manner. Knowledge of the username and OwnerID details would enable identification of SkyDrive accounts, to preserve and secure potential evidence. It was observed that SkyDrive retains a record of computers that are used to access and synchronize with an account. This information would be beneficial to determine whether a particular computer was synchronized to a SkyDrive account, and also may identify other computers with data of evidential value or other avenues for investigation.

In addition, a (spreadsheet) timeline of events can be created using the identified data and information from the various sources, which can assist to explain the course of events. Merging the information from the hard drive, network captures, memory, and the SkyDrive account into one timeline may also be of assistance during the analysis process to gain an understanding of the sequence of events. This will be demonstrated in the Case Study section.

Table 3.14 Summary of Analysis Findings

Control (Base-VM)	Data Artifacts Found
Username, Password, Software, URL, Enron Sample filenames or files	Nil
KWS terms	Nil
	Nil
	Matches to "*skydrive*" relating to icon files (Internet Explorer Base-VM)
Client Software (Upload-VM)	**Data Artifacts Found**
Username	Cookie files "*cloud@login.live*", *$MFT*, and *$LogFile. Memory capture* files "*&login=*"
OwnerID	OwnerID found in SkyDrive software installation *.dat* and *.ini* files
Password	Located in RAM—search for *&login=* and *&passwd=*
Software	*SkyDriveSetup.exe* file located when downloaded.
	SkyDrive Software installation under *User \AppData\Local\Microsoft*
	SyncDiagnostics.log file includes OwnerID and file information, dates and times
URL	When software downloaded, URLs included https://skydrive.live.com and http://www.skydrive.com
Enron sample filenames	Multiple locations, including *Prefetch, Link files, $MFT, Registry*. Filenames in *Network PCAP* files.
Enron sample files	Located in Sync folder under *User\SkyDrive*.
KWS terms	"*EnableDogFood*" found in SkyDrive client software files
Browser Access (Access-VM)	**Data Artifacts Found**
Username	FF and GC History; "*formhistory.sqlite*" and "*Web Data.*" *Memory capture* files "*&login=*"
OwnerID	Observed in URL https://skydrive.live.com/? cid=XXXXXXXXXXXXXXX# (FF and GC) + RAM
Password	Nil
Software	Nil
URL	Multiple locations; *cookie, history, icons, pagefile. sys, and unallocated*
Enron sample filenames	Sufficient to identify files accessed with references to the filenames in *Registry* and *Browsing History*
Enron sample files	Full text in *RAM* and *System Volume Information*
KWS terms	Multiple matches to KWS terms

(Continued)

Table 3.14 (Continued)

Browser Download (Download-VM)	Data Artifacts Found
Username	FF and GC History; *"formhistory.sqlite"* and *"Web Data."* Memory capture files *"&login="*
OwnerID	Observed in URL https://skydrive.live.com/? cid=XXXXXXXXXXXXXXXX# (FF and GC) + RAM
Password	Nil
Software	Nil
URL	Multiple locations; *cookie, history, icons, pagefile. sys, and unallocated*
Enron sample filenames	Sufficient to identify files accessed with references in *$MFT, Link, Registry,* and *Prefetch* files
Enron sample files	Via uncompressed zip; *"skydrive-YYYY-MM-DD. zip"* or folder name *"Documents.zip"*
KWS terms	Full text in *RAM* and *System Volume Information*
Eraser (Eraser-VM)	**Data Artifacts Found**
Username	FF and GC History; *"formhistory.sqlite"* and *"Web Data"* Memory capture files *"&login="*
OwnerID	Observed in URL https://skydrive.live.com/? cid = XXXXXXXXXXXXXXXX# (FF and GC) + RAM
Password	Nil
Software	Nil
URL	Multiple locations; *cookie, history, icons, pagefile. sys, and unallocated*
Enron sample filenames	Sufficient to identify files accessed with references to the filenames in *$MFT, Link,* and *Prefetch* files
Enron sample files	Full text in *RAM* and *System Volume Information*
KWS terms	Multiple matches to KWS terms
CCleaner (CCleaner-VM)	**Data Artifacts Found**
Username	FF and GC History; *"formhistory.sqlite"* and *"Web Data"* Memory capture files *"&login="*
OwnerID	Observed in URL https://skydrive.live.com/? cid = XXXXXXXXXXXXXXXX# (FF and GC) + RAM
Password	Nil
Software	Nil
URL	Multiple locations; *cookie, history, icons, pagefile. sys, and unallocated*
Enron sample filenames	Sufficient to identify files accessed with references to the filenames in *$MFT, Link,* and *Prefetch* files
Enron sample files	Full text in *RAM* and *System Volume Information*

(Continued)

Table 3.14 (Continued)	
KWS terms	Multiple matches to KWS terms
DBAN (DBAN-VM)	**Data Artifacts Found**
Username	
Password	
Software	
URL	All data erased, no information located
Enron sample filenames	
Enron sample files	
KWS terms	

SkyDrive forensics: Apple iPhone 3G

Traditional forensic analysis is undertaken on computer hard drives and common storage, such as USB devices and optical media. There is a growing shift toward the greater use of mobile devices which increasingly use cloud storage, as internal storage on each device can be limited. A report from Gartner, for example, highlights the trend in client computing is shifting from a focus on PCs to include portable devices and also predicts that personal cloud storage will replace the PC as the main method of users' storage by 2014 (Kleynhans, 2012). This presents challenges to forensic practitioners and methodologies for a number of reasons, such as the technical differences between the devices and the increase in the use of cloud storage. The variety and difference between operating systems and file systems among portable devices present technical difficulties for practitioners (Taylor, Haggerty, Gresty, & Lamb, 2011).

Since its launch in 2007, Apple has sold over 42 million iPhones, making it one of the most successful mobile phone products (Laugesen & Yuan, 2010). The Apple iPhone can be used to access SkyDrive cloud storage either using the built-in Safari browser or installing the Microsoft SkyDrive application (App). Analysis of portable devices is a growing area for forensic practitioners, and there are both hardware and software solutions to assist this process, such as MicroSystemation .XRY, Cellebrite UFED, and Radio Tactics Aceso. Although current mobile phone forensic tools, such as Microsystemation XRY and Oxygen Forensics, are able to extract increasing amounts of data from smartphones, evidence in relation to cloud storage may not be able to be extracted (Zhu, 2011). In the scope of this research, it is relevant to consider what information can be determined from a portable device in relation to the use of SkyDrive. This also serves to further assess the suitability of the framework being applied in a variety of circumstances.

SkyDrive accounts could be used and accessed for criminal purposes for a range of reasons, such as to host illicit data. Files in SkyDrive accounts can be shared with other users, and links to the shared files could be disseminated via email or SMS messages, or a user could send another user the account name and password, granting them access to an account. There is a need to determine what remnants are left after a user has accessed a SkyDrive account via the browser or via the application, separate from other remnants in email or SMS stored areas.

Commence (Scope)

The scope of this part of the research is to examine the data remnants on an iPhone 3G running iOS 4.2.1 when used accessing SkyDrive via a browser and when using the SkyDrive iOS application (app). Analysis also needs to determine if there are any remnants prior to accessing SkyDrive on a standard device.

Preparation

An iPhone 3G was selected which had not been used to access SkyDrive previously. The device usage was known to the authors, and MicroSystemation .XRY 6.2.1 was used to extract a logical image of the contents, excluding audio and video files, prior to accessing SkyDrive or installing the SkyDrive application. This first extract was analyzed to confirm there was no SkyDrive related data on the device prior to undertaking the research. The inbuilt Apple Safari iOS browser was used to access the SkyDrive user account created for this research and view the Enron files stored remotely. A logical extract was then conducted using .XRY. The Microsoft SkyDrive iOS app was then downloaded and installed to the iPhone 3G. The research account was then accessed using the Application, and the files stored in the SkyDrive account were viewed. A third logical extract with.XRY was then conducted.

Evidence source identification and preservation

In the context of this research, files were identified which would contain the information needed to conduct the analysis, in this instance being the .XRY extract files and the output of the .XRY software, including PDF reports and the files exported using .XRY. These were identified for each of the extracts: Base, Browser, and Application.

Collection

To observe the principles of digital forensic analysis (ACPO, 2006; NIJ, 2008), a forensic copy was made of the .XRY extract files, the file output, and the reports. As these were logical files, this was done in the Encase Logical format (L01) and the X-Ways Evidence File Container format (ctr). MD5 hash values were used to ensure the forensic integrity of the data.

Examination and analysis

For this research, each of the forensic logical files was examined using forensic tools, including X-Ways Forensic 16.5 and EnCase 6.19.4. PList Explorer v1.0 was used to examine the contents of the Apple plist files extracted by .XRY.

Control—Base-XRY

Analysis of the control Base-XRY extract confirmed there was no data originally present relating to the Enron sample test data or the SkyDrive app. In addition, no references were located for the term "skydrive" or the web site URLs (skydrive .live or skydrive.com).

SkyDrive accessed via the iOS Safari browser

The username was not located in the Browser-XRY extracts; however, the Client ID number was located in a URL for skydrive.live.com (`https://skydrive .live.com`) in the `History.plist` file. This information was also extracted by XRY in the `Web-History.txt` file (output listed in Table 3.15). PList Explorer 1.0 was also used to view the data in the plist files to verify the information in the XRY report. The SkyDrive OwnerID was also located in `Cookies.binarycookies` file.

Filenames for the Enron test files were located in the `History.plist`, for the txt, rtf, and docx files. This information was also extracted by XRY in the `Web-History.txt` file. A full picture file was located in `/private/var/mobile/Media/ DCIM/102APPLE/` within the XRY extract (Table 3.16).

SkyDrive application used to access the research account

Analysis of the third XRY extract was able to determine the username used to access SkyDrive account. This was located in the "`keychain-backup.plist`" near the text: `useridentity`, `windows live`, and "`.com.microsoft.skydrive`." This information appears to be parsed by XRY in the file "`Device-Accounts.txt`." However, the information is listed by .XRY as a Windows Live ID without mention of SkyDrive for the entry. To determine if the application is present, information in the "`com.apple.AppStore.plist`" file lists "`http://itunes.apple.com/ au/app/skydrive`." Information is also stored in the "`IconState.plist`" file as "`com.microsoft.skydrive`." The text from the Enron files was not located in any of the extracts. No password was located in any of the extracts or files.

Presentation
Analysis findings

In this research, several data remnants were located when searching for evidence of SkyDrive use on the test item (iPhone 3G). Recall that the aim was to determine what data remnants were left to identify if SkyDrive was accessed, and

Table 3.15 Output from .XRY Web-History.txt file

Web-History #	6
Application:	Safari (Apple)
Web Address:	**https://skydrive.live.com/browse.aspx/Dataset?cid=FDXXXXXX89F707D0**
Page Title:	Dataset - SkyDrive
Access Count:	1
Accessed:	4/07/2012 3:24:05 AM UTC (Device)

Table 3.16 Output from.XRY Web-History.txt File

Web-History #	5
Application:	Safari (Apple)
Web Address:	https://goq98w.sn2.livefilestore.com/y1pnjQfg9cr138aplsHGoP8vBe4CqfSfUO-2INcwF2eGQ8ovO09LCPWbDffF5CeeHl4aGyyhoaxPRmYGl0QXTMlzPVowvoGrVG0/ **Enron3111.rtf**?download&psid=1
Access Count:	1
Accessed:	4/07/2012 3:25:25 AM UTC (Device)

whether this was via the browser or an installed application. Initial analysis of the control extract identified no matches to the term "skydrive," but matches in the subsequent extracts indicating that conducting a keyword search for the word "skydrive" could indicate if skydrive has been used.

When the browser was used to access the SkyDrive account, entries were left in the History.plist file, which is also listed in the .XRY Web-History.txt file. The SkyDrive OwnerID was listed in the Cookies.binarycookies file, but the username was not located in the extract. The filenames accessed were listed in the History.plist file and in the .XRY Web-History.txt file. A full picture file was located in within the.XRY extract.

When the SkyDrive application was installed and used to access the SkyDrive research account, the username was able to be determined from the keychain-backup.plist file and in the XRY "Device-Accounts.txt" file. Information in the "com.apple.AppStore.plist" file lists "http://itunes.apple.com/au/app/skydrive," and in the "IconState.plist" file was "com.microsoft.skydrive." However, the text from the Enron files was not located in any of the extracts, nor was it possible to locate the password for the SkyDrive account.

In typical use scenarios, there could potentially be additional data available on a device, such as emails or SMS messages relating to the creation of a SkyDrive account, or messages from a user to another user disseminating links to a SkyDrive account and shared files.

Complete

This research was limited by not being able to jailbreak the iPhone. Microsystemation XRY and other iPhone extract solutions require an iPhone to be jailbroken to undertake a physical extract. A future research opportunity is to undertake a physical extract of an iPhone and compare this to a logical extract to determine what information is available in comparison with the logical extract. Also there may be more comprehensive results possible when compared to other iPhone forensic tools, which we were unable to undertake due to licensing restrictions. In addition, there are opportunities for further experiments to be conducted using an iOS 5 or 6 device, and other mobile phone operating systems and devices, such as Google Android devices and the various versions currently in operation, and Microsoft Windows phone operating systems.

Case study

To illustrate the relevance of the research, the following case study outlines where the information previously identified can assist in an investigation and also follows the cloud (storage) forensic framework (Figure 2.1). The circumstances relate to a hypothetical case of an employee suspected of copying intellectual property from Acme Corp (a fictional organization), the type of situation a business could experience. The circumstances of the case study are greatly simplified for the purposes of this chapter:

> IT Security in Acme Corp observed unapproved IP addresses, including 70.37.10.100 and 70.37.179.232, in network logs originating from the Marketing Department. A "whois" lookup determined these IP addresses to be associated with Microsoft Global Online Services and are suspected of being associated with cloud storage. This network traffic was flagged as unusual, as the Marketing Department do not have a need to use online cloud services, nor are they permitted to in the user agreement. Discreet enquiries were made with the manager of the marketing department, who confirmed that no-one had asked for permission to use cloud storage. It was determined that an investigation was necessary to confirm whether company data had been released without authority.

Step 1—Commence (Scope)

Authority and approval to undertake an investigation was received from the chief information officer (CIO), with the scope and limitation being to determine and identify any unauthorized use of cloud storage within the marketing department and any workstation/s and person/s involved.

Step 2—Preparation

The IT Security section manager gathered the forensic response kit, which contained software and hardware including a laptop with forensic software, network cables, hardware write blockers, and other associated equipment. The manager had undertaken forensic training and had the knowledge to undertake first response identification and preservation.

Step 3—Evidence source identification and preservation

Analysis of the network log files identified the computer associated with the IP addresses identified. Encase® Enterprise had been previously deployed throughout the organization as a security measure and was used to conduct analysis of the computer in the marketing department. Conducting a keyword search across the computer identified SkyDrive URL references ("www.skydrive.com" and "https:// skydrive.live.com") in Pagefile.sys.

Memory and network traffic for the identified computer was forensically copied using Encase and Wireshark. This data is the most volatile and should be preserved as soon as reasonably possible (ACPO, 2006; NIJ, 2008). IT Security liaised with the senior HR manager to attend the marketing department to identify who was using the computer. The workstation was located and was unattended. The power plug was disconnected from the back of the PC (ACPO, 2006; NIJ, 2008; SAI, 2003), with the understanding that in this case the volatile data had already been preserved, and no encryption was in use. The PC was immediately sealed in an exhibit bag and signed by IT security with HR witnessing this.

Step 4—Collection

A forensic expert was contracted to undertake analysis to determine if any breaches of the company policy had occurred. The forensic expert reviewed the process undertaken thus far to ensure the process was legally and forensically sound. The expert then commenced exhibit logs and chain of custody sheets to document the process. A forensic copy of the PC hard drive was then made using a Tableau T35es-R2 eSATA Forensic Bridge (hardware write blocking) and verified with MD5 and SHA1 hashes. Appropriate entries were made in the exhibit log relating to access to the PC and hard drive by the expert. Forensic copies were also made of the memory capture and network traffic in Encase Logical format (L01) and verified with hash values.

Step 5—Examination and analysis

Analysis was then undertaken on the forensic copies of the data. A username and password were located in the memory capture, after searching for the terms "&login=" and the term "&passwd=." SkyDrive client software was also located under "`C:\Users\SmithT\AppData\Local\Microsoft\SkyDrive\`." Filenames of files associated with the SkyDrive account were located in link files and prefetch files such as `dllhost.pf`. The contents of the files were able to be discerned from data carving of unallocated space, and the metadata within the files further identified the computer and user account used to create the documents and pictures. Dates and times were able to be discerned from the SkyDrive `syncdiagnostics.log` file and the `$MFT` to indicate when the SkyDrive software had been installed, and when the files had been created and accessed.

A company-issued iPhone was located on the desk near the workstation and placed in a faraday bag[6] to prevent network interaction. It was conveyed to the forensic expert who undertook a logical extract using Microsystemation .XRY. A physical extract was considered, but this requires the phone to be jailbroken, which is in breach of company policy and hence was not undertaken. Analysis of the logical extract locates the SkyDrive application and the username in the `keychain-backup.plist` file and in the .XRY "`Device-Accounts.txt`" file. A picture file was located in `/private/var/mobile/Media/DCIM/ 102APPLE/` within the .XRY extract. This picture was a jpg file which appeared to be a screenshot of a confidential company document.

The employee was interviewed by HR and when shown the information located so far agreed to cooperate. The employee allowed the forensic expert to access the SkyDrive account, providing the password and written permission to access the account for the purposes of the investigation. The expert created a VM and recorded the VMWare Player window as a video file. The expert logged in to the SkyDrive account and examined the account information. The computers linked to the account were listed on the browser screen and included the company computer as being linked to the account. This however did not rule out other persons accessing the account in addition to the linked computers.

Step 6—Presentation

A report was prepared for the HR director and the CIO outlining the process and the findings of the analysis. A meeting was held with the forensic expert where the findings were outlined in a manner that both the CIO and the HR director were able to understand. A timeline of the data from the various sources was used to demonstrate interaction with the files from the tower PC and the iPhone (Figure 3.2). In the timeline, it is possible to see when the documents were initially created via the metadata, when the documents were copied to the work PC, link files related to the documents are created, SkyDrive is accessed,

---

[6]"A 'Faraday bag' is intended to shield a mobile phone or similar small device to prevent unwanted applications being invoked remotely, such as wiping the memory or to prevent possible problems with veracity of evidence" (Duffy, 2010).

Source	Key Date	Event type	Comment
IEF RAM	14/06/2011 14:22:00	Last Modified	enron_with_categories.tar.gz
IEF RAM	9/02/2012 15:23:00	Last Modified	Enron3111.jpg
IEF RAM	9/02/2012 15:24:00	Last Modified	Enron3111.docx
X-Ways Docx Metadata	9/02/2012 15:24:00	Doc created metada	Enron3111.docx
IEF RAM	25/02/2012 11:02:00	Last Modified	Enron3111.rtf
X-Ways Docx Metadata	25/02/2012 12:02	Doc created metada	Enron3111.rtf
Event Log Explorer	9/06/2012 12:27:09	Logon	cloud' user
IEF Firefox	9/06/2012 12:34:00	Date Visited	http://www.mozilla.com/en-US/firefox/13.0/firstrun/
IEF Firefox	9/06/2012 12:34:00	Date Visited	http://www.mozilla.org/en-US/firefox/13.0/firstrun/
Encase file list	9/06/2012 12:41:49	Created	3111.txt
Encase file list	9/06/2012 12:41:49	Created	enron_with_categories.tar.gz
Encase file list	9/06/2012 12:41:49	Created	Enron3111.docx
Encase file list	9/06/2012 12:41:49	Created	Enron3111.jpg
Encase file list	9/06/2012 12:41:49	Created	Enron3111.rtf
X-Ways Link Data	9/06/2012 12:41:49	Target Created	3111.lnk
X-Ways Link Data	9/06/2012 12:41:49	Target Created	Enron3111.lnk
Encase file list	9/06/2012 12:41:55	Created	3111.lnk
Encase file list	9/06/2012 12:42:03	Created	NOTEPAD.EXE-EB1B961A.pf
Encase file list	9/06/2012 12:42:08	Created	Enron3111.lnk
IEF Firefox	9/06/2012 12:45:00	Date Visited	http://www.google.com/search?q=skydrive%20preview%20for%20windo
IEF Firefox	9/06/2012 12:45:00	Date Visited	http://www.google.com.au/search?q=skydrive%20preview%20for%20wi
IEF Firefox	9/06/2012 12:45:00	Date Visited	https://apps.live.com/skydrive/app/9a65e47d-606a-4816-a246-90f54bf7a
IEF Firefox	9/06/2012 12:45:00	Date Visited	https://apps.live.com/skydrive/go/9a65e47d-606a-4816-a246-90f54bf7a3
IEF Firefox	9/06/2012 12:45:00	Date Visited	http://g.live.com/8SESkydrive/WinDownload
Encase Internet	9/06/2012 12:46:00	Start Date	SkyDriveSetup.exe
IEF Firefox	9/06/2012 12:46:00	Date Visited	https://g.live.com/1rewlive5skydrive/skydrivesetup
IEF Firefox	9/06/2012 12:46:00	Date Visited	http://wl.dlservice.microsoft.com/download/C/9/1/C910D7E6-EB8E-45F3
Encase file list	9/06/2012 12:46:20	Created	CollectSkyDriveLogs.bat
Encase file list	9/06/2012 12:46:26	Created	SKYDRIVESETUP.EXE-FCECAE9C.pf
Encase file list	9/06/2012 12:46:34	Created	Microsoft SkyDrive.lnk
Encase file list	9/06/2012 12:46:34	Created	SkyDrive
Encase file list	9/06/2012 12:46:34	Created	SkyDrive.exe
Encase file list	9/06/2012 12:46:34	Created	SkyDrive.lnk
Encase file list	9/06/2012 12:46:34	Created	SKYDRIVECONFIG.EXE-1F11320F.pf
Encase file list	9/06/2012 12:46:34	Created	SkyDriveSetup.exe
X-Ways Link Data	9/06/2012 12:46:34	Target Created	Microsoft SkyDrive.lnk
X-Ways Link Data	9/06/2012 12:46:34	Target Created	SkyDrive.lnk
X-Ways Prefetch Data	9/06/2012 12:46:34	Prefetch last run	SKYDRIVE.EXE-76AB3CF5.pf
Encase file list	9/06/2012 12:46:44	Created	SKYDRIVE.EXE-76AB3CF5.pf
Encase file list	9/06/2012 12:47:01	Created	cloud@login.live[1].txt
Encase file list	9/06/2012 12:47:55	Created	fd79e4bb87f909d0.dat
Encase file list	9/06/2012 12:47:55	Created	fd79e4bb87f909d0.ini
Encase file list	9/06/2012 12:48:34	Created	SyncDiagnostics.log
Encase file list	9/06/2012 12:50:16	Accessed	3111.lnk
X-Ways Prefetch Data	9/06/2012 12:50:16	Prefetch last run	NOTEPAD.EXE-EB1B961A.pf
Encase file list	9/06/2012 12:50:25	Accessed	Enron3111.lnk
Encase file list	9/06/2012 12:50:28	Created	Enron3111 (2).lnk
Encase file list	9/06/2012 12:50:35	Created	WORDPAD.EXE-1BCC3DB7.pf
Encase file list	9/06/2012 12:50:36	Created	Enron3111 (3).lnk
X-Ways Prefetch Data	9/06/2012 12:50:36	Prefetch last run	WORDPAD.EXE-1BCC3DB7.pf
Encase file list	9/06/2012 12:51:30	Accessed	SkyDrive
iPhone XRY extract	4/07/2012 12:54:05	accessed	Dataset - SkyDrive
iPhone XRY extract	4/07/2012 12:55:25	accessed	Enron3111.rtf download

FIGURE 3.2

Example of Timeline (for Case Study).

SkyDrive software is installed onto the PC, and files read on the PC and the iPhone.

Step 7—Complete

The forensic expert reviewed the entire process and was concerned about the lack of documentation from Acme Corp in relation to the seizure of the PC. The expert contacted the ACME CIO and forwarded a recommendation relating to the use of notes, exhibit logs, and chain of custody forms by Acme IT Security in future, in accordance with the NIST First Responders Guidelines (NIJ, 2008) and Standards Australia HB171 recommended practices (SAI, 2003). A training package was prepared and forwarded to the company to ensure IT staff could be trained in appropriate forensic response procedures to ensure potential evidence would be secured in accordance with best practice for future incidents. Not adhering to these recommended practices could jeopardise the chance of having information admitted as evidence in a court or tribunal.

The forensic expert was notified that the matter was finalized and ensured the forensic copies, notes, and other material related to the investigation was appropriately stored in case of future unfair dismissal claims or legal action was undertaken. As this could potentially be many years later, the data and information was stored in a manner that could be retrieved in future if required, such as storing the forensic copies on both optical and magnetic media, and relevant reports were also printed out in hardcopy.

CONCLUSION

When investigating the storage of data using cloud service providers, the initial stages of an investigation include the identification of a cloud service and user account details. This will enable practitioners to identify the potential location of data and act to secure this data in a timely manner. In our case study, we found that a practitioner can identify SkyDrive account use by undertaking keyword searches, hash comparison, and examine common file locations in Windows 7 systems to locate relevant information (as detailed in Table 3.8).

We found that a SkyDrive username can be determined from forensic images. Of great interest is that a SkyDrive account password can, in some instances, be located as plain text in memory captures. As outlined, there are a wide range of investigation points for a practitioner to determine the use of SkyDrive, such as directory listings, prefetch files, link files, thumbnails, registry, browser history, and memory captures. A future research opportunity would be to undertake the experiments with the Windows 8 operating system to determine if the same data remnants are present.

The next chapter consists of research into the remnants of the cloud storage service Dropbox (see Quick & Choo, 2013b). This will assist to determine data remnants from other cloud storage service providers and encompass a methodology that can be used to identify cloud storage providers and cloud computing providers. The aim is to encompass future developments in the field of remote storage and developing a consistent digital forensic framework, such as the one proposed in this research.

References

ACPO. (2006). Good practice guidelines for computer based evidence v4.0, from <www.7safe.com/electronic_evidence> Accessed 26.01.13.

Chung, H., Park, J., Lee, S., & Kang, C. (2012). Digital forensic investigation of cloud storage services, from <http://www.sciencedirect.com/science/article/pii/S1742287612000400> Accessed 26.01.13.

Duffy, A. (2010). Faraday Bag testing in a reverberation chamber — a preliminary study, from <http://www.faradaybag.com/faraday-bag-testing/demontfort-university-faraday-bag-testing.html> Accessed 26.01.13.

Kleynhans, S. (2012). The New PC Era- The Personal Cloud, from <http://www.gartner.com/resId=1890215> Accessed 26.01.13.

Klimt, B., & Yang, Y. (2004). *Introducing the Enron corpus.* Paper presented at the First conference on email and anti-spam (CEAS).

Laugesen, J., & Yuan, Y. (2010). *What Factors Contributed to the Success of Apple's iPhone?* Paper presented at the Mobile Business and 2010 Ninth Global Mobility Roundtable (ICMB-GMR), 2010 Ninth International Conference on.

McClain, F. (2011, 31 May 2011). Dropbox Forensics, from <http://www.forensicfocus.com/dropbox-forensics> Accessed 26.01.13.

Microsoft. (2008). How NTFS reserves space for its Master File Table (MFT), from <http://support.microsoft.com/kb/174619> Accessed 26.01.13.

Microsoft. (2012a). Shortcuts: frequently asked questions', from <http://windows.microsoft.com/en-us/windows-vista/Shortcuts-frequently-asked-questions> Accessed 26.01.13.

Microsoft. (2012b). What is the prefetch folder? from <http://windows.microsoft.com/en-AU/windows-vista/What-is-the-prefetch-folder> Accessed 26.01.13.

Mueller, L. (2010). Windows 7 Forensics — Part IV — Thumbcache_*.db' Retrieved 29 March, 2013, from <http://www.forensickb.com/2010/01/windows-7-forensics-part-iv.html> Accessed 26.01.13.

NIJ. (2008). Electronic crime scene investigation: A guide for first responders (2nd ed.), from <http://www.nij.gov/pubs-sum/219941.htm> Accessed 26.01.13.

NIST. (2012). NIST computer forensic tool testing, from <http://www.cftt.nist.gov/disk_imaging.htm> Accessed 26.01.13.

Quick, D., & Choo, K.-K. R. (2013a). Digital droplets: Microsoft SkyDrive forensic data remnants. *Future Generation Computer Systems, 29*(6), 1378–1394.

Quick, D., & Choo, K.-K. R. (2013b). Dropbox analysis: Data remnants on user machines. *Digital Investigation, 10*(1), 3–18.

SAI. (2003). HB 171-2003 Guidelines for the management of IT evidence. Sydney, Australia: Standards Australia.

Taylor, M., Haggerty, J., Gresty, D., & Lamb, D. (2011). Forensic investigation of cloud computing systems. *Network Security, 2011*(3), 4–10.

USDoD. (1995). DoD 5220.22-M-Sup 1, National Industrial Security Program Operating Manual Supplement, from <http://www.dtic.mil/whs/directives/corres/pdf/522022 MSup1.pdf> Accessed 26.01.13.

W3Counter. (2012). Browser Statistics July 2012, from <http://www.w3counter.com/globalstats.php?year = 2012&month = 7> Accessed 26.01.13.

Zhu, M. (2011). *Mobile Cloud Computing: implications to smartphone forensic procedures and methodologies.* AUT University.

Dropbox Analysis: Data Remnants on User Machines

4

INFORMATION IN THIS CHAPTER

- Dropbox forensic analysis
- Evidence source identification and preservation
- Collection of evidence from cloud storage services
- Examination and analysis of collected data

In the previous chapters, the cloud (storage) forensic framework was outlined (based on our earlier work—see Martini & Choo, 2012; Quick & Choo, 2013a; Quick & Choo, 2013b), and Microsoft SkyDrive analysis was undertaken using the framework (see Quick & Choo, 2013a). This chapter focuses on Dropbox cloud storage and explores the process of determining data remnants using the framework to guide the research (see Quick & Choo, 2013b).

INTRODUCTION

Dropbox is a file hosting service that enables users to store and share files and folders. At the time of this research, there is a free service which allows 2 GB of data storage, and additional storage space can be acquired by referring or signing up new users. Users can subscribe to a paid service of 100 GB for US$99 per year, with options for 200 Gb or 500 GB with Dropbox Pro and for business users starts at 1 TB for five users and can be expanded to "as much as needed." The service can be accessed using a web browser (e.g., Internet Explorer) or client software. Dropbox client software is available for Microsoft Windows operating system (OS), Apple Mac OSX, Linux, Apple iOS, Android, Blackberry, and Windows phone devices.

This research focuses on identifying data remnants of the use of cloud storage; in this chapter, the storage examined is Dropbox, on a Windows 7 PC, and an Apple iPhone 3G. This was undertaken to determine the remnants a practitioner should search for when cloud storage, and in particular Dropbox, is suspected. This research also included the circumstances of a user employing anti-forensic methodology to hide evidence of cloud storage usage and whether remnants remain to identify cloud storage use. The aim is to identify the cloud storage used, any usernames or passwords, files or data associated with a cloud account, and any other remnants that may assist an investigation.

In this study, a standard personal computer (PC) environment with Windows 7 OS installed is used to locate data remnants. It was determined that the use of a virtual computer with a standard installation of the Windows 7 OS would enable different configurations to be quickly set up and analyzed, without having to reconfigure and copy physical hard drives, memory, or undertake external network capture. This allowed the examination of a variety of test PCs in several configurations to facilitate forensic analysis of the Dropbox client software and different browsers, namely Microsoft Internet Explorer®, Google Chrome™, Mozilla Firefox®, and Apple Safari®.

When conducting analysis with data stored with cloud services, one of the main issues is to identify where potential data resides. The previous Director of US Department of Defence (DoD) Computer Forensics Laboratory and the previous Chief Scientist at US Air Force Research Laboratory Information Directorate posited that "[m]ore research is required in the cyber domain, especially in cloud computing, to identify and categorize the unique aspects of where and how digital evidence can be found. End points such as mobile devices add complexity to this domain" (Zatyko & Bay, 2012). To that end, our research focuses on identifying data remnants of the use of cloud storage, namely Dropbox, on a Windows 7 PC, and an Apple iPhone 3G. This is undertaken to determine the remnants a practitioner should search for when cloud storage is suspected, and in particular Dropbox. Our research also includes the circumstances of a user employing anti-forensic methodology to hide evidence of cloud storage usage and whether remnants remain to identify cloud storage use.

In the following chapter, the process of locating data remnants of a user accessing Dropbox in a variety of ways, and also undertaking anti-forensics to hide the use of cloud storage, on a Windows 7 PC is undertaken, using the framework. The framework is then applied in the research and analysis of an Apple iPhone 3G to determine the data remnants when using the inbuilt browser and when installing the Dropbox iOS Application. A case study is used to demonstrate application of the research findings. The chapter concludes with a summary of the findings and recommends areas for future research.

Dropbox forensics: Windows 7 PC

The framework in Chapter 2 is again used to guide the research process. This is now applied to Dropbox cloud storage to further validate the framework and ensure that it is forensically sound and is flexible enough to work with different cloud storage services. In our first experiment, we examined data remnants from the use of Microsoft SkyDrive and were able to find a vast range of information which will assist a practitioner to identify the presence of data being stored in a cloud account (see Chapter 3). We found that a practitioner can identify SkyDrive use by undertaking hash analysis and examine common file locations to locate software and files. We found that a SkyDrive username can be determined from browser history when web access has been undertaken with Mozilla Firefox and Google Chrome, and when a user has stored their username with Microsoft Internet Explorer. We also found a wide range of investigation points for a practitioner to determine the use of SkyDrive, such as directory listings, prefetch files, link files, thumbnails, registry, browser history, and memory captures.

Commence (Scope)

The scope of this research is to determine the data remnants on a Windows 7 PC for the use of Dropbox, such as username, password, browser or software access, files stored within the account, data remnants from the files stored, and the associated dates and times. As the research aims to locate data remnants, four control (base) files are used to compare subsequent processes to determine changes. There is a need to undertake known interactions with Dropbox, such as creating and accessing accounts in a range of ways including different browsers and client software use. There is also a need to undertake anti-forensic processes and be able to compare this with the control (base) data. There will be a large amount of data created to be analyzed, and this needs to be undertaken in a timely manner. This all needs to be documented and reported.

Preparation

To gather the data required to answer the research questions in relation to the use of Dropbox, a variety of virtual machines (VMs) were created. It was decided to examine a variety of circumstances of a user accessing Dropbox and also to examine any differences when using different browsers. Multiple scenarios are explored to make use of Dropbox with a different browser, namely Internet Explorer (IE), Mozilla Firefox (FF), Apple Safari (AS), and Google Chrome (GC). Multiple VMs were created for each browser to replicate different circumstances of usage, as outlined in Table 4.1. This resulted in 28 VMs representing 28 physical computer systems available for analysis, with different circumstances and data remnants available for analysis on each VM. Had this been attempted using physical hardware, the expense and time to undertake setup, erasing, copying, and reinstalling would have been onerous.

The base systems were set up with small amounts of memory and hard drive space for a variety of reasons. Firstly, to reduce the storage space required for the many virtual devices and forensic images created during the experiments. Secondly, to reduce the time required to analyze the data resulting from the

Table 4.1 Configurations of VMs

VMs	Details
Base-VM IE, FF, AS, and GC	Windows 7 Home Basic SP1, 1 GB RAM, 20 GB hard disk drive. Browser for each test installed; Microsoft Internet Explorer (IE), Mozilla Firefox (FF), Apple Safari (AS) and Google Chrome (GC).
Upload-VM IE, FF, AS, and GC	Dropbox Windows client software (version 1.2.52) was downloaded and installed. Test account accessed. Enron sample data were uploaded to user Dropbox account.
Uninstall-VM IE, FF, AS, and GC	Using the Upload-VM, uninstall the Dropbox client software using the option from the Windows Start Menu.
Access-VM IE, FF, AS, and GC	Browser used to access the Dropbox web site at www.dropbox.com and sign in to the user test account. Each file stored in the Dropbox account storage was opened but was not purposely downloaded.
Download-VM IE, FF, AS, and GC	Browser used to access the Dropbox web site at www.dropbox.com and sign in to the user test account. Each file was downloaded to the VM Hard Drive Desktop and opened.
Eraser-VM IE, FF, AS, and GC	Using each copy of the Download-VMs, the Dropbox and Enron files were erased using Eraser software.
CCleaner-VM IE, FF, AS, and GC	Using each copy of the Eraser-VMs, CCleaner was downloaded, installed, and run with default options.

experiments. Thirdly, it was considered that if data of relevance was able to be located on smaller systems, there would be a greater chance of remnants on typically larger systems.

The UC Berkeley Enron Email subset data file was used as the sample data and was downloaded from the project web site (http://bailando.sims.berkeley.edu/enron_email.html) on the February 9, 2012. The text of email 3111 was copied and used to create a text file saved in the "rtf" format. The text was also copied and used to create a Word 2010 document saved in the "docx" format. A picture file in "jpg" format was created from the Enron data to further test if any differences were observed for different file types. MD5 values were calculated for these files and key terms were selected to enable searching and location of the data and files in subsequent analysis.

In the first series of experiments, SysInternals Process Monitor v3.03 (previously Filemon and Regmon) was used to monitor system changes in the VMs (Russinovich & Cogswell, 2012). However, this resulted in the forensic images and memory captures being tainted with a large amount of data: on both the memory captures and hard drive images. The first experiments were redone without Process Monitor running, and analysis was then conducted. Analysis was undertaken to compare the base (control) image files to subsequent image files to determine the changes made, and it was possible to observe the changes to registry files and file systems.

VMs were created using VMware® Player 4.0.1. For each browser scenario, a base image was created, and Windows 7 Home Basic was installed on a 20 GB virtual hard drive with 1 GB RAM. The Base-VM files were used as control media to determine the files created when user activity was undertaken in each scenario. The different actions undertaken were as follows (also outlined in Figure 4.1):

1. The first step was to install the browser software into separate Base-VMs for each browser: Mozilla Firefox (FF) 10.0.2, Internet Explorer (IE) 9.0.8112.16421IC, Apple Safari (AS) 5.1.7 for Windows 7, and Google Chrome (GC) 18.0.1025.162m.

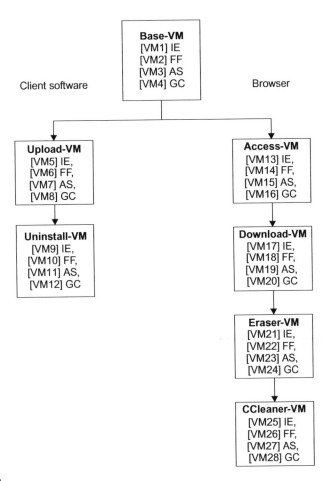

FIGURE 4.1

VMs created for this research.

2. Next was to make a copy of the Base-VM for each browser. These four VMs were labeled IE, FF, AS, or GC Upload-VM and were then used to access the Dropbox web site and download and install the Dropbox client software (version 1.2.52). Previously, a Dropbox account was created for this research on a separate computer. While the creation of an account may leave data residue, this was not part of the testing protocol, which in this case is to test the process of uploading data to an existing account. Sign-in was undertaken with the client software and the Enron sample files were copied to the User Desktop of the VM hard drive from the host PC and then were uploaded to the Dropbox account. The files were left on the hard drive to simulate the situation of a typical user loading files to a Dropbox account from a PC, without attempting to hide or mask the presence of the files. The location of the files on the Desktop was known, and so any other copies or remnants of the files observed during analysis would be the result of the client software interaction.

3. Copies of the Upload-VMs for each browser were made, labeled Uninstall-VM. These were used to uninstall the Dropbox client software using the option in the Start Menu folder.

4. Additional copies of the Base-VM for each browser were made, labeled Access-VM. These were used to access the Dropbox web site using each installed browser. The sign-in option was used to log in to the research user account. Each of the stored files were opened within the browser, but not deliberately downloaded.

5. The Access-VMs were then copied to be used in this next step, which examines the process of accessing and downloading files from a web account, rather than just accessing and viewing files in an account. Copies were made of the Access-VMs, labeled Download-VM. The browser was used to access the Dropbox web site. The sign-in option was used to log in to the research user account. All of the files in the Dropbox cloud storage account were downloaded to the Desktop of the VM hard drive as a compressed zip file. The contents of the zip file were extracted to the Desktop and then each file was opened and closed.

6. Copies were made of the Download-VMs, labeled Eraser-VM. Eraser 5.8.8 was installed with the default settings. Eraser was then used to erase each of the Enron data files and the Dropbox sample files from the Desktop. The USDoD 5220.22-M setting was used to erase the data. According to the DoD publication, this is an overwrite of *"all locations three (3) times (first time with a character, second time with its complement, and the third time with a random character)"* (USDoD 1995).

7. Copies were made of the Eraser-VMs, labeled CCleaner-VM. CCleaner v3.17.1689 was installed and run across the VM hard drives to remove the browsing history and file references in relation to the use of Dropbox and the presence of the Enron files. The Eraser-VMs were used to simulate the process of a user undertaken a variety of anti-forensic processes which build

upon each other. In this case, the use of eraser to erase the files on the desktop and the downloaded files. CCleaner was used to remove browsing remnants, which Eraser does not address. This experiment was not undertaken to test the capability of either Eraser or CCleaner, but to assess each step of a user undertaking anti-forensic methodology to remove data, commencing with erasing known files, then removing other information such as browsing history.

While preparing each VM, Wireshark 1.6.5 was run on the host computer to capture network traffic from the VM network interface. Memory capture was facilitated by copying the Virtual Memory (VMEM) files created by VMWare. The 28 VMEM files were copied while the VM was running, just prior to shutdown. The network capture files were saved at various points while the VMs were running, and after shutdown.

Evidence source identification and preservation

In the context of our research, we identified files which would contain the information needed to conduct the analysis—the VMDK files in each VM folder for the hard drive, each VMEM file for the memory capture, and each saved network capture file (PCAP) for the network captures. These were identified for each VM. Initial experiments were undertaken using FTK Imager to capture memory from within the virtual system. Analysis of the memory captures from within the VM detected remnants of FTK Imager in the memory data. This was then compared with the VMEM files captured prior to using FTK Imager. It was determined that the VMEM file represented a capture of memory which was not tainted with the use of FTK Imager and was deemed to be appropriate for analysis with less data remnants from interaction with the system. This consideration was also made in relation to running FTK Imager within the virtual system to make a forensic copy of the hard drive. When FTK Imager was run inside the virtual system, data remnants of FTK Imager were found on the image of the hard drive. A variety of commercial and free solutions exist in relation to memory capture and should be tested on known systems by a practitioner to determine data remnants left on live systems prior to use. The analysis of the VMDK file was undertaken with common forensic software such as Encase and FTK, which treat the VMDK as a physical hard drive and was not tainted with remnants from using FTK Imager from within the virtual system.

Collection

One of the basic tenets of a digital forensic investigation is the ability to conduct analysis on a forensic copy, rather than interacting with or altering the original source (ACPO, 2006, NIJ, 2004, 2008). For this research, a forensic copy was made of each virtual hard drive (vmdk file) using AccessData FTK Imager CLI

2.9.0 in the E01 container format. A forensic copy of each memory file (vmem) and network capture (pcap) file was made in the AccessData Logical Image (AD1) format, and an MD5 hash value for each original file was calculated and verified with each forensic copy.

Examination and analysis

For this research, each of the forensic copies of the VM hard drives, memory, and network captures were examined using a range of tools, such as Guidance Software EnCase version 6.19.4, AccessData FTK version 1.81.6, and version 4.01. A standard analysis process was developed for this research, and the process was applied for each captured VM, memory file, and network capture. This included a step-by-step process to examine a range of data, such as the MFT, prefetch files, link files, registry files, running keyword searches, and using Magnet Forensics Internet Evidence Finder.

Web browser Dropbox account information

While accessing the Dropbox accounts to create the VMs, it was observed that the Dropbox web account retains a record of computers used to access and synchronize with an account. The information is shown when using a web browser to access the Dropbox account and is available under a tab labeled "My Computers" and also displays the time stamp of the last activity, the IP address for the last connection, and the version of the client software used on the linked computer. There is the ability to alter the computer name when first linked, and also to later rename and unlink a linked computer. IP addresses can be obfuscated by users, e.g., by using a proxy or The Onion Router (TOR) connection; hence any IP address information should be investigated and verified prior to taking further action.

Accessing a Dropbox account via a web browser also has an option to show deleted files, which are available for 30 days for free accounts and unlimited time for paid accounts (McClain, 2011). When a file is deleted, it is not visible unless the option to "Show Deleted Files" is selected; however, the last modified date is not visible. The deleted files can be restored or permanently deleted from the browser. Dropbox retains a snapshot of a file each time it is modified and the history of a file can be viewed. A timeline of previous events can also be viewed, such as when files were uploaded, deleted, restored, or other computers were linked to the account, including the date and time for the event.

The information listed above may be crucially important to an investigation, and consideration needs to be made in relation to preserving this information. As it is not necessarily stored on the computer used to access an account, other methods of preservation will be required. This could entail undertaking a legal process to preserve the information via the Dropbox legal contact points (Dropbox, 2012). Some legal jurisdictions have legislation allowing data to be preserved at the time of serving a seizure warrant, such as in Australia with Section 3L of the *Crimes Act 1914 (Cth)*, which includes a provision for the executing officer of a search and seizure warrant to access data which includes data not held at the premises, i.e., accessible from a computer or data storage device. This may not be the case in a number of jurisdictions, including the United States.

Control—Base-VMs

Analysis of the control Base-VM hard drives confirmed there was no data originally present relating to the Enron sample test data and Dropbox files. References were found for the term "Dropbox" in "index.dat" files, "msjint40.dll.mui," "pagefile.sys," and unallocated clusters. This should be borne in mind, as this indicates the presence of the keyword term "dropbox" on a hard drive does not necessarily indicate that Dropbox has been used. As is usual for a digital forensic examination, the context of a search result needs to be analyzed to determine the reason for a keyword match, rather than drawing a conclusion at face value of the presence of data. The control VMs in this case have shown that data matches will occur, even when user activity in relation to Dropbox has not been undertaken.

Dropbox client software

In the four Upload-VMs, it was observed that the Dropbox client software installed under Windows 7 does not install into the "C:\Program Files\" folder, and instead installs into the Users "C:\Users\[username]\AppData\Roaming\" folder. Dropbox sample files and folders were observed on the hard drive, at the default Dropbox folder location ("C:\Users\[username]\Dropbox"). These included files "Getting Started.pdf," two "How to use" text files, and three sample pictures. The files, locations, and MD5 values for the software and sample files are listed in Table 4.2 and allow a practitioner to identify known files based on the MD5 values. When a new release of the Dropbox Windows client software is released, the hash values of the standard files and sample files will need to be recalculated as these may change.

Analysis of the time stamps of the files indicated, including those which change with usage, may lead a practitioner to conclusions relating to when these files were created on a system, and when software was last run. To locate information relating to the files synchronized, and whether these were shared with other users requires analysis of any client software log files. According to McClain (2011), the Dropbox (Windows) client software available in 2011 included a filecache.db file, which contained a history of filenames synchronized with Dropbox. In the Dropbox client software used for this research (version 1.2.52), this file was not present. However, there was a file with a DBX extension (filecache.dbx), which appears to be encrypted and was not able to be interpreted. According to the Magnet Software web site (2013), "IEF Triage" is able to decrypt the filecache.dbx file when run on a live system, but not a forensic image or mounted drive. In addition, analysis identified the "host.db" file which included the path for Dropbox file storage in Base64 string encoded text. For example, the following string was located: "QzpcVXNlcnNcY2xvdWRcRHJvcGJveA==." Converting this as a Base64 string results in the text "C:\Users\cloud\Dropbox."

Table 4.2 Dropbox Windows Software Files with MD5 Values

File	MD5
Dropbox Windows client software: **Dropbox 1.2.52.exe**	c05a03f72386b7c9d5cc7dcefa8555da
File: \Dropbox**Getting Started.pdf**	d0a31650c916d07316458ad11e4093c3
File: \Dropbox\Photos**How to use the Photos folder.txt**	e6655fb94380d9afa943c5d1397f6253
File: \Dropbox\Photos\Sample Album**Boston City Flow.jpg**	5fcd8abc87de2629a3e75598999944da
File: \Dropbox\Photos\Sample Album**Costa Rican Frog.jpg**	30bf1fadcfc52c796d143563a9d4484f
File: \Dropbox\Photos\Sample Album**Pensive Parakeet.jpg**	b44d238643412e46d5ec7a6fe95d5e8f
File: \Dropbox\Public**How to use the Public folder.txt,**	12313c2e338ee010a8ddc97ed33d9158
File: \AppData\Roaming\Dropbox\bin\ **Dropbox.exe,**	9ed3cfe54cd2e797dc9a04397c001e89
File: \AppData\Roaming\Dropbox\bin\ **DropboxExt.14.dll,**	6d74290856347cf8682277a54b433d4b
File: \AppData\Roaming\Dropbox\bin\ **msvcp71.dll,**	561fa2abb31dfa8fab762145f81667c2
File: \AppData\Roaming\Dropbox\bin\ **msvcr71.dll,**	86f1895ae8c5e8b17d99ece768a70732
File: \AppData\Roaming\Dropbox\bin\ **Uninstall.exe,**	6420486a64af043b5b0e0a11b15c3e23
Hash values are not included for these as they will change according to usage:	
File: \AppData\Roaming\Dropbox\bin\ **Dropbox.exe.log**	
File: \AppData\Roaming\Dropbox\bin**itag**	
File: \AppData\Roaming\Dropbox**config.db**	
File: \AppData\Roaming\Dropbox**config.dbx**	
File: \AppData\Roaming\Dropbox**filecache.dbx**	
File: \AppData\Roaming\Dropbox**host.db**	
File: \AppData\Roaming\Dropbox**host.dbx**	
File: \AppData\Roaming\Dropbox**sigstore.dbx**	
File: \AppData\Roaming\Dropbox**unlink.db**	

Software to parse the client software files (Dropbox Reader 1.1) was previously available from Architecture Technologies Corporation Cyber Marshal utilities web page (not available when checked on January 23, 2013). Dropbox Reader 1.1 consists of six command line tools to parse Dropbox client software files, including config.db and filecache.db (Architecture Technologies, 2011). As stated above, previous versions of Dropbox included these files; however, the client software used in this research (version 1.2.52 and onward) included .dbx files which appear to be encrypted. The dbx and db files from version 1.2.52 examined in this research were not able to be read or parsed by Dropbox Reader 1.1 when tested.

It is possible in a typical use situation that there may be other data which may point a practitioner to the use of Dropbox. This could include emails from Dropbox relating to the creation of an account, or emails from a user to another user directing them to the presence of a Dropbox account, or a shared link to data within a Dropbox account. The use of the Dropbox accounts in this research was quite minimal, and in typical use over an extended period of time and user sessions, there may be a greater amount of data remnants. This research has highlighted that with even minimal use, there are many data remnants to examine.

Uninstallation of Dropbox client software
Step 3 of this research was undertaken to assess the results of a user uninstalling the client software using the link contained in the Windows 7 Start Menu. Analysis of the Uninstall-VMs revealed that only the Dropbox.exe file within the AppData folder structure was marked as deleted, and other client software files remained, including "dll," "bat," and other "exe" files. Of note was that the Dropbox sync folder and file contents in "Users\[username]\Dropbox\" remained on the hard drive and was not affected by the uninstallation. All other remnants of the client software also remained present and unaffected.

Keyword search terms
Keyword search terms were determined from the filenames observed, and the text from within the Enron data files. These included the following:

- "www.dropbox.com," "dropbox"
- "Getting Started.pdf," "Boston City," "Costa Rican Frog," "Pensive Parakeet"
- "How to use the Photos," "How to use the Public"
- The username and password of the Dropbox account created for this research
- "filecache.dbx," "dataset.zip," "Enron," "3111.txt," "enron3111," and "Enron Wholesale Services"

Directory listings
For each of the VM hard drives, a directory listing was produced using AccessData FTK Imager 3.1.0. Analysis was also conducted using Encase to view the filenames. Analysis of the directory and file listings of the four control

Base-VM hard drives revealed no references to the Enron sample data filenames, Dropbox files, or Dropbox sample files. It was concluded that references to Dropbox and the Enron sample files were not present in the control media directory listings prior to installing the software or accessing the files.

There were many references in the other VMs. In the four Upload-VMs, there was a substantial amount of filenames seen, including on the User's Desktop, in the Downloads folder, and in the Dropbox folder: "C:\User\[username]\Dropbox." Dropbox URL references were also observed in the four Upload-VMs file listings, but not seen in the four Access-VMs or the Download-VMs, indicating this URL reference was created as part of the Dropbox client software installation.

When a browser was used to access a Dropbox account, there were less filename references, in comparison with when the Dropbox client software was used to access cloud storage. However, with the browser being used to access the Dropbox account stored files, there were sufficient file name references remaining on the hard drives to identify the filenames that were accessed, including the Enron sample data files and the Dropbox sample files. When the files were downloaded from the Dropbox cloud storage, there were additional filename references observed on the hard drive, including link files. This indicates when a user uses Dropbox, there will be references in the $MFT and directory listing to indicate this, and also to determine the filenames associated with Dropbox use.

Analysis of the four Eraser-VMs and four CCleaner-VM hard drives identified references to link files for the Enron sample files and Dropbox sample files. When all options were used for Eraser and CCleaner, the references to the filenames were removed. The use of Darik's Boot and Nuke (DBAN) completely erased the hard drives, and there was no data to analyze in these VMs.

Prefetch files

Prefetch files are used by Windows to store information in relation to software activity, including the number of times software has run and associated files used by the software. Analysis of the VM hard drives identified that prefetch files contained information relating to the filenames of the Dropbox executable, Dropbox sample files, and Enron test data filenames in all the VM hard drives except the control Base-VM hard drives. It was observed that even after erasing with both Eraser and CCleaner, there was enough information in prefetch files, such as notepad.exe.pf, wordpad.exe.pf, explorer.exe.pf, and dllhost.exe.pf to indicate the presence and path of the Enron sample data files and the sample Dropbox files.

Link files

There were no Dropbox associated link files found within the four control Base-VMs. Link files relating to Dropbox and the Enron sample data files were observed for all Upload-VM, Download-VM, Eraser-VM, and CCleaner-VM hard drives. The link files observed related to the filenames and folder names for the Dropbox executable, Dropbox sample files, such as "Boston City Flow.lnk," "Photos.lnk," and "Dropbox.lnk," and the Enron test data. These were located in the "Windows\Recent" and "Windows\Start" folders in the Users "AppData" directory. There were no Dropbox or Enron link files within the four Access-VM hard drives, indicating that if files were not downloaded from Dropbox to the computer, link files were not created.

Registry

Registry files were analyzed using AccessData Registry Viewer 1.6.3.34 and RegRipper version 20080909. Analysis revealed there were no references to Dropbox or the Enron sample files in the four control Base-VM hard drives. In the Upload-VM, Access-VM, and Download-VM registry files, there were references to the Dropbox URL, Dropbox software files and folders, the Dropbox sample files, and the Enron test files. For example, the "RecentDocs" key in the NTUSER.dat registry file provided a list of Dropbox and Enron related files and folders, and a sample RegRipper output is listed as follows:

```
- - - - - - - - - - - - - - - - - - - - - - - - - - - - - - - - - - - - -
RecentDocs - recentdocs
**All values printed in MRUList\MRUListEx order.
Software\Microsoft\Windows\CurrentVersion\Explorer\RecentDocs
LastWrite Time Fri Apr 20 12:13:24 2012 (UTC)
    14 = Public
    13 = How to use the Public folder.txt
    12 = Photos
    11 = How to use the Photos folder.txt
    8 = Sample Album
    10 = Pensive Parakeet.jpg
    9 = Costa Rican Frog.jpg
    7 = Boston City Flow.jpg
    3 = Dataset
    5 = Enron3111.rtf
    2 = Enron3111.jpg
    6 = Enron3111.docx
    4 = 3111.txt
- - - - - - - - - - - - - - - - - - - - - - - - - - - - - - - - - - - - -
```

There were no references to the Dropbox username within the registry files in any of the VMs. Deleted Dropbox information was located within the NTUSER .dat registry files in the Chrome and IE CCleaner-VMs, such as filenames and URL references, but not in the Firefox CCleaner-VM. Dropbox software file references were located in the SOFTWARE and SYSTEM registry hives when the Dropbox client software was installed, but not when a browser was used to access or download data from Dropbox. References were also found within the UsrClass.dat registry files when the Dropbox client software was used, but not when a browser was used to access Dropbox.

Thumbcache

Analysis of the thumbnails stored within the thumbcache files within the four control Base-VMs determined that there were no Dropbox sample pictures or Enron sample picture thumbnails present prior to installing or accessing Dropbox. Thumbnails for the Dropbox sample pictures and the Enron sample picture were located in the Upload-VM, Download-VM, and Eraser-VMs; however, none were found in the Access-VMs or the CCleaner-VMs. This indicates that the thumbnail cache is a source for possible data relating to Dropbox use, but results may not be definitive. Dropbox can be used in certain circumstances without leaving any trace in thumbnails, such as accessing files using a browser but not downloading the files to a computer.

Event logs

Event log files were examined with the inbuilt Windows viewer and also with external software: event log Explorer and EvtParser. The analysis process included reading through the event entries for the times of particular events on each VM, and keyword searches were conducted. However, there were very few entries in relation to the Dropbox activity. The keyword term "dropbox" was found within Windows "Windows Firewall.evtx" event log files when client software was installed and run. For example, the text "a rule has been added to the Windows Firewall exception list" was located in the log file. There were also references within "GroupPolicy_Operational.evtx" files relating to Dropbox and Enron sample data files when Internet Explorer was used to download data from a Dropbox web account. Similar entries were not seen when the Google Chrome, Apple Safari, or Mozilla Firefox browser were used.

Browser analysis

Internet browsing information was analyzed using Encase 6.19.4, Magnet Forensics Internet Evidence Finder (IEF) v5 Standard Edition, Digital Detective NetAnalysis v1.53, and SQLite Database Browser v1.3. It was confirmed there was no Dropbox or Enron sample data in the Internet history of the four control Base-VM files. The Dropbox account username could be determined when Mozilla Firefox and Google Chrome were used, but there was no record of this when Internet Explorer or Apple Safari was used. However, if the username and password were stored when using IE version 9, the details were able to be retrieved by using Nirsoft IE PassView v1.26. The username was stored in Firefox in the "formhistory.sqlite" database and in Chrome in the Autofill "Web Data" file.

Dropbox web site information was located in Cookie files, web history, FavIcons, and in the FileSlack of other files, when Internet Explorer, Mozilla Firefox, or Google Chrome was used to access Dropbox. Filenames for files downloaded, including the Dropbox sample files, were also located in the web history for the browsers. When using the Dropbox client software, references to the Enron sample data filenames and file path were located in the Internet

Explorer History when Mozilla Firefox was used. Using all options with CCleaner removed all references in the Mozilla Firefox and Internet Explorer VMs, but information remained in the Google Chrome FavIcon history to identify Dropbox usage, which included dates and times for last access.

Network traffic (PCAP) analysis

Network traffic capture is a potential source of relevant information and is a process available to a range of government agencies which have the legal authority to undertake this type of monitoring and interception of data (Kisswani, 2010). Analysis of the network traffic capture files was undertaken using Network Miner v1.0 and Wireshark Portable 1.6.5 to determine what data remnants were available when Dropbox is used in the circumstances of the research. Network traffic was seen on TCP Port 80 (HTTP) and 443 (HTTPS) only. When accessing Dropbox accounts using the client software or a web browser, a session with an IP in the range 199.47.216.0–199.47.219.255 (registered to Dropbox), was first established on Port 80, and then a session with an IP in the range 199.7.48.0–199.7.63.255 or 199.16.80.0–199.16.95.255 on Port 80 then Port 443, which is registered to VeriSign/Thawte. Certificates were observed from VeriSign/Thawte services. The next IPs accessed were in the range of 74.125.0.0–74.125.255.255 (which are registered to Google) and indicate Google Analytics services. IP numbers allocated to AmazonAWS, the Amazon Web Services (EC2) service, were then observed. See Table 4.3 for a list of IP number ranges and the registered owner for the range.

When the Dropbox Windows client software was downloaded, the URL name made reference to Amazon Cloudfront. Amazon Web Services EC2 was also listed for many URLs, with additional information referencing Dropbox, such as "photos1.dropbox," "photos2.dropbox," and "photos3.dropbox." IP numbers also observed in the packet captures are registered to SoftLayer Technologies and

Table 4.3 Observed IP and Registered Organization from Network Traffic Captures	
DROPBOX	199.47.216.0–199.47.219.255
VERISIGN	199.7.48.0–199.7.63.255
	199.16.80.0–199.16.95.255
GOOGLE	74.125.0.0–74.125.255.255
AMAZON-AWS	23.20.0.0–23.23.255.255
	50.16.0.0–50.19.255.255
	107.20.0.0–107.23.255.255
	184.72.0.0–184.73.255.255
	174.129.0.0–174.129.255.255
	204.246.160.0–204.246.191.255
SoftLayer Technologies Inc.	75.126.0.0–75.126.255.255
WestHost, Inc.	69.36.160.0–69.36.191.255

WestHost Inc. and according to the URL name were related to client-stats. Dropbox.com and ocsp.digicert. OCSP is the Online Certificate Status Protocol, used by VeriSign/Thawte.

Viewing the network data, it appeared there were different URL names when using Dropbox client software in comparison with using a web browser, even if the same IP number was used. When the client software was used, the URL name seen in the network capture commenced with "v-client" or "client." When a browser was used, the URL commenced with "v-www" or "dl-web." This appears to be an indicator that when a Dropbox cloud account is accessed with client software, the URL displays "client," and when a browser was used, "www" or "web" was displayed.

Network Miner was used to rebuild files from the captured packets, and Dropbox webpage icon files, such as "landingboxbig.png," were observed. However, no Enron sample data files or the Dropbox sample files were seen in the network traffic. There was no evidence of the filenames for the Enron or Dropbox sample files, nor any Dropbox user credentials seen in the network traffic. On examining the captured network data, it appeared to be encrypted, with no readable text observed after a Dropbox user account logged in.

Memory analysis

Memory capture is another potential source of important information (ACPO, 2006). Analysis of the memory captures (VMEM files) was undertaken using Encase 6.19.4 and AccessData FTK 4.01. The term "dropbox" was located in the memory captures of the Internet Explorer and Google Chrome control Base-VM files. None were located in the Mozilla Firefox or Apple Safari control Base-VM files. The entries in the Chrome and Explorer memory appeared with lists of other web sites, such as "drugstore.com."

Observed within the memory captures when client software was used was the Dropbox username near to text "u'email": as listed in Table 4.4. This text can be used to search and locate potential usernames for Dropbox accounts. Also observed near this text was "u'displayname": and following this was the computer name of the VM. This information would be of interest when seeking to identify data relating to a specific computer, such as in log files available from a service provider. When a browser was used to access a Dropbox account, the text "login_email" was observed preceding the username. However, when the Safari browser was used, the username was only recovered in the Upload-VM memory capture.

Table 4.4 Data Observed in Client Software Memory (VMEM)

34.553|AUTHENTICATE:u'displayname': **'WIN-B1EGOBJP23T'**,

34.553|AUTHENTICATE:u'email': **'username@hotmail.com'**,

34.553|AUTHENTICATE:u'excserver':u'dl-debug1.Dropbox.com',

Surprisingly, the password in cleartext for the user account was able to be located in memory captures when the client software was installed, which serves to highlight the importance of capturing memory when possible, rather than unplugging a live machine and potentially losing this information. Password information was located in Upload-VM memory captures near to the following extracted text (Figure 4.2):

- "... $0.00 free name periods $0.00..." (Safari),
- "... name 2 GB | periods $99.00 Free ..." (Chrome)

Observed within memory captures were Dropbox and Enron filename references in all VMs except the control Base-VM and the DBAN-VM. Web site details such as "www.dropbox.com" were recovered in all Upload-VMs, and the majority of the Access-VMs, Download-VMs, and CCleaner-VMs. The full text of the Enron data files and the Dropbox sample files was recovered in the Upload-VM, Access-VM, and Download-VM memory captures. Data carving was undertaken and resulted in the recovery of thumbnail pictures and partial picture files of the Dropbox sample files and the Enron sample pictures from the memory captures for Access-VM, Upload-VM, and Download-VM files.

Analysis of Pagefile.sys files was not as conclusive as the memory capture files. Undertaking data carving of the pagefile.sys files produced no matches to Dropbox sample files or Enron data pictures or thumbnails. Some thumbnail icons were located within the Mozilla Firefox Upload-VM, and a partial screen capture of the Dropbox web site was found in the Google Chrome Access-VM pagefile, indicative of a thumbnail icon used in the Google Chrome navigation tab. The username was located only in the Apple Safari Upload-VM, with no text associated with this that would enable future searches. The password was not located in any pagefile.sys files. It is possible in a typical use situation that the size of pagefile may be larger, and hence there may be a better chance of data remnants being present. This would also apply to the contents of hiberfil when a user puts a system into hibernation and the contents of memory are stored on a hard drive.

Results of applying anti-forensic techniques (Eraser, CCleaner)

Remnants indicating the use of Dropbox were located after Eraser and CCleaner were used. This indicated that Eraser or CCleaner did not necessarily remove all data remnants in relation to the use of Dropbox or completely remove the information relating to the previous presence of the Enron sample files or the Dropbox sample files.

Presentation

In our case study, a variety of data remnants were located when a user used Dropbox to store or access data. Dropbox client software, sample data files, and common locations were outlined in Table 4.3. This information enables a

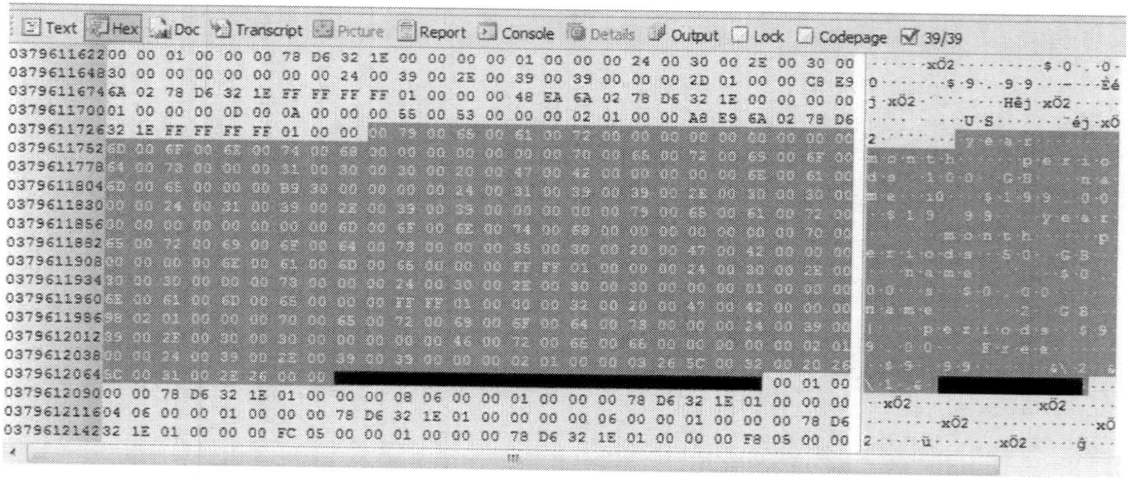

FIGURE 4.2

Hex display of memory capture (GC Upload-VM) password redacted for "name 2 GB" text.

practitioner to conduct hash analysis and keyword searches for the filenames listed, and will assist to determine if Dropbox client software (in this case version 1.2.52) has been used.

Artifacts from windows client

From the analysis undertaken, the task of identifying whether a Dropbox account has been accessed either using client software or a web browser can be determined in several ways. Information such as a Dropbox username, URLs in the network traffic, filename data in prefetch and link files, filename references in directory listings, RecentDocs and typed URLs in registry files, browser history, and information recovered from memory files all proved conclusive to identify Dropbox use, filenames, and actual data from the files of interest. Once forensic analysis has determined that a Dropbox account has potential evidence of relevance to an investigation, the practitioner can communicate this to relevant persons to enable them to respond to secure evidence in a timely manner. The findings are summarized in Table 4.5.

Table 4.5 Summary of Analysis Findings

Control (Base-VM)	Data Artifacts Found
Username, password,	Nil
software, URL, Enron	Nil
KWS terms	Matches to *"dropbox"* in *"index.dat"* files, *"msjint40.dll.mui,"* *"pagefile.sys,"* *unallocated clusters*, and memory captures.
Client Software (Upload-VM)	**Data Artifacts Found (Also Found in the Uninstall-VM)**
Username	*Memory capture* files near: "u'email":
Password	Located in RAM—search for "free name periods"
Software	*Dropbox 1.2.52.exe* file located when downloaded.
	Dropbox software installation under "*[User]\AppData \Roaming\Dropbox*"
	Dropbox sample files and folders at location "*C:\Users \username]\Dropbox*"
URL	When software downloaded, URLs included *www.dropbox. com*
Enron sample filenames	Multiple locations, including *Prefetch, Link files, $MFT, Registry*.
Enron sample files	Located in Sync folder under *User\Dropbox*. Thumbnail pictures in *Thumbcache*
KWS terms	"dropbox" in event logs
	Data Artifacts Found

(Continued)

Table 4.5 (Continued)

Browser Access (Access-VM)	
Username	FF and GC history: *"formhistory.sqlite"* and *"Autofill."* *Memory capture* files "login_email"
Password	Nil
Software	Nil
URL	Multiple locations: *cookie, history, icons, pagefile.sys, and unallocated*
Enron sample filenames	Sufficient to identify files accessed with references to the filenames in *Registry* and *Browsing History*
Enron sample files	Full text in *RAM*
KWS terms	Multiple matches to KWS terms
Browser Download (Download-VM)	**Data Artifacts Found**
Username	FF and GC History: *"formhistory.sqlite"* and *"Autofill."*
Password	Nil
Software	Nil
URL	Multiple locations: *cookie, history, icons, pagefile.sys and unallocated*
Enron sample filenames	Sufficient to identify files accessed with references in *$MFT, Link, Registry,* and *Prefetch* files
Enron sample files	Via uncompressed zip or folder name, *"Documents.zip"*
KWS terms	References in *event logs* (IE)
Eraser (Eraser-VM)	**Data Artifacts Found**
Username	FF and GC History: *"formhistory.sqlite"* and *"Autofill."*
Password	Nil
Software	Nil
URL	Multiple locations: *cookie, history, icons, pagefile.sys, and unallocated*
Enron sample filenames	Sufficient to identify files accessed with references to the filenames in *$MFT, Link,* and *Prefetch* files
Enron sample files	Thumbnail pictures in *Thumbcache*
KWS terms	Multiple matches to KWS terms
CCleaner (CCleaner-VM)	**Data Artifacts Found**
Username	Nil
Password	Nil
Software	Nil
URL	Google Chrome *Favicon* history
Enron sample filenames	Sufficient to identify files accessed with references to the filenames in *Prefetch* and *Link* files
Enron sample files	Nil
KWS terms	Multiple matches to KWS terms

Volatile data capture

Analysis of the RAM captures recovered full files, filenames, the Dropbox username and password, and other data. Network analysis determined that most of the network traffic was encrypted, and the file information was not recovered. Some of the network traffic was not encrypted, and hence when available would be useful to identify Dropbox access, and also to identify if Dropbox client software or a browser was used to access cloud storage. This indicates that network traffic and memory capture is important, and when possible should be undertaken.

Artifacts from browser

It was also observed that Dropbox retains a record of computers used to access and synchronize with an account, including the IP number. This information would be important to determine whether a particular computer was synchronized to a Dropbox account and should be a consideration, bearing in mind that IP addresses can be spoofed or obfuscated through proxies or TOR services. There is a timeline history of files and computer synchronization, and previous versions of files are also available through the Dropbox account when accessed with a browser. This information needs to be identified and preserved through a legal process to ensure the data is available to an investigation.

Complete

During this research, one finding was that conducting research using virtual computers was beneficial to compare a range of different configurations of software and data access. The addition of the steps of "prepare" and "feedback" to a forensic analysis framework was beneficial to adequately prepare for analysis and also to incorporate lessons learnt into subsequent investigations. It is important to consider the positive and negative experiences during an examination and incorporate these into future examinations. It is also important to report any issues or improvements to other practitioners, and the digital forensic community in general.

The final step is the completion of an investigation. For the purposes of this research, it was determined that analysis of other cloud storage services, Microsoft SkyDrive and Google Drive, will serve to widen the scope of the research and further assess the framework. The files created for this research were archived, and working copies were available to compare when undertaking the next stages of the research.

In summary, it has been demonstrated that it is possible to determine the username, password, method of access, filenames, contents, and dates and times of access when Dropbox is used to store, access, or download data from cloud storage. Memory captures and Network files were an important source of information, especially locating the username and password in memory files when the client software was set up and used.

Dropbox forensics: Apple iPhone 3G

As discussed earlier, the previous Director of USDoD Computer Forensics Laboratory stated that mobile devices add complexity to the identification of digital evidence associated with cloud computing (Zatyko & Bay, 2012). To explore this in the context of this research, an Apple iPhone 3G was selected to determine the data remnants on a portable device. An iPhone can be used to access a Dropbox account via the inbuilt browser, or client software (Dropbox App) can be used to access an account. Both processes will be tested for data remnants in this research.

Commence (Scope)

An iPhone 3G running iOS 4.2.1 was selected which had not been used to access Dropbox previously as the device usage was known to the authors.

Preparation

Micro Systemation (MSAB) .XRY 6.2.1 was used to extract a logical image of the contents, excluding audio and video files, prior to undertaking the research. This extract was analyzed to confirm there was no Dropbox related data on the device. Next, the inbuilt Apple Safari iOS browser was used to access the Dropbox user account created for this research and view the Dropbox sample files and Enron files stored remotely. A logical extract was then conducted using .XRY. The Dropbox iOS Application was then downloaded and installed to the iPhone 3G. The Dropbox account was then accessed using the Application, and the files stored in the account were viewed. A third logical extract with .XRY was then conducted.

Evidence source identification and preservation

In the context of this research, files were identified which would contain the information needed to conduct the analysis, in this instance being the .XRY extract files and the output of the .XRY software, including PDF reports and the files exported using .XRY. These were identified for each of the extracts: Base, Browser, and Application.

Collection

To observe the principles of forensic computer analysis (ACPO, 2006, NIJ, 2004), a forensic copy was made of the logical .XRY extract files, the data and files output from XRY, and the reports generated by XRY. As these were logical files, this was done in the X-Ways Evidence File Container format (ctr) and could also be preserved using Encase (L01) or AccessData FTK (AD1) logical file containers. MD5 hash values were calculated to ensure the forensic integrity of the data.

Examination and analysis

Each of the forensic files was examined using forensic tools including X-Ways Forensic version 16.5 and Guidance Software EnCase version 6.19.4. PList Explorer v1.0 was used to examine the contents of the Apple plist files extracted by .XRY. SQLite Database Browser 2.0 was used to examine the sqlite files.

Control—Base-XRY

Analysis of the control Base-XRY extract confirmed there was no data originally present relating to the Dropbox sample files, the Enron sample test data, or the Dropbox application. In addition, no references were located for the term "dropbox" or the web site URL (www.dropbox.com).

Dropbox accessed via the iOS Safari browser

The research username or account password was not located in the Browser-XRY extracts. Filenames for the Dropbox sample files and Enron test files were located in History.plist. This information was also extracted by XRY in the Web-History.txt file, as displayed in Table 4.6.

The dropbox web site URL was also located in the History.plist and Web-History.txt files. An example is listed in Table 4.7. The URL was also located in the Cookies.binarycookies file.

Table 4.6 Output from .XRY Web-History.txt File

Web-History #	2
Application:	Safari (Apple)
Web Address:	https://dl-web.dropbox.com/get/Getting%20Started.pdf?w=7d8bf985
Access Count:	1
Accessed:	16/08/2012 1:38:57 AM UTC (Device)

Table 4.7 Output from .XRY Web-History.txt File

Web-History #	14
Application:	Safari (Apple)
Web Address:	https://www.dropbox.com/m/home?path=/Dataset
Page Title:	Dropbox files
Access Count:	1
Accessed:	16/08/2012 1:22:56 AM UTC (Device)

Dropbox application used to access the research account

Analysis of the third XRY extract was able to determine the username used to access Dropbox account. This was located in the "com.getdropbox.Dropbox .plist" file near the text "=]DBAccountInfo" (see Figure 4.3) and also in the "keychain-backup.plist." This information does not appear to be parsed by XRY as it was not present in the XRY report. To determine if the application is present, information in the "iTunesstored2.sqlitedb" file also included references to "dropbox." Surprisingly, the text from the Enron files was not located in any of the extracts. No password was located in any of the extracts or files.

Presentation

In this research, several data remnants were located when searching for evidence of Dropbox use on the test item (iPhone 3G). Initial analysis of the control experiment extract identified no matches to the term "dropbox," but matches in the subsequent extracts indicating that conducting a keyword search for the word "dropbox" could indicate if Dropbox had been used. It is possible in a typical use situation that there may be other data which may point a practitioner to the use of Dropbox. This could include emails or SMS messages relating to the creation of an account, or emails or SMS messages from a user to another user directing them to the presence of a Dropbox account, or a shared link to data within a Dropbox account. The use of the Dropbox accounts in this research was quite minimal, and in typical use over an extended period of time and user sessions, there may be a greater amount of data remnants. This research has highlighted that with even minimal use, there are many data remnants to examine.

Artifacts from iOS browser

When the browser was used to access the Dropbox account, entries were left in the History.plist file, which is also listed in the .XRY Web-History.txt file. The username and password were not located in the extract. The filenames accessed were listed in the History.plist file and in the .XRY Web-History.txt file.

Artifacts from Dropbox iOS client software

When the Dropbox application was installed and used to access the research account, the username was able to be determined from the "com.getdropbox. Dropbox.plist" file. Information in the "com.apple.AppStore.plist" file lists "http://itunes.apple.com/au/app/dropbox/id327630330." However, the text from the Dropbox sample files or the Enron files was not located in any of the extracts, nor was it possible to locate the password for the account.

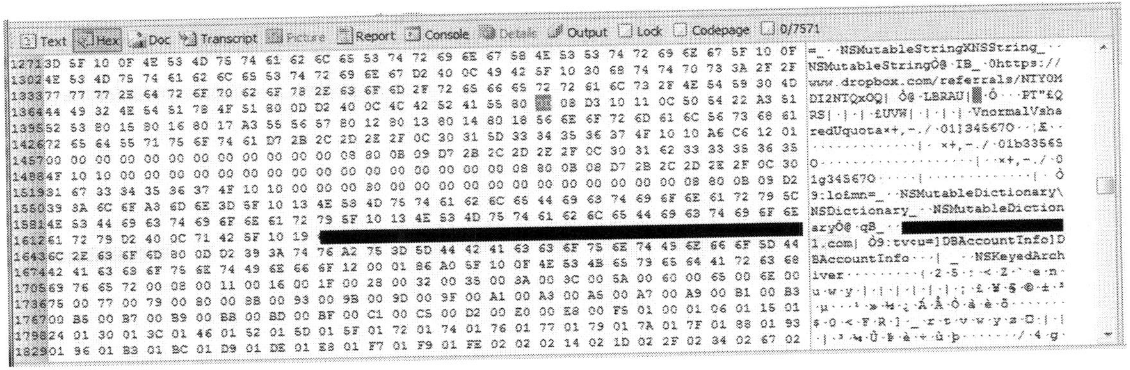

FIGURE 4.3

Hex display of username (redacted) near to "DBAccountInfo" text.

Complete

This research was limited by not being able to jailbreak the iPhone. At the time of this research, Micro Systemation (MSAB) XRY and other iPhone extract solutions require the iPhone to be jailbroken to undertake a physical extract. A future research opportunity is to undertake a physical extract of an iPhone and compare this to a logical extract to determine what information is available in comparison with the logical extract, and also to compare other mobile forensic tools. In addition, there are opportunities for further experiments to be conducted using other mobile phone OSs and devices, such as Google Android devices and the various versions currently in operation, and Microsoft Windows phone OSs.

Case study

To illustrate an application of the research findings, the following hypothetical case study outlines where the information identified in this chapter can assist in an investigation. The circumstances relate to a hypothetical case of a person suspected of managing a botnet. The circumstance of the case study is greatly simplified for the purposes of this chapter and explores a possible response using currently available software and hardware forensic solutions:

> Police receive confidential information that Bob Smith has been seen managing a botnet. A close acquaintance was visiting Bob, and observed files relating to a "Poseidon" botnet on the screen of a computer in Bob's study.
>
> An investigation case file was raised, and issued to IO Jones. IO Jones undertook background enquiries and determined that there had been prior allegations about Bob being involved in botnet offences, and that he had previous convictions for these offences. A Warrant was issued by the Court for IO Jones to attend the premises, and search and seize evidence to investigate these allegations.
>
> IO Jones attended Bob's home address and seized a PC, laptop, mobile phone, and some USB devices. These items were submitted to the Police Forensic Computing Section (FCS) for analysis.

Step 1—Commence (Scope)

IO Jones completed a Request for Analysis form, outlining the scope of the investigation, namely to search for evidence of material related to the "Poseidon" botnet.

Step 2—Preparation

As this type of analysis is a process undertaken by the FCS on a regular basis, the practitioners are trained and experienced in the analysis of the type of devices seized by IO Jones. A Standard Operating Procedure (SOP) relating to the analysis of computers and mobile devices is documented and referred to by practitioners and outlines the process. Notes are an important aspect of the SOP, and all practitioners maintain accurate notes of the process they undertake.

Step 3—Evidence source identification and preservation

The devices submitted for analysis included a custom tower PC with two hard disk drives, a generic laptop with one hard disk drive, and an Apple iPhone 3G. The USB devices were identified as wireless adapters with no data stored within them. The USB devices were photographed and details were noted for future reference.

Step 4—Collection

The details of the hard drives were documented, including make, model, and serial number. A forensic copy of the hard drives was then made using FTK Imager 3.1.0 and a Tableau T35es-R2 eSATA Forensic Bridge (hardware write blocking), and verified with MD5 and SHA1 hashes. Micro Systemation (MSAB) .XRY was used to extract the logical data from the iPhone. Appropriate entries were made in the exhibit log relating to access to the evidence by the practitioner.

Step 5—Examination and analysis

Analysis was then undertaken on the forensic copies of the data using X-Ways Forensic 16.5. "Poseidon" botnet related files were located on the second hard drive in the tower PC, and were extracted and reports created relating to the information located.

A search was conducted using the filenames identified, and references were located indicating the files were also associated with a Dropbox account. Further analysis was undertaken and URLs relating to Dropbox access were located, as was a username *bob@badstuff.com*. Dropbox client software was located under "C:\Users\bob\AppData\Roaming\Dropbox\." Additional names of further files associated with the Dropbox account were located in link files and prefetch files, such as dllhost.pf, indicating additional evidence was stored within the Dropbox account.

Analysis of the logical extract of the iPhone locates the Dropbox application and the username in the "com.getdropbox.Dropbox.plist" file and in the "keychain-backup.plist" file. Filenames associated with Dropbox were located in the "History.plist" file, and the information was also reported in the .XRY "Web-History.txt" file.

IO Jones communicated with the legal section at Dropbox to ensure the data in the account was preserved and made available in relation to the investigation.

Step 6—Presentation

A report was prepared, outlining the process and the findings of the analysis. The selected files were copied to DVD, along with the associated reports for each file, outlining creation and access dates, file details, and hash values. A timeline was used to demonstrate interaction with the files from the tower PC and the iPhone, as listed in Figure 4.4. In the timeline, it is possible to see when the documents were created via the metadata, when the documents were copied to the tower PC, link files related to the documents are created, Dropbox is accessed in relation to Poseidon, Dropbox software is searched and installed onto the PC, and files read on the PC and the iPhone.

Step 7—Complete

The practitioner was concerned that Bob may have used other cloud storage services to store copies of the "Poseidon" files and communicated this with IO Jones. IO Jones interviewed Bob, but Bob would not disclose if other accounts existed. The practitioner undertook additional searches for common cloud storage providers, such as Microsoft SkyDrive and Google Drive, identifying additional accounts held by Bob. Further enquiries were undertaken with the legal sections of the identified service providers to determine if these accounts held any relevant data.

At the completion of the original examination, the extracted data, notes, and other material related to the investigation were appropriately stored in preparation for future legal action.

CONCLUSION

With the increasing use of cloud computing, particularly cloud storage services, by both public and private sectors, the continued development of the digital forensic discipline is more important than ever. In relation to the storage of data using cloud service providers, the determination of the provider and user details is a necessary aspect of an investigation. This will enable practitioners to identify the potential location of data and act to secure this data in a timely fashion. In our case study, we found that a practitioner can identify Dropbox use by undertaking hash analysis and examine common file locations to locate software and files. We found that a Dropbox username can be determined from browser history when web access has been undertaken with Mozilla Firefox and Google Chrome, and when a user has stored their username with Microsoft Internet Explorer. By searching for a range of keyword terms, a practitioner can determine whether Dropbox has been used on seized hardware. As outlined, there are a wide range of investigation points for a practitioner to determine the use of Dropbox, such as directory listings, prefetch files, link files, thumbnails, registry, browser history,

Source	Key Date	Event type	Comment
X-Ways Docx Metadata	9/02/2012 15:24:00	Doc created metada	Poseidon.docx
X-Ways Docx Metadata	25/02/2012 12:02	Doc created metada	Poseidon.rtf
Event Log Explorer	9/06/2012 12:27:09	Logon	cloud' user
IEF Firefox	9/06/2012 12:34:00	Date Visited	http://www.mozilla.com/en-US/firefox/13.0/firstrun/
IEF Firefox	9/06/2012 12:34:00	Date Visited	http://www.mozilla.org/en-US/firefox/13.0/firstrun/
X-Ways file list	9/06/2012 12:41:49	Created	Poseidon.txt
X-Ways file list	9/06/2012 12:41:49	Created	Poseidon.tar.gz
X-Ways file list	9/06/2012 12:41:49	Created	Poseidon.docx
X-Ways file list	9/06/2012 12:41:49	Created	Poseidon.jpg
X-Ways file list	9/06/2012 12:41:49	Created	Poseidon.rtf
X-Ways Link Data	9/06/2012 12:41:49	Target Created	Poseidon.lnk
X-Ways Link Data	9/06/2012 12:41:49	Target Created	Poseidon.lnk
X-Ways file list	9/06/2012 12:41:55	Created	Poseidon.lnk
X-Ways file list	9/06/2012 12:42:03	Created	NOTEPAD.EXE-EB1B961A.pf
X-Ways file list	9/06/2012 12:42:08	Created	Poseidon.lnk
iPhone XRY extract	9/06/2012 12:43:30	accessed	Poseidon - Dropbox
IEF Firefox	9/06/2012 12:45:00	Date Visited	http://www.google.com/search?q=Dropbox%20preview%20for%20wind
IEF Firefox	9/06/2012 12:45:00	Date Visited	http://www.google.com.au/search?q=Dropbox%20preview%20for%20wi
Internet History	9/06/2012 12:46:00	Start Date	DropboxSetup.exe
X-Ways file list	9/06/2012 12:46:34	Created	Dropbox.lnk
X-Ways file list	9/06/2012 12:46:34	Created	Dropbox
X-Ways file list	9/06/2012 12:46:34	Created	Dropbox.exe
X-Ways file list	9/06/2012 12:46:34	Created	Dropbox.lnk
X-Ways Link Data	9/06/2012 12:46:34	Target Created	Dropbox.lnk
X-Ways Link Data	9/06/2012 12:46:34	Target Created	Dropbox.lnk
X-Ways file list	9/06/2012 12:47:01	Created	cloud@login.live[1].txt
iPhone XRY extract	9/06/2012 12:48:30	accessed	Poseidon.rtf download
X-Ways file list	9/06/2012 12:50:16	Accessed	Poseidon.lnk
X-Ways Prefetch Data	9/06/2012 12:50:16	Prefetch last run	NOTEPAD.EXE-EB1B961A.pf
X-Ways file list	9/06/2012 12:50:25	Accessed	Poseidon.lnk
X-Ways file list	9/06/2012 12:50:28	Created	Poseidon (2).lnk
X-Ways file list	9/06/2012 12:50:35	Created	WORDPAD.EXE-1BCC3DB7.pf
X-Ways file list	9/06/2012 12:50:36	Created	Poseidon (3).lnk
X-Ways Prefetch Data	9/06/2012 12:50:36	Prefetch last run	WORDPAD.EXE-1BCC3DB7.pf
X-Ways file list	9/06/2012 12:51:30	Accessed	Dropbox

FIGURE 4.4

Example of Timeline (Dropbox Case Study).

and memory captures. Our research has identified the locations of data and files to determine user details and cloud storage information relating to Dropbox usage. Areas for further research include the relationship of time stamps to identified files, additional experiments relating to mobile devices, and examining other popular cloud storage services[1], employing the same methodology undertaken in this research.

The outcomes of this research proved to be beneficial for a current police investigation when information was located which identified the use of Dropbox cloud storage to store illicit material. The details of the investigation cannot be expanded as it is ongoing, but it is important to highlight the real-world application of this research is already achieving the goals of expanding the information and methodology available in forensic examinations to identify when cloud storage services are being used.

References

Architecture Technologies. (2011). *Dropbox Reader V1.1* 2011 (Google Cache), viewed 23 January 2013, <http://webcache.googleusercontent.com/search?q=cache:http://cybermarshal. com/index.php/cyber-marshal-utilities/dropbox-reader&hl=en&tbo=d&strip=1> Accessed 10.02.13.

Association of Chief Police Officers (ACPO). (2006). Good Practice Guidelines for Computer Based Evidence v4.0. <www.7safe.com/electronic_evidence> Accessed 10.02.13.

Dropbox. (2012). *Contact web page — legal inquiries.* <https://www.dropbox.com/contact/> Accessed 10.02.13.

Kisswani, N. M. (2010). *Telecommunications (Interception and Access) and its regulation in arab countries* (Vol. 5, p. 225). J. Int'l Com. L. & Tech.

Martini, B, & Choo, K.-K. R. (2012). An integrated conceptual digital forensic framework for cloud computing. *Digital Investigation, 9*(2), 71−80.

McClain, F. (2011). Dropbox Forensics. *Forensic Focus,* <http://www.forensicfocus.com/ Dropbox-forensics> Accessed 10.02.13.

National Institute of Justice (NIJ). (2004). *Forensic examination of digital evidence: A guide for law enforcement.* <http://nij.gov/nij/pubs-sum/199408.htm> Accessed 10.02.13.

National Institute of Justice (NIJ). (2008). *Electronic crime scene investigation: A guide for first responders,* (2nd ed.). <http://www.nij.gov/pubs-sum/219941.htm> Accessed 10.02.13.

MagnetSoftware. (2013). *'IEF Triage',* viewed 10 February 2013, <http://www. magnetforensics.com/products/internet-evidence-finder/ief-triage> Accessed 10.02.13.

---

[1]For example, we have examined data remnants from the use of Microsoft® SkyDrive® and were able to find a vast range of information which will assist a practitioner to identify the presence of data being stored in a cloud account (see Quick and Choo, 2013).

Quick, D., & Choo, K.-K. R. (2013a). Digital droplets: Microsoft SkyDrive forensic data remnants. *Future Generation Computer Systems*, *29*(6), 1378–1394.

Quick, D., & Choo, K.-K. R. (2013b). Dropbox analysis: Data remnants on user machines. *Digital Investigation*, *10*(1), 3–18.

Russinovich, M., & Cogswell, B. (2012). *Microsoft sysinternals process monitor*, viewed 23 January 2013, <http://technet.microsoft.com/en-au/sysinternals/bb896645.aspx> Accessed 10.02.13.

USDoD. (1995). *Dod 5220.22-M-Sup 1, National industrial security program operating manual supplement*. <http://www.dtic.mil/whs/directives/corres/pdf/522022MSup1.pdf> Accessed 10.02.13.

Zatyko, K., & Bay, J. (2012). The digital forensics cyber exchange principle. *Forensic Magazine*. December 2011 - January 2012, pp. 13–15.

Google Drive: Forensic Analysis of Cloud Storage Data Remnants

5

INFORMATION IN THIS CHAPTER

- Google Drive forensic analysis
- Evidence source identification and preservation
- Collection of evidence from cloud storage services
- Examination and analysis of collected data

In the previous two chapters, the forensic analysis of cloud storage using Dropbox and SkyDrive was explored when a user uploads, accesses, or downloads data using a Windows 7 PC or an Apple iPhone 3G (see Quick & Choo, 2013a; Quick & Choo, 2013b). This was achieved using the cloud (storage) forensic framework, and data remnants were located in numerous locations. In this chapter, the focus is on Google Drive (see Quick & Choo, 2013c). The framework is again used to step through the process in a logical manner.

INTRODUCTION

The focus of this chapter is to discover the remnants left on client devices, in this case a computer and an iPhone, after a user accesses Google Drive, and to examine the benefits of using a framework to guide an investigation when undertaking forensic analysis of a cloud computing environment.

Using Google Drive as a case study, the following questions are examined:

1. What data remains on a computer hard drive after a Google Drive user has used client software or accessed cloud storage via a browser, and the location within the Windows 7 operating system of data remnants?
2. What data can be seen in network traffic, and what data remains in memory?
3. What data remains on an Apple iPhone running iOS version 4.2.1 after a user has used the inbuilt browser to access Google Drive cloud storage?

The following discussion explains first the preparation and analysis of Google Drive access using a virtual computer (VM) running Windows 7. Following this, the analysis of Google Drive access using an iPhone 3G running iOS version 4.2.1 is then discussed. The findings are then outlined, and a hypothetical case study is then used to demonstrate the relevancy of the research findings. Finally, potential future research opportunities are outlined.

Google drive forensics: Windows 7 PC

This section discusses the application of the framework (Figure 2.1) when conducting research into the data remnants on a Windows 7 computer. This serves to outline the steps of the framework, and the process used to conduct research into Google Drive data remnants. Each step is discussed in turn, as follows.

Commence (Scope)

The first step in the framework is to outline the scope of the investigation or research. The focus of this research is to determine what data remnants are locatable after a user has uploaded, accessed, or downloaded data from Google Drive using either the Google Drive client software or a browser. Popular browsers include Microsoft Internet Explorer, Mozilla Firefox, Google Chrome, and Apple Safari (W3Counter, 2012). These four browsers are used in this research to determine any differences in the ability to retrieve data remnants. The goal is to determine data remnants such as username, password, filenames, dates and times, or the presence of client software, to indicate which cloud service, if any, had been used on a Windows 7 PC. In addition, circumstances were created to simulate a user running Eraser or CCleaner to remove evidence of using Google Drive (i.e., anti-forensics). Memory capture and analysis is included as this is an important source of evidence which should be captured and examined when possible (Association of Chief Police Officers (ACPO), 2006; National Institute of Justice (NIJ), 2008). Network data capture is another potential source of information which will form part of the scope to determine what data is present within the network traffic from a host PC.

Preparation

To gather the data required to answer the research questions in relation to the use of Google Drive, a variety of VMs were created. It was decided to examine a variety of circumstances of a user accessing Google Drive and also to examine any differences when using different browsers. Multiple scenarios were explored, each making use of Google Drive with the various browsers: Internet Explorer (IE), Mozilla Firefox (FF), Google Chrome (GC), and Apple Safari (AS). Ultimately there were 36 VMs created which replicate different circumstances of usage. A benefit of using virtual machines is the ease of capturing memory, by copying the "VMEM" files as a virtual machine (VM) was running. It was also easy to capture network traffic by running Wireshark on the host PC and monitoring and capturing network traffic on the VM interface. Attempting this using physical hardware would have been difficult, and the time and equipment required undertaking this would have reduced the scope of the research.

The UC Berkeley Enron Email subset data file was used as the sample data and was downloaded from the project web site (http://bailando.sims.berkeley.edu/enron_email.html) on the February 9, 2012. Hash values (MD5) were calculated for these files, and keyterms were identified to enable searching and location of the data and files in subsequent analysis.

Virtualized PCs were created using VMware Player 4.0.1. For each scenario, a Base image was created, and Windows 7 Home Basic was installed on a 20 GB virtual hard drive with 1 GB RAM. The Base-VMs were used as control media to determine the files created when user activity was undertaken in each scenario. The different actions undertaken were as follows:

1. The first step was to install the browser software into separate Base-VMs for each browser: Mozilla Firefox 13.0.1, Internet Explorer 9.0.8112.16421IC, Google Chrome 19.0.1084.56m, and Apple Safari 5.1.7 for Windows 7.
2. Next was to make a copy of the Base-VM for each browser. These four VMs were labeled IE, FF, GC, and AS Upload-VM, and were used to access the Google Drive web site, and download and install the client software ("googledrivesync.exe" version 1.2.3101.4994 and 1.3.3209.2688). A Google Drive account was created for this research, and sign-in undertaken using the client software. The Enron sample files were uploaded to the Google Drive account using the client software.
3. Additional copies of the Base-VM for each browser were made, labeled Access-VM. These were used to access the Google Drive web site (https://drive.google.com) using each installed browser. The sign-in option was used to log in to the user account created in step 2. Each of the stored files was opened within the browser, but not deliberately downloaded.
4. Copies were made of the four Base-VMs, labeled Download-VM. Each installed browser was used to access the Google Drive website. The sign-in option was used to log in to the user account created in step 2. All of the files in the Google Drive cloud storage account were downloaded to the virtual machine hard drive as a zip file. The contents of the zip file were extracted to the Desktop and then each file was opened and closed.
5. Copies were made of the four Download-VMs, labeled Eraser-VM. Eraser v6.0.10.2620 was installed and used to erase each of the Enron data files and the zip files.
6. Copies were made of the four Eraser-VMs, labeled CCleaner-VM. CCleaner v3.19.1721 was installed and run across the virtual machine hard drives to remove the browsing history and file references.
7. Copies were made of the four CCleaner-VMs, labeled DBAN VM. Darik's Boot and Nuke (DBAN) version 2.2.6 Beta was used to boot each

DBAN-VM. DBAN was run with the option to erase the entire 20 GB hard drive with the "USDoD level 3" setting.

While preparing each VM, Wireshark 1.6.5 was run on the host computer to capture network traffic from the virtual machine network interface. Memory capture was facilitated by copying the Virtual Memory (VMEM) files created by VMware just prior to shutdown. The network capture files were saved at various points while the VMs were running, and also after shutdown.

Evidence source identification and preservation

In the context of this research, files were identified which would contain the information needed to conduct the analysis: the virtual hard drives (VMDK files) in each VM folder, each memory instance (VMEM files), and each saved network capture file (PCAP). These were identified for each of the VMs.

Collection

To observe the principles of forensic computer acquisition (Association of Chief Police Officers (ACPO), 2006; National Institute of Justice (NIJ), 2008), a forensic copy was made of each virtual hard drive (VMDK file) using AccessData FTK Imager CLI 2.9.0 in the Encase Evidence format (E01). In regard to the each memory file (VMEM) and network capture (PCAP) file, a forensic copy was made using Encase version 6.19.4, in the Logical Evidence format (L01), and the X-Ways Evidence File Container format (ctr). Hash values (MD5) were used to ensure the forensic integrity of the data.

Examination and analysis

For this research, each of the forensic copies of the VM hard drives, memory, and network captures was examined using a range of forensic analysis tools, including X-Ways Forensic version 16.5, Guidance Software EnCase version 6.19.4, AccessData FTK version 1.81.6 and version 4.01, Network Miner 1.0, Wireshark 1.6.5, Magnet Software (formerly JADSoftware) Internet Evidence Finder 5.52, and RegRipper version 20080909. Many of these tools are widely used for digital forensic analysis by law enforcement agencies and the private sector. In addition, Encase 6.5 and FTK Imager 2.5.3.14 have been tested by the Office of Law Enforcement Standards of the National Institute of Standards and Technology (Office of Law Enforcement Standards, 2012).

Control—Base-VMs

Analysis of the four control Base-VM hard drive images confirmed there was no data originally present relating to the Enron sample test data and Google Drive client software files. References were only located for the web site address details "drive google com" in the Google Chrome Base-VM, in the "chrome.dll" file and "chrome.7z." No references were located in the other VMs.

Google drive client software

Analysis of the four Upload-VMs locates the "googledrivesync.exe" file that was downloaded from the Google Drive web site to the Users "Downloads" folder. When run, the executable file "googledrivesync.exe" was copied to "C:\Program Files\Google\Drive\" folder, and "googledrivesync32.dll" was created. Different hash values were observed for the executable files, the only consistent hash value was "1de85d9907bb78b381d1433b8330880d" for the executable installed to the Program Files folder, created on June 13, 2012 at 4:30 p.m. (ACST). The installation executable files downloaded from Google at different times had varying hash values, suggesting changes are made regularly, and hence the hash values were different. For a practitioner to use hash values to locate client software files, there would be a need to maintain a database of hash values, including historical software hash values for the different client software releases.

Created in the Users folder is a directory as follows: "C:\Users\[username]\ AppData\Local \Google\Drive\". Within this folder were two files of interest: "sync_config.db" and "snapshot.db." Both files are SQLite format 3 database files and are able to be viewed in SQLite reader software such as the SQLite Manager Application for Mozilla Firefox (https://code.google.com/p/sqlite-manager/). Data stored in the sync_config.db file includes the local path for the sync folder where the files in the account are downloaded and synchronized (\\?\C:\ Users\[username]\Google Drive) and the user email is used to access the Google Drive account. Data stored in the snapshot.db file included the file details for files stored in the Google Drive account. Information such as filenames, modified and created times, URL, size, resource ID, and a checksum value matches the MD5 value for the associated file. Example data from one of the snapshot.db files is included in Table 5.1 with the data for the Enron.jpg test file. The modified and created times appear to be Unix Numeric time format, which can be decoded using DCode (www.digital-detective.co.uk) and were found to match the times of the files stored in the sync folder. The information in the snapshot.db file is of particular importance to a forensic investigator.

Google Drive synchronized files and folders were observed at the default Google Drive folder location ("C:\Users\[username]\Google Drive\"). Within this folder was a "desktop.ini" file with the following contents: "InfoTip = Your Google Drive folder contains files you're syncing with Google." and "IconFile = C:\Program Files\Google\Drive\googledrivesync.exe." A Prefetch file was also created in the Windows Prefetch folder with the name "GOOGLEDRIVESYNC.EXE-XXXXXXXX.pf." Client software filename references were also located in a variety of locations, such as $LogFile, $MFT, $UsnJrnl, hiberfil. sys, and pagefile.sys. Link files were created on the Windows Desktop and in the Windows Start Menu.

Table 5.1 Example of Snapshot.db SQLite File Contents for enron.jpg File

Resource_id:	"file:XXwUTD1c9KXiMXXJCVXFsZEIqRkE"
Filename:	"Enron3111.jpg"
Modified:	"1328766794" (DCode Unix Numeric Value = Thu, 09 February 2012 15:23:14. +0930)
Created:	"1339309046" (DCode Unix Numeric Value = Sun, 10 June 2012 15:47:26. +0930)
Acl_role:	"0"
Doc_type:	"1"
Removed:	"0"
URL:	"https://docs.google.com/file/d/XXwUTD1c9KXiMXXJCVXFsZEIqRkE/edit"
Size:	"315868"
Checksum:	"77638319ea64cc1b70d4d4f20a56295d"
Shared:	"0"

Also of note is that the **password** for the Google Drive user account was located in **cleartext** within the file "`C:\Users\[username]\AppData\Local \Microsoft\Internet Explorer\Recovery\Last Active\ {F9C06D05-B2C2-11E1- B53F-000C29985EDE}.dat`" near the text "&Passwd =," such as:

```
&ktl = &ktf = &Email = username@mail.
com&Passwd = XXXXXXXX&PasswdAgain = XXXXXXX
```

This information was located within the IE Upload-VM and also in System Volume Information Restore Points. The password in the file was not observed when the other browsers were used. While this may be beneficial to a forensic investigation, this also presents a security risk to users. Subashini and Kavitha (Subashini et al., 2011) explained that "[m]alicious users can exploit weaknesses in the data security model to gain unauthorized access to data." A password and username stored within files on a hard drive could easily be discerned by a criminal user who has gained remote access to a victim's computer using a common exploit, and could be used to extract data from an account or to store illicit data in the victim's account.

When installed, the Google Drive client software ran automatically when the Windows operating system started and logged in to the user account without prompting for a password. This can be of assistance in an investigation, as a forensic copy of a seized computer hard drive can be used with software which will allow the forensic copy of a hard drive to be run within a virtual environment. Software such as Virtual Forensic Computing or LiveView will scan the forensic image of a hard drive and prepare the requisite files to run an operating system on a hard drive within VMware Player. In tests conducted, when the forensic copy of a hard drive contains the Google Drive client software with a user account and password already stored, the PC when started in a VM automatically signed in to the Google Drive account. This process will provide a practitioner access to the files stored within the Google Drive user account (once synchronized). In addition, there was an option with the Google Drive client software from the Google Drive icon at the bottom right of the Desktop on Windows 7 labeled "**visit Google Drive on the web**" which when selected resulted in the opening of the default browser and provided full access to the Google Drive account, including the ability to view user activity, all items, and view the modified, edited, and last opened dates for files. In a forensic environment, care would need to be taken when connecting a forensic image to the Internet. Legal authority would be required to ensure a practitioner has the appropriate authority within their jurisdiction to examine the data stored within the cloud storage account, which could potentially be stored overseas or in another jurisdiction. For example in Australia, Section 3L of the *Crimes Act 1914* (Cth) has a provision for the executing officer of a warrant to access data which includes data not held at the premises, i.e., accessible from a computer or data storage device. Where assistance is required in operating the equipment and the executing officer believes on reasonable grounds that the material is liable to be destroyed, modified, or tampered with they may "do whatever is necessary to secure the equipment, whether by locking it up, placing a guard or otherwise" (see Section 3L(4)) for a period of up to 24 hours or until expert assistance can be obtained, whichever happens first (see Subsection 3L(6)). This period may be extended under Section 3L(7), and notice of these arrangements must also be given to the occupier under Sections 3L(5) and 3L(8). Section 3LA also makes it an offence for persons with knowledge of computers or computer networks of which computers form a part, or measures applied to protect data held in, or accessible from, computers, to fail to provide any information or assistance that is reasonable and necessary to allow access to data held in, or accessible from, a computer that is on warrant premises, to copy the data to a data storage device, or to convert the data into documentary form. Failure to comply carries a maximum penalty of two years' imprisonment. Provisions such as Section 3LA of the *Crimes Act 1914* (Cth) are designed to overcome the efforts of accused persons to conceal data through the use of passwords or encryption, including in cloud storage services.

In addition, the files contained within the installed Google Drive folders were copied to another PC; however, this did not allow access to the Google Drive account without knowing the username and password. The process of copying the software files from a PC was previously worked with Dropbox client software (Chung et al., 2012; McClain, 2011).

Google drive account when accessed via a browser

It was observed that the Google Drive web account (accessed via `https://drive.google.com`) displays the username at the top right of the browser. When selecting a file in a Google Drive account using a browser, there is an option to display the metadata for a file by clicking on the "Manage Revisions" link using the right-mouse-button (RMB). Folder information is also displayed and includes the last modified time.

When downloading files from Google Drive via the browser, the folders and files are packed into a compressed ZIP file. There is an option to download "All Items" and the ZIP file is named "documents-export" with the date, e.g., "`docu-ments-export-2012-08-29.zip`." When a download is undertaken from a folder, the ZIP is named with the folders name and the date, e.g., "`Dataset-2012-08-29.zip`."

Keyword search terms

Keyword search terms were determined from the filenames observed and the text from within the Enron data files. These included the following:

- the username and password of the Google Drive account created for this research
- "https://drive.google.com/," "Google Drive," and "googledrivesync.exe"
- "dataset," "3111.txt," "enron3111," and "Enron Wholesale Services"

Directory listings

Analysis was conducted using X-Ways Forensic 16.5 and Encase 6.19.4 to view the filenames stored within the VMs, determined from the directory listing ($MFT[1] files) and keyword searches across the forensic image files. Analysis of the directory and file listings of the four control Base-VM hard drives revealed no references to the Enron sample data filenames or Google Drive client software filenames. It was concluded that references to Google Drive and the Enron sample files were not present in the control media directory listings prior to installing the software or accessing the files.

Not surprisingly, there were references to the Google Drive client software in the Upload-VMs, which correlated to the VMs where the client software was used. This included the downloaded installation program "googlesdrivesync.exe" and the previously mentioned database files "sync-config.db" and "snapshot.db." There were no references to the client software in the other VMs. There were references to the filenames for the Enron sample files in the VMs (excluding the Base-VMs), and when the files were downloaded via the browser from the root folder. In the Upload-VMs, there was a substantial amount of filenames seen, including from the source folder and in the default Google Drive folder "`C:\User\[username]\Google Drive`."

When a browser was used to access a Google Drive account, there were less filename references for the Enron files (in comparison with when the client software was used to access cloud storage). However, with a browser being used to access the Google Drive account stored files, there were sufficient file name

---

[1]"*The NTFS file system contains at its core a file called the master file table (MFT). There is at least one entry in the MFT for every file on an NTFS volume, including the MFT itself*" (Microsoft, 2008).

references remaining on the hard drives to identify the filenames that were accessed, such as the Enron sample data filenames. In the circumstances when the files were downloaded and opened from the Google Drive cloud storage, there were additional filename references observed on the hard drive, including link files. This indicates when a user accesses Google Drive, there will potentially be references in the $MFT directory listing and in a variety of locations (such as pagefile.sys and prefetch files) to indicate this, and also to potentially determine the filenames associated with Google Drive use by searching for Google Drive filename entries in the $MFT.

Link file references remained after Eraser and CCleaner had been used to remove the files and "clean" the hard drive. Using CCleaner with all options selected removed the link files (however sufficient information remained in other locations such as prefetch files, relating to Google Drive and the Enron sample files, discussed in the next section). The use of DBAN completely erased the hard drives, and there was no data to analyze in these VMs.

Prefetch files

Analysis of the VM hard drives identified that prefetch[2] files stored information relating to the filenames of the Google Drive executable and Enron test data filenames. This was located in all the VM hard drives except the control Base-VM hard drives and the Access-VM hard drives. It was observed that even after running CCleaner, there was enough information in prefetch files, such as `notepad. exe.pf`, `wordpad.exe.pf`, and `dllhost.exe.pf`, to indicate the presence and path of the Enron sample data files. Also located were `googledrivesync.exe.pf` prefetch files when the client software was installed. Information located within the prefetch files included the file and folder path, the number of times run, and last run time and date. This information may be important in an investigation.

Link files

Analysis of link[3] files was undertaken using Encase 6.19.4. No Google Drive associated link files were found within the four control Base-VMs or the Access-VMs. Link files relating to Google Drive and the Enron sample data files were observed for all Upload-VM, Download-VM, Eraser-VM, and CCleaner-VM hard drives. When CCleaner was used with all options selected, there were no logical link files containing Google Drive or the Enron sample data filenames (however the information from the deleted Link files was still present and recoverable from the hard drives).

---

[2]*"Windows keeps track of the way a computer starts and which programs are commonly opened. Windows saves this information as a number of small files in the prefetch folder."* (Microsoft, 2012b).
[3]A link file is a shortcut to a file or program (Microsoft, 2012a).

The link files observed related to the filenames and folder names for the Google Drive executable, such as `C:\Program Files\Google\Drive\googledrive sync.exe` with the description `Your Google Drive folder contains files you're syncing with Google`. Link files relating to the Enron test data were also located. These were located in the "Windows\Recent" and "Windows\Start" folders in the Users "AppData" directory, such as "`C\Users\[username]\AppData\Roaming \Microsoft\Windows\Recent\3111.lnk`." There was no Google Drive or Enron link files within the four Access-VM hard drives, indicating that if files were not downloaded from Google Drive to the computer and opened, link files were not created. The presence of a link file may indicate the prior presence of a file, even if the logical file has been deleted, which may be of importance in an investigation.

Thumbcache files

Analysis of the thumbnail pictures stored within the thumbcache[4] files within the four control Base-VMs determined that there were no Enron sample picture thumbnails present prior to installing or accessing Google Drive. Thumbnails for the Enron sample picture were located in "`thumbcache_256.db`" files in the Upload-VM, Download-VM, and Eraser-VMs; however, none were found in the Access-VMs or the CCleaner VMs. This indicates that the thumbnail cache is a source for possible data relating to Google Drive use, but results may not be definitive. It is possible for Google Drive to be used in certain circumstances without leaving thumbnails, e.g., accessing files using a browser but not down-loading the files to a computer. Thumbcache data may be of assistance to determine whether a file was present on a drive, even if the file has been deleted or erased. It is possible that even if a file has been erased, enough information may remain within a thumbcache file to show the contents of a picture file, conclude a file was present, and associated dates and times may also be of assistance.

Event log files

Event log files are sources of information relating to system, software, and other events recorded by Windows operating systems. In this research, there were two records relating to Google Drive within the event log files. These were in the IE Upload-VM "Microsoft-Windows-Diagnostics-Performance Operational.evtx" file and related to the googledrivesync.exe file. However, the details of these entries could not be interpreted with Event Log Explorer, EvtParser, or the inbuilt Windows Event Viewer. Similar entries were not seen when the Google Chrome, Mozilla Firefox, or Apple Safari browser were used. No entries were located in the Base-VM images nor in the other VM images. Therefore, data in an event log file may indicate if the Google Drive client software was installed on a PC, even

---

[4]"*Windows 7 creates small thumbnail images of graphic files. There are files named Thumbcache_32.db, Thumbcache_96.db, Thumbcache_256.db, and Thumbcache_1024.db which correspond to the thumbnails stored for that specific user account and size*" (Mueller, 2010).

if the software has been uninstalled. Examining the entries in context may indicate dates and times when the software was in use.

Registry files

Windows registry files were parsed using RegRipper version 20080909 and parsed and analyzed with X-Ways 16.5. Encase 6.19.4 was also used to analyze the registry files and RegRipper output. Analysis revealed there were no references to Google Drive or the Enron sample files in the four control Base-VM hard drives. There were no references to the Google Drive username or password within the registry files in any of the VMs. When the Google Drive client software was used, there were references found in the Upload-VMs for all browsers in NTUser.dat, UsrClass.dat, SOFTWARE, and SYSTEM registry files. This information was located using keyword searches for the term "googledrivesync.exe" across the registry files and also the parsed text from the registry files (output from RegRipper). Specific keys were created when the client software was installed, such as "SOFTWARE\Google\Drive\" with the key "InstallLocation," listing the path to the executable C:\Program Files\Google\Drive\ googledrive sync.exe.

There were no references to the filenames when a browser was used to access the Google Drive account files. However, when a browser was used to download and open files from Google Drive accounts, there were references to the filenames of the files in the Download-VM registry files for all browsers. For example, the "RecentDocs" key in the NTUSER.dat registry file provided a list of the Enron related files and folders, and a sample RegRipper output is listed as follows:

```
- - - - - - - - - - - - - - - - - - - - - - - - - - - - - - - - - - - - - - - -
RecentDocs — recentdocs
**All values printed in MRUList\MRUListEx order.
Software\Microsoft\Windows\CurrentVersion\Explorer\RecentDocs
LastWrite Time Sun Jun 17 02:31:14 2012 (UTC)
            1 = Dataset
            4 = Enron3111.rtf
            3 = Enron3111.jpg
            2 = Enron3111.docx
            0 = 3111.txt
- - - - - - - - - - - - - - - - - - - - - - - - - - - - - - - - - - - - - - - -
```

Deleted information regarding Google Drive and the Enron files and folders was located within the NTUSER.dat registry files after CCleaner was run, such as the previously observed filenames and URL references. References were also found within the UsrClass.dat registry files when the Google Drive client software was used.

$Recycle.Bin

Files that were deleted were easily located in the $Recycle.Bin folder in a folder with the SID of the user. The information files (beginning with $I) included the data relating to the original file and when it was deleted, such as the following example relating to the Google Drive Dataset folder deleted from the default Google Drive sync location (Table 5.2).

Also located in the Recycle Bin were the file contents files (beginning with $R), which contained the original folder and file contents. In the scope of this research, this included the files synchronized from Google Drive account using the client software.

Data carve

Data carving is the process of searching through allocated or unallocated data to locate files based on known headers and footers, such as 0xFFD8 and 0xFFD9 for a jpg file. This was undertaken using Encase 6.19.4 File Finder Signature Search and X-Ways 16.5 File Header Signature Search across all VMs created for this research. Thumbnail icons and partial full size pictures were carved from all VMs, except the Base-VMs.

Browser analysis

Internet browsing information was analyzed using Magnet Software (formerly JADsoftware) Internet Evidence Finder (IEF) v5.52 Standard Edition, X-Ways Forensic 16.5, and SQLite Database Browser v2. It was confirmed there were no references to Google Drive or Enron sample data in the Internet history of the four control Base-VMs. References were located for the Google Drive web site ("drive google com") in the Google Chrome Base-VM. The Google Drive account username could be determined when Mozilla Firefox, Google Chrome, and Internet Explorer were used to access the account using the browser, but the username was not located when Apple Safari was used. The username was stored in Firefox in the "formhistory.sqlite" database and in Chrome in the Autofill "Web Data" file.

The Google Drive web site URL (drive.google.com) was located in a range of areas, such as Cookie files, web history, FavIcons, in the FileSlack of other files, unallocated space, and Pagefile.sys. This occurred for all browsers. Filenames for files downloaded were located in the web history of all hard drives, except for the Base-VMs. Data was located in Browser history files, such as index.dat files

---

Table 5.2 $Recycle.Bin $I Information for Deleted Google Drive Dataset Folder (X-Ways 16.5)

Size: 4.7 MB
Moved to recycle bin: 01/10/2012 14:23:44
C:\Users\cloud\Google Drive\Dataset

and `downloads.sqlite`. When using the Google Chrome browser to access Google Drive, references were located in a range of browser system files, such as `Top Sites`, `History`, `Shortcuts`, `Preferences`, `History Provider Cache`, `FavIcons`, `Current Tabs`, and `Current Sessions`.

When storing files in Google Drive, a unique Resource-ID identifier is assigned to a file and is included in a URL reference for the file. For example, for the file 3111.txt, Google Drive (and Google Docs) assigned the following URL:

https://docs.google.com/file/d/XXwUTD1c9KXiMXXNERGJKV1FTUUE/

Examining multiple URLs, it appears the Resource-ID identifier consists of the first part relating to the user, and the second part relates to the file, as for multiple files the initial 13 characters are the same, and the subsequent 15 characters are different depending on the file. This information is stored within the snapshot. db file, and IEF also outputs the information for the URL and the filename from the web browsing history in the format listed in Table 5.3. A practitioner can conduct searches for a known filename or Resource-ID identifier to locate instances of the file or URL being used. Searches conducted across the network captures (PCAPS) also locate the Resource-ID identifiers, associated with drive.google. com cookie files.

IEF 5.5 introduced the ability to report information relating to cloud storage, including Google Drive related data. Using this option, some data was located in some Upload-VM files, but not for all instances when the software or access was

---

Table 5.3 Example of snapshot.db SQLite File Contents and IEF Output

`Firefox` (`snapshot.db`)
`16/06/2012 20:48:46`
`3111.txt` - `Google Docs`
`https://docs.google.com/file/d/XXwUTD1c9KXiMXXNERGJKV1FTUUE/edit?`
`pli=1`
`Internet Explorer` (`snapshot.db`)
`10/06/2012 16:01:40`
`httpsdocs.google.com file/d/XXwUTD1c9KXiMXXNERGJKV1FTUUE/edit?pli=1`
`3111.txt` - `Google Docs`
`Chrome Web History` (`IEF`)
`2012-06-17 02:19:47`
`https://docs.google.com/file/d/XXwUTD1c9KXiMXXNERGJKV1FTUUE/edit`
`3111.txt` - `Google Docs`
`2012-06-17 02:19:56`
`https://docs.google.com/file/d/XXwUTD1c9KXiMXXNERGJKV1FTUUE/edit`
`3111.txt` - `Google Docs`

undertaken and not all potential data was reported. Data was recovered from the Internet Explorer, Google Chrome, and Apple Safari Upload-VMs, but not the Firefox Upload-VM. Data located included filenames, the user name and the file URL Identifiers, associated file dates and times, and file sizes. Information was also located in the Internet Explorer Access-VM. Information was reported from the Google Drive "snapshot.db" file, Pagefile.sys, Unallocated Clusters, and File Slack. The information recovered was of benefit, but was not all the available information from the VMs. Additional information was viewable from the "snapshot.db" files in each of the Upload-VM files, using the SQLite Manager Application for Mozilla Firefox. Using CCleaner with standard options and then all options did not remove the references previously located in relation to Google Drive use.

Metadata

Using X-Ways 16.5, it is possible to extract metadata from files, such as the EXIF data from JPG files or information from documents. This can then be used to conduct analysis. It was possible to determine the picture files which related to the Enron test data by searching on the metadata contents. It was also possible to locate the rtf document files based on the author information stored within the file.

Network analysis

Analysis of the network traffic capture files was undertaken using Network Miner v1.0, Wireshark Portable 1.6.5, and Encase 6.19.4. The network traffic was observed on Port 80 (HTTP) and 443 (HTTPS). When accessing Google Drive accounts using the client software or a browser, it appears login sessions are established with Google using IP numbers such as 74.125.237.133, 134, 135, and 144 (in the range registered to Google: 74.125.0.0−74.125.255.255), with URLs of "www.google.com." Verification is then undertaken on IP 199.7.55.72, which is registered to Verisign Global Registry Services, with the URL "ocsp.verisign. net." Security certificates appeared to be approved using VeriSign/Thawte ser- vices, in the 199.7.48.0−199.7.63.255 range. The URL "ocsp.verisign.net" was observed in the network traffic, OCSP is the Online Certificate Status Protocol, used by VeriSign/Thawte. When downloading the client software, IPs 173.194.72.84 and 173.194.72.190 (which are registered to Google) were observed, with the URLs "accounts.google.com" and "dl-ssl.google.com." The client software download of "gsync.msi" then occurred via an ISP cache location (in this case 150.101.13.84 which is registered to Internode). When the client soft- ware was run and synchronized with an account, IPs in the range 74.125.237.128−142 were observed, with URLs of "docs.google.com." These are registered to Google in the range 74.125.0.0−74.125.255.255.

When accessing files or data in an account via a browser, the process of acces- sing IPs in the ranges previously mentioned for the client software were observed: (1) "www.google.com," (2) "verisign," (3) "account.google," and (4) "docs.

google." An IP (173.194.72.189) with the URL of "drive.google.com" was also observed. Table 5.4 lists the IP number ranges observed in the captured network traffic and the registered owner for the range, and in the order observed when connecting to an account and accessing data within the account. The same URL names were observed when using either the Google Drive client software or accessing via a browser. Previous analysis of Dropbox network traffic determined Dropbox uses different URLs when using a browser compared to when using the client software.

The username for the Google Drive account was observed in cleartext in the network traffic when Internet Explorer was used, but not when other browsers were used. The contents of the Enron sample data files were not seen in the network traffic, suggesting the data was encrypted. No password information was observed in cleartext in the network traffic. The web site URL "drive.google. com" was observed in network traffic when an account was accessed, but not in the control Base-VM, the Eraser-VM, or CCleaner-VM network traffic.

System volume information

When Eraser or CCleaner were used, information was still located in various System Volume Information files, also known as Restore Points or Volume Shadow Copies. The information included the username for the Google Drive account, the URLs for the Google Drive web site (https://drive.google.com), the filenames, and full text of the Enron files. When limited information was located during analysis, such as filenames only, the System Volume Information files contain a wider range of information, such as file contents or deleted URLs. System Volume Information was highlighted as an important source of information when anti-forensic methods had been used, in this research Eraser and CCleaner.

Table 5.4 IP Addresses Observed in Network Traffic

Step	Registered Owner	IP Start	IP Finish	URLs Observed in Network Traffic
1	Google Inc.	74.125.0.0	74.125.255.255	www.google.com
2	Verisign Global Registry	199.7.48.0	199.7.63.255	ocsp.verisign.net
3	Google Inc.	173.194.0.0	173.194.255.255	accounts.google.com and dl-ssl.google.com
4	Google Inc.	74.125.0.0	74.125.255.255	docs.google.com and large-uploads.google.com
5	Google Inc.	173.194.0.0	173.194.255.255	drive.google.com

Memory (RAM) analysis

Analysis of the memory captures (VMEM files) was undertaken using X-Ways 16.5 and Encase 6.19.4. The term "Google Drive" was located in all the memory captures excluding the control Base-VM memory files. The URL (drive.google.com) was not located in the control Base-VM memory files but was located in all other memory capture files. The Google Drive account username was located in all Upload-VMs, and in the Firefox, Google Chrome, and Internet Explorer Access-VM and Download-VMs (not in the Safari Access-VM or Download-VM). The Google Drive username was located in memory capture files near the text; "? —Email," "?? Email," and "<email>." The **password** was located in **freetext** in the Upload-VM memory files for Firefox, Internet Explorer, and Safari browsers, near the text "&passwd = [password]" and "&passwdagain = [password]."

The username was also located in the Eraser-VM memory captures, in the Firefox and Google Chrome CCleaner-VM memory captures, and also in the Google Chrome memory capture file when CCleaner was used with all options. However, when the Safari browser was used, the username was only recovered in the Upload-VM memory capture.

The full text of the Enron data files was recovered in the Upload-VM, Access-VM, and Download-VM memory captures. In addition, the text was located in the Google Chrome Erase-VM memory file. No text was located in the control Base-VM memory files. Observed within memory captures were Enron filename references in all VM memory files, except the control Base-VM memory files.

Data carving was undertaken across the memory capture files and resulted in the recovery of thumbnail pictures, partial and full picture files of the Enron sample pictures, and Google Drive logos from the memory captures for all Upload-VM and Download-VM memory files. No picture files were recovered from the Base-VM memory files, or when Eraser or CCleaner had been used.

Analysis of Pagefile.sys files was also undertaken. The username was located in the Safari Access-VM pagefile.sys file and the Internet Explorer Upload-VM pagefile. The web site URL ("https://drive.google.com") was located in the Internet Explorer and Safari browser pagefile.sys files, but not the Firefox or Google Chrome browser pagefile.sys files. The filenames for the Enron test files were located in Upload, Download, Erase, and CCleaner-VM pagefile.sys files when Chrome and Safari browsers were used, but not when Firefox was used. Filenames were located in the Internet Explorer Upload-VM pagefile.sys file, but no other Internet Explorer VM files. Filenames were located after Eraser and CCleaner were used, again highlighting pagefile.sys as an area for examination if anti-forensic methods are suspected of being used. The full text of the Enron email was found in the pagefile.sys file in the Google Chrome Erase and CCleaner-VM files only.

Eraser, CCleaner, and DBAN

As discussed, many remnants indicating the use of Google Drive and the presence of the Enron sample files were located after Eraser and CCleaner were used.

This indicated that Eraser or CCleaner did not necessarily remove all data remnants in relation to the use of Google Drive or completely remove the information relating to the presence of the Enron sample files. The use of a full erasing tool, in this case DBAN, was found to remove all traces, but this also erased the operating system and user files. The operating system and user files would need to be reinstalled, which could be a lengthy process and may dissuade the average user from undertaking this process to remove evidence of Google Drive usage.

Presentation

Analysis findings

A variety of data remnants were located when Google Drive was used to store or access data. The focus (or scope) was to determine what data remnants were left to identify if Google Drive had been used on a Windows 7 PC. Conducting a search for the web site "drive google com" was shown to be inconclusive to demonstrate use, as it was shown that the term is present even when Google Drive has not been accessed, as outlined in the analysis of the control Base-VMs in the Google Chrome Base-VM "chrome.dll" file and "chrome.7z."

The Google Drive username was able to be discerned from a variety of locations, such as cookie files, memory captures (searching for "&Email="), in pagefile.sys, from SQLite database files, and IEF output. The username was also observed in cleartext in the network traffic when the Internet Explorer browser was used, but not when other browsers were used.

Surprisingly, the **password** for the Google Drive account was able to be located **unencrypted** in an Internet Explorer .dat file, as follows:

"C\Users\[username]\AppData\Local\Microsoft\Internet Explorer\Recovery \Last Active\ {F9C06D05-B2C2-11E1-B53F-000C29985EDE}.dat" near the text "&Passwd=," such as:

&ktl=&ktf=&Email=username@mail.com&Passwd=XXXXXXXX&PasswdAgain= XXXXXXX

This was not observed when the other browsers were used. This information was also located within System Volume Information Restore Point data on the IE Upload-VM image file. The cleartext password was also located in the memory captures from the Upload-VMs for Mozilla Firefox, Internet Explorer, and Apple Safari browsers, pagefile.sys from the Safari Access-VM, and the Internet Explorer Upload-VM pagefile. The password was located in freetext near the text "&passwd=[password]" and "&passwdagain=[password]."

Passwords are commonly used in a variety of locations, and when conducting analysis to determine a password to view encrypted files, one practice is to build an index of words from a forensic image to use with password analysis tools such as AccessData Password Recovery Toolkit, Passware, or Elcomsoft password analysis tools. With the actual password stored in cleartext, this would vastly speed up the process of password discovery. Hence, memory capture and analysis should be a key consideration when determining the possible sources of data in step 3 of the framework (identify and collect) for indexing purposes.

If the password is not located in memory, or if memory capture is not possible, it is still possible to access a Google Drive account using the forensic image of a hard drive where the Google Drive client software has been used to access an account. This can be achieved by running the hard drive forensic image as a virtual machine. When the VM starts up, it automatically synchronizes with the Google Drive cloud service and updates files in the local Google Drive folder. The Google Drive client software also includes the ability to connect to the account via a browser, without requiring the username or password. There is an option from the Google Drive icon at the bottom right of the Desktop on Windows 7 labeled "**visit Google Drive on the web**" which when selected results in the opening of a browser with full access to the Google Drive account, including the ability to view user activity, all items, and view the modified, edited, and last opened dates for files. Appropriate legal authority would be required to ensure the account and information can be accessed and used for analysis.

Analysis to determine the method of access, whether the client software was used, a browser used to upload, access, or download, or a combination of both, is possible. When the client software was downloaded, there was a GoogleDriveSync.exe file downloaded to the local hard drive. In addition, registry entries may indicate the use of the setup software or the client software, as will link files. Prefetch files were observed for the client software and also included the number of times run, and associated dates and times.

When using a browser to access a Google Drive web account, the username was displayed at the top right of the browser. When selecting a file in a Google Drive account using a browser, there was an option to display the metadata for a file by clicking on the "Manage Revisions" link using the RMB. Folder information was also displayed and included the last modified time. This information may be important in an investigation and should be recorded, either as handwritten notes, screen captures, or video recording a browser window using software such as Microsoft Expression Encoder 4. There were many references in the output from IEF for browser access to a Google Drive account. When bulk files were downloaded using the web account from the root folder, a compressed ZIP file was created and downloaded with the name of the folder and the date in the filename, such as "Dataset-2012-08-29.zip."

When using the client software, files of interest are created in the Users folder at the following location: "C:\Users\[username]\AppData\Local\Google\Drive\." Within this folder were two files of interest: "sync_config.db" and "snapshot.db." Both files are SQLite format 3 database files. Data stored in the sync_config.db file includes the local sync root path (\\?\C:\Users\[username]\Google Drive) and the user email is used to access the Google Drive account. Data stored in the snapshot. db file includes the file details for files stored in the Google Drive account. Information such as filenames, modified and created times, Resource-ID, File Size, and a checksum value matching the MD5 value for the associated file.

Filenames were also observed in the Registry "RecentDocs" keys, $MFT entries, and Prefetch files such as DLLHost.pf, Wordpad.pf, and Notepad.pf. Link files and the IEF output also list the filenames. The contents of the files were also recovered from temporary Internet files, thumbcache, memory captures, pagefile. sys, system volume restore points, and unallocated space. Eraser and CCleaner were not effective in removing all data remnants, and information was able to be determined from VMs relating to the Google Drive accounts, filenames, dates and times, and file contents.

In total, it has been demonstrated that it is possible to determine the username, password, method of access, filenames, contents, and dates and times of access when Google Drive is used to store, access, or download data from cloud storage. Memory captures and network files were an important source of information, including locating the username and password in memory files when the client software was set up and used. The various access points are listed in Table 5.5.

Table 5.5 Summary of Analysis Findings

Control (Base-VM)	Data Artifacts Found
Username, password Search terms	Nil software, URL, Enron sample filenames or files located Matches to "*drive google com*" when Google Chrome installed (Google Chrome Base-VM)
Client Software (Upload-VM)	**Data Artifacts Found**
Username Password Software URL Enron sample filenames Enron sample files KWS terms	Users\AppData\Local\Google\Drive**sync_config.db**; *Memory capture* files "*? -Email = *" Located on HD (IE) \AppData\Local\Microsoft\Internet Explorer\Recovery\Last Active\{FC4656}.dat Located in RAM—search for **&Email =** and **&Passwd =** and **&PasswdAgain =** *GoogleDriveSync.exe* file located when downloaded. Google Drive software installation under **C:\Program Files \Google\Drive** Users\AppData\Local\Google\Drive**sync_config.db** and **snapshot.db** includes file information When software downloaded, URLs include **https://drive. google.com** Multiple locations, including *Prefetch, Link files, $MFT, Registry.* Located in Sync folder under ***User\Google\Drive.*** Multiple matches to KWS terms
Browser Access (Access-VM)	**Data Artifacts Found**
Username Password Software URL	FF and GC history: "*formhistory.sqlite*" and "*Web Data*"; *Memory capture* files "*? -Email = *" Nil Nil

(Continued)

Table 5.5 (Continued)

Enron sample filenames	Multiple locations: *cookies, history, icons, pagefile.sys, and*
Enron sample files	*unallocated*
KWS terms	Sufficient to identify files accessed with references to the filenames in *Registry* and *Browsing history*
	Full text in *Temporary Internet Files, RAM,* and *System Volume Information*
	Multiple matches to KWS terms
Browser Download (Download-VM)	**Data Artifacts Found**
Username	FF and GC history: *"formhistory.sqlite"* and *"Web Data"*;
Password	*Memory capture* files "? -Email = "
Software	Nil
URL	Nil
Enron sample filenames	Multiple locations: *cookies, history, icons, pagefile.sys, and*
Enron sample files	*unallocated*
KWS terms	Sufficient to identify files accessed with references to the filenames in *Registry* and *Browsing history*
	Full text in *Temporary Internet Files, RAM,* and *System Volume Information*
	Multiple matches to KWS terms
Eraser (Eraser-VM)	**Data Artifacts Found**
Username	FF and GC history; *"formhistory.sqlite"* and *"Web Data"*;
Password	*Memory capture* files "? -Email = "
Software	Nil
URL	Nil
Enron sample filenames	Multiple locations; *cookies, history, icons, pagefile.sys, and*
Enron sample files	*unallocated*
KWS terms	Sufficient to identify files accessed with references to the filenames in *Registry* and *Browsing history*
	Full text in *Temporary Internet Files, RAM,* and *System Volume Information*
	Multiple matches to KWS terms
CCleaner (CCleaner-VM)	**Data Artifacts Found**
Username	FF and GC history: *"formhistory.sqlite"* and *"Web Data"*;
Password	*Memory capture* files "? -Email = "
Software	Nil
URL	Nil
Enron sample filenames	Multiple locations: *cookies, history, icons, pagefile.sys, and*
Enron sample files	*unallocated*
KWS terms	Sufficient to identify files accessed with references to the filenames in *Registry* and *Browsing history*
	Full text in *Temporary Internet Files.*
	Multiple matches to KWS terms
DBAN (DBAN-VM)	**Data Artifacts Found**
	All data erased, no information located

Once forensic analysis has determined, a Google Drive account has potential evidence of relevance to an investigation, and the practitioner can communicate this to relevant persons to enable them to respond to secure evidence in a timely manner. Knowledge of the username details would enable identification of Google Drive accounts, to preserve and secure potential evidence.

Complete

Important information discovered in this research was the ease of locating a Google Drive username, the discovery of the password stored in cleartext in multiple locations, the ability to gain full access on account without knowing the username or password, and the vast amount of information able to be located in relation to Google Drive use, either via a browser or client software. It is important to share this information with the wider IT community, for both forensic analysis purposes and information security purposes, to enable practitioners to locate information when required and to ensure security issues are understood when using cloud storage services. The addition of the steps of "prepare" and "feedback" to a forensic analysis framework was beneficial to adequately prepare for analysis and also to incorporate lessons learnt into subsequent investigations. It is important to consider the positive and negative experiences during an examination and incorporate these into future examinations. It is also important to report any issues or improvements to other practitioners, and the digital forensic community in general.

The final step is the completion of an investigation. A decision is made whether further analysis is required, based on the feedback from those involved in the process. If further enquires are required, the process returns to the "prepare and respond" step. If there are no further avenues for investigation, the case can be completed, data archived, and backed up as required. In the context of this research, the data created and used may be required in future research opportunities, and hence has been stored on multiple hard drives to enable future use.

Google drive forensics: Apple iPhone 3G

The use of portable devices to access cloud stored data is increasing. A report from Gartner, for example, highlights the trend in client computing is shifting from a focus on personal computers to include portable devices and also predicts that personal cloud storage will replace the PC as the main method of users' storage by 2014 (Kleynhans, 2012). The Apple iPhone is one such device that can be used to access Google Drive cloud storage either using the built-in Safari browser or installing the Google Drive application (App). Analysis of portable devices is a growing area for forensic practitioners, and there are hardware and software solutions to assist this process, such as MicroSystemation .XRY, Cellebrite UFED, and Radio Tactics Aceso. In the scope of this research, it is relevant to consider what information can be determined from a portable device in relation to the use of Google Drive. This also serves to further assess the suitability of the framework being applied in a variety of circumstances. This section also serves to further explore the potential of data remnants on a mobile device when cloud storage is accessed.

Commence (Scope)

The scope of this next part of the research is to examine the data remnants on a mobile device. An iPhone 3G running iOS 4.2.1 was available to be used for testing Google Drive access via a browser. The data remnants for the Google Drive iOS application were also to be tested; however, the application will only work with iOS 5 or above. iOS5 is not able to be installed onto an iPhone 3G, which prevented testing of the Google Drive application. This research first examined whether there were any remnants prior to accessing Google Drive on the Apple iPhone 3G, i.e., prior to accessing Google Drive.

Preparation

An iPhone 3G was selected which had not been used to access Google Drive previously. The device usage was known to the authors, and MicroSystemation .XRY 6.2.1 was used to extract a logical image of the contents, excluding audio and video files, prior to accessing Google Drive. This first extract was analyzed to confirm there was no Google Drive related data on the device prior to undertaking the research. The inbuilt Apple Safari iOS browser was used to access the Google Drive user account created for this research and to view the Enron files stored remotely. A logical extract was then conducted using .XRY.

Evidence source identification and preservation

In the context of this research, files were identified which would contain the information needed to conduct the analysis, in this instance being the .XRY extract files and the output of the .XRY software, including PDF reports and the files exported using .XRY. These were identified for each of the extracts: Base and Browser.

Collection

To observe the principles of forensic computer analysis (Association of Chief Police Officers (ACPO), 2006; National Institute of Justice (NIJ), 2008), a forensic copy was made of the .XRY extract files, the file output, and the reports. As these were logical files, this was done in the Encase Logical format (L01) and the X-Ways Evidence File Container format (ctr). MD5 hash values were used to ensure the forensic integrity of the data.

Examination and analysis

For this research, each of the forensic logical files was examined using forensic tools including X-Ways Forensic 16.5 and EnCase 6.19.4. PList Explorer v1.0 was used to examine the contents of the Apple plist files extracted by .XRY.

Control—Base-XRY

Analysis of the control Base-XRY extract confirmed there was no data originally present relating to the Enron sample test data. In addition, no references were located for the term "Google Drive" or the web site URL (drive.google.com).

Google drive accessed via the iOS Safari browser

The Google Drive username was located in a "cookies.binarycookies" file near the text "m.google.com." Filenames for the Enron test files were located in the History.plist, for the txt, rtf, and docx files. This information was also extracted by XRY in the Web-History.txt file. The text from the Enron files was not located in any of the extracts, nor was it possible to locate the password for the Google Drive account.

Presentation

Analysis findings

In this research, several data remnants were located when searching for evidence of Google Drive use on the test item (iPhone 3G). Recall that the aim was to determine what data remnants were left to identify if Google Drive was accessed. Initial analysis of the control extract identified no matches to the keyword search terms, such as "Google Drive" and "drive.google.com." When the browser was used to access the Google Drive account, entries were left in the History.plist file, which is also listed in the .XRY Web-History.txt file. The Google Drive username was listed in the "cookies.binarycookies" file. The filenames accessed were listed in the History.plist file and in the .XRY Web-History.txt file.

Complete

This research was limited by not being able to install the Google Drive application or to jailbreak the iPhone. At the time of conducting this research, Microsystemation XRY and other iPhone extract solutions require the iPhone to be jailbroken to undertake a physical extract. A future research opportunity is to undertake similar research using an iOS 5 later device and also expand the type of devices examined to include other popular mobile device operating systems, such as Google Android or Microsoft Windows. Future research could also include the comparison of a physical extract of an iPhone to a logical extract to determine the information available and also a comparison with other iPhone forensic software and hardware.

In the context of this research, the data created and used may be required in future research opportunities, and hence has been stored on multiple hard drives to enable future use.

Google drive case study

To illustrate the relevancy of our research findings (including the framework described in Figure 2.1), the following hypothetical case study outlines where the information identified in this chapter can assist in an investigation. The circumstances relate to a hypothetical case of a person suspected of importing steroids. The circumstances of the case study are greatly simplified for the purposes of this chapter and only explore one of several possible responses using currently available software and hardware forensic solutions.

> *Police receive confidential information that Suspect has been importing and selling steroids. A close acquaintance was visiting Suspect and observed computer files relating to steroid sales on the screen of a computer in Suspect's study.*
>
> *An investigation case file was raised and issued to investigating officer (IO) Jones. IO Jones undertook background enquiries and determined that there had been prior allegations about Suspect being involved in steroid importation offences, and that he had previous convictions for these offences. A Warrant was issued by the Court for IO Jones to attend the premises, and search and seize evidence to investigate these allegations.*
>
> *IO Jones liaised with the Police Forensic Computing Section (FCS), to arrange for a Specialist to attend the search and provide assistance to IO Jones under the terms of the warrant.*

Step 1—Commence (Scope)

IO Jones completed a FCS Request for Assistance form, outlining the scope of the investigation, namely to attend at the addresses identified and provide assistance in relation to search and seizure of evidence of material related to the importation of steroids.

Step 2—Preparation

As this type of attendance is a process undertaken by the FCS on a regular basis, the practitioners are trained and experienced in the examination of the computers and electronic devices. A Standard Operating Procedure (SOP) relating to the on-scene examination of computers and mobile devices is documented and referred to by practitioners and outlines the process. Notes are an important aspect of the SOP, and all practitioners maintain accurate notes of the process they undertake.

Step 3—Evidence source identification and preservation

On the nominated day, Specialist Perry attended the address of Suspect in the company of IO Jones and the response team. IO Jones secured the scene and initially identified a tower PC (running) in the study, a generic laptop in the lounge room (off), and an Apple iPhone 3G (on) in a bedroom. Specialist Perry was then called in to provide assistance in searching the PC, Laptop, and iPhone for evidence.

Specialist Perry photographed all items *in situ* and made written notes about the items, including make, model, and serial numbers of hard drives and the hardware. Exhibit sheets were started for each item to record information relating to access. The iPhone was placed in a Faraday bag.[5]

Preservation (PC on scene)

A video camera was set up to record the PC screen during the examination. Data capture of the running PC was undertaken with LiveDetector (http://h11dfs.com/live-detector.php) from a CD to preserve the contents of memory and running processes. Data was saved to a USB which had been erased prior to responding.

Analysis (PC on scene)

Helix3 (http://www.e-fense.com/helix3pro.php) on a CD was then used to run AccessData FTK Imager and examine key files of interest. References were located indicating potential customer data files associated with a Google Drive account in the file "C:\Users\Suspect\AppData\Local\Google\Drive\ **snapshot.db**." A username was located in "C:\Users\Suspect\AppData\Local\Google\ Drive **\sync_config.db**" indicating the username "suspect@badstuff.com." An icon for Google Drive client software was observed running in the system tray. Specialist Perry understood that any further interaction with the live PC may make changes to current or historical data, and (with the knowledge that live data had been preserved) pulled the power plug to immediately shut off the system. The hard drive was removed from the PC and connected to a Tableau T35es-R2 eSATA Forensic Bridge (hardware write blocking). This was connected to Specialist Perry's laptop computer to enable on-scene analysis to continue without altering the contents of the hard drive. Virtual Forensic Computing software (http://www.virtualforensic-computing.com/) was then used to run the physical write blocked hard drive as a VM. When the VM finished the start-up process, it was ready to continue analysis.

The option "**visit Google Drive on the web**" was selected from the Google Drive icon previously observed in the System Tray. A browser window opened with access to the Google Drive account of Suspect. The details of the files in the account were recorded, including the dates and times listed, filenames, and owner

---

[5]A "'Faraday bag' is intended to shield a mobile phone or similar small device to prevent unwanted applications being invoked remotely, such as wiping the memory or to prevent possible problems with veracity of evidence" (Duffy, 2010).

details where listed. The files were selected and downloaded to the USB as a compressed ZIP file. As the live data had been preserved and on-scene analysis had identified evidence stored on the PC, the PC was seized by IO Jones.[6]

Collection (iPhone on scene)

Microsystemation .XRY was used to extract the logical data from the iPhone.

Analysis (iPhone on scene)

On-scene analysis of the logical extract of the iPhone locates filenames associated with the previously identified Google Drive account in the "History.plist" file, and the information was also reported in the .XRY "Web-History.txt" file. As relevant evidence was stored on the iPhone, it was seized by IO Jones.

Preservation (laptop on scene)

As the laptop was in a powered off state, the hard drive was removed and connected to a Tableau T35es-R2 eSATA Forensic Bridge (hardware write blocking). This was connected to Specialist Perry's laptop computer to enable on-scene analysis to be undertaken without altering the contents of the hard drive.

Analysis (laptop on scene)

On-scene analysis of the laptop hard drive was undertaken with X-Ways 16.5. Link file references were located for the previously identified Google Drive files in the Start menu. As relevant evidence was stored on the laptop, it was also seized by IO Jones.

Transportation to lab

All the items were transported by IO Jones and lodged for examination with the FCS.

Step 4—Collection

IO Jones communicated with the legal section of Google in relation to the data identified in the Google Drive account to ensure the data in the account was preserved and made available in relation to the investigation. The identified data was collected from Google through MLAT process.

---

[6]Practitioners should be aware that when accessing a cloud storage, account that changes could be made to the data stored in an account. For example, if files are deleted from a synchronized folder on a computer while offline, any cloud files will remain until the computer is booted and connects to the account. Therefore, connecting a computer that has folders synchronized to a cloud storage account could cause deleted files on the computer or client device to delete from the cloud storage service. Accessing an account via a web browser from a computer or client device that is not synchronized will minimize this situation, and, if possible, the contents of a synchronized folder and cloud stored files should be compared to determine differences prior to connecting a computer, client device, or virtual machine with client software to the Internet.

A forensic copy of the hard drives was made using AccessData FTK Imager 3.1.0 and a Tableau T35es-R2 eSATA Forensic Bridge (hardware write blocking), and verified with MD5 and SHA1 hashes. Appropriate entries were made in the exhibit log relating to access to the evidence by the specialist.

Step 5—Examination and analysis

Analysis was then undertaken on the collected data from Google to compare to the previously preserved forensic copies.

Step 6—Presentation

A report was prepared, outlining the process and the findings of the analysis. The selected files were copied to CD, along with the associated reports for each file, outlining creation and access dates, file details, and hash values. An extract from a sample examination report is included in Appendix A.

Step 7—Complete

The specialist was concerned that Suspect may have used other cloud storage services to store information about other drug importation and sales, and communicated this with IO Jones. IO Jones interviewed Suspect, but Suspect would not disclose if other accounts existed. The specialist undertook additional searches for common cloud storage providers, such as Microsoft SkyDrive and Dropbox, identifying additional accounts held by Suspect. Further enquiries were undertaken with the legal sections of the identified service providers in relation to the identified user account files and data.

At the completion of the examination, the extracted data, notes, and other material related to the investigation were appropriately stored in preparation for future legal action.

CONCLUSION

When investigating the storage of data using cloud service providers, the initial stages of an investigation include the identification of a cloud service and user account details. This will enable practitioners to identify the potential location of data and act to secure this data in a timely manner. In this research, it was found that a practitioner can identify Google Drive account use by undertaking keyword searches and examine common file locations to locate relevant information (as detailed in Table 5.5).

A Google Drive username and password was also determined from the preserved forensic images. It is of great interest (and also a security concern) that a Google Drive account password can in some instances be located as plain text stored on a hard drive or in memory captures or pagefile.sys files. It was also possible to access a Google Drive account without knowing the username or password, by using Virtual Forensic Computing software to create a VM from a forensic image which previously had the Google Drive client software installed and synchronized with an account. By running the forensic image as a VM and selecting the "visit Google Drive on the web" option from the client software, it was possible to connect to the account without entering the username or password. There are a wide range of investigation points for a practitioner to determine the use of Google Drive, such as directory listings, prefetch files, link files, thumbnails, registry, browser history, and memory captures.

Information was able to be located on an Apple iPhone to identify the use of Google Drive, including the username and the filenames for the files accessed. It has been identified that conducting research into physical extracts of data from an iPhone would be of relevance, with a comparison of this to the information obtained from a logical extract.

The use of the cloud (storage) forensic framework (see Chapter 2) was of assistance to ensure all aspects of an investigation were followed, from initially defining the scope to remain on-track, following the standard process of identifying, preserving, analyzing, and reporting, with the ability to return to a previous step while analysis or other steps were progressing was of benefit. In addition, considering feedback was important to ensure any new processes or information was documented and reported, and the final step of completing the process ensured the data used throughout the process was stored appropriately. It is important to develop and use a consistent digital forensic framework, such as the one examined in this research, to ensure investigations are thorough, all issues are encompassed, and the process is flexible enough to apply in different situations.

Summary of Microsoft SkyDrive, Dropbox, and Google Drive findings

It was found that there were data remnants from cloud storage services on Windows 7 computer systems and on the Apple iPhone 3G. In addition, remnants were located when anti-forensic processes were undertaken, including erasing files, and cleaning browsing and file history information.

These findings are similar to those for other cloud storage services: Microsoft SkyDrive (Quick and Choo, 2013a) and Dropbox (Quick and Choo, 2013b); in that the client software has relevant data remnants in files on a hard drive. Username and password information is able to be located in a variety of locations, and browsing history provides a range of information of interest to a forensic practitioner. The findings for Microsoft SkyDrive (Quick and Choo, 2013a), Dropbox (Quick and Choo, 2013b), and Google Drive are summarized in Table 5.6.

Table 5.6 Summary of Cloud Storage Data Remnants from Google Drive, Microsoft SkyDrive (Quick and Choo 2013a), and Dropbox (Quick and Choo 2013b)

Service	Client Software Config Files	Username	Password	Mobile Device
Dropbox (Quick and Choo 2013b)	Versions prior to October 2011; **config.db** and **filecache.db**. From version 1.2.48 the files **config.dbx** and **filecache.dbx** are encrypted.	Located near text; u'email':	Located in memory; free name periods login_email	Client software: **com. getdropbox. Dropbox.plist**
SkyDrive (Quick and Choo 2013a)	**SyncDiagnostics. log** and **OwnerID. dat**	Located near text; &login =	Located in memory; &passwd =	Client software: **keychain-backup.plist'**
Google Drive	**sync_config.db** and **snapshot.db**	Located near text; ? —**Email** ?? Email <email>	Located in memory and on hard drive; &passwd = &passwdagain =	Browser; **History.plist** and **cookies. Binarycookies**

References

Association of Chief Police Officers (ACPO). (2006). *Good practice guidelines for computer based evidence v4.0.* <www.7safe.com/electronic_evidence> Accessed 02.10.12.

Chung, H., Park, J., Lee, S., & Kang, C. (2012). *Digital forensic investigation of cloud storage services, digital investigation.* <http://www.sciencedirect.com/science/article/pii/S1742287612000400> Accessed 02.10.12.

Duffy, A. (2010). *'Faraday bag testing in a reverberation chamber – a preliminary study'.* <http://www.faradaybag.com/faraday-bag-testing/demontfort-university-faraday-bag-testing.html> Accessed 02.10.12.

Kleynhans, S. (2012). *The new PC Era- the personal cloud.* Gartner Inc. <http://www.gartner.com/resId = 1890215> Accessed 02.10.12.

McClain, F. (2011). Dropbox Forensics. *Forensic Focus,* <http://www.forensicfocus.com/dropbox-forensics> Accessed 02.10.12

Microsoft. (2008). *How NTFS reserves space for its master file table (MFT).* <http://support.microsoft.com/kb/174619> Accessed 02.10.12.

Microsoft. (2012a). *Shortcuts: frequently asked questions.* <http://windows.microsoft.com/en-us/windows-vista/Shortcuts-frequently-asked-questions> Accessed 02.10.12.

Microsoft. (2012b). *What is the prefetch folder?* <http://windows.microsoft.com/en-AU/windows-vista/What-is-the-prefetch-folder> Accessed 02.10.12.

Mueller, L. (2010). *Windows 7 Forensics - Part IV - Thumbcache_*.db.* <http://www.forensickb.com/2010/01/windows-7-forensics-part-iv.html> Accessed 02.10.12.

National Institute of Justice (NIJ). (2004), *Forensic examination of digital evidence: A guide for law enforcement.* <http://nij.gov/nij/pubs-sum/199408.htm> Accessed 02.10.12.

National Institute of Justice (NIJ). (2008), *Electronic crime scene investigation: A guide for first responders,* 2nd ed. <http://www.nij.gov/pubs-sum/219941.htm> Accessed 02.10.12.

Office of Law Enforcement Standards of the National Institute of Standards and Technology (NIST). (2012). *NIST computer forensic tool testing.* <http://www.cftt.nist.gov/disk_imaging.htm> Accessed 02.10.12.

Quick, D., & Choo, K. (2013a). Digital droplets: microsoft SkyDrive forensic data remnants. *Future Generation Computer Systems, 29*(6), 1378−1394.

Quick, D., & Choo, K. (2013b). Dropbox analysis: data remnants on user machines. *Digital Investigation, 10*(1), 3−18.

Quick, D., & Choo, K. (2013c). Google drive: forensic analysis of data remnants. *Journal of Network and Computer Applications,* In press.

Subashini, S., & Kavitha, V. (2011). A survey on security issues in service delivery models of cloud computing. *Journal of Network and Computer Applications, 34*(1), 1−11 ISSN 1084-8045, doi:10.1016/j.jnca.2010.07.006

W3Counter. (2012). *Browser statistics July 2012.* <http://www.w3counter.com/globalstats.php?year = 2012&month = 7> Accessed 02.10.12.

Appendix A

Example of examination report (adapted from National Institute of Justice (NIJ), 2004)

REPORT OF MEDIA ANALYSIS
MEMORANDUM FOR: Police Investigator Jones
SUBJECT: Forensic Media Analysis Report
            SUBJECT: SUSPECT
            Case Number: 012345

1. **Status:** Complete.
2. **Summary of Findings:**
   * 3 document files containing information relating to importation and sales of steroids.
   * 14 shortcut files that pointed to files stored in Google Drive account with the username "suspect@badstuff.com."
   * Internet History containing links to files stored in Google Drive.
3. **Items Analyzed:**

Tag Number:	Item Description:
012345	One Generic laptop, Serial # 123456789
012346	One Tower PC, Serial # not listed
012347	Apple iPhone 3G, Serial # 123456780

4. **Details of Findings for Item 012345:**

Findings in this paragraph related to the Generic Hard Drive, Model ABCDE, Serial # 3456ABCD, recovered from Tag Number 012345, One Generic laptop, Serial # 123456789.

1) The examined hard drive was found to contain a Microsoft Windows 7 operating system.

2) The directory and file listing for the media was saved to "012345 LT HD File Listing.csv."

3) The Internet History at C:\USERS\SUSPECT\APPDATA\LOCAL \MICROSOFT\WINDOWS\INTERNET EXPLORER\HISTORY\INDEX. DAT was found to contain URL references to files stored in a Google Drive account with the filenames; "steroid customers.docx," "steroid importations.docx," and "steroid sales.docx." The last accessed dates for the references disclosed the date and times as July 5, 2012 between 11:23 p.m. and 11:57 p.m.

5. **Details of Findings for Item 012346:**

Findings in this paragraph related to the Generic Hard Drive, Model ABCDF, Serial # 3456ABCE, recovered from Tag Number 012346, One Tower PC, Serial # not listed.

1) The examined hard drive was found to contain a Microsoft Windows 7 operating system.

2) The directory and file listing for the media was saved to "012346 PC HD File Listing.csv."

3) Google Drive client software was installed on the PC, located at C:\Program Files\Google\Drive\. During an examination on scene, the client software was used to connect to the stored client account details using the link option "**visit Google Drive on the web**." The following files were observed stored in the Google Drive account:

   * File 1 **"steroid customers.docx":** the files' modified date and times are July 5, 2012 11:33 p.m. (ACST).
   * File 2 **"steroid importations.docx":** the files' modified date and times are July 5, 2012 11:35 p.m. (ACST).
   * File 3 **"steroid sales.docx":** the files' modified date and times are July 5, 2012 11:57 p.m. (ACST).

   These files were downloaded at the time of on-scene access to a compressed ZIP file; "012346 GD.ZIP."

4) These three files were also located in the default Google Drive synchronization folder on the hard drive, located at "C:\Users\Suspect \Google\Drive\."

5) The Internet History at C:\USERS\SUSPECT\APPDATA\LOCAL \MICROSOFT\WINDOWS\ INTERNET EXPLORER\HISTORY\INDEX. DAT was found to contain URL references to files stored in a Google Drive account with the filenames; "steroid customers.docx," "steroid importations.docx," and "steroid sales.docx."

6. **Details of Findings for Item 012347:**

   Findings in this paragraph related to the Apple iPhone 3G logical evidence extract, recovered from Tag Number 012347, Apple iPhone 3G, Serial # 123456780.

   1) The examined iPhone was found to contain iOS 4.2.1 operating system.
   2) The Microsystemation XRY extract file was saved to "012347 Apple iPhone.xry."
   3) The Internet History at "Web History.txt" was found to contain URL references to files stored in a Google Drive account with the filenames; "steroid customers.docx," "steroid importations.docx," and "steroid sales. docx."

7. **Glossary:**

   ACST: Australian Central Standard Time

   Shortcut File: A file created that links to another file.

8. **Items Provided:** In addition to this hard copy report, one compact disk (CD) was submitted with an electronic copy of this report. The report on CD contains hyperlinks to the above-mentioned files and directories.

   SPECIALIST PERRY   Released by_____
   Computer Forensic Specialist

Open Source Cloud Storage Forensics: ownCloud as a Case Study

6

INFORMATION IN THIS CHAPTER

- ownCloud forensic analysis
- Client and server artifact hypothesis
- Technical artifact discussion

INTRODUCTION

Recently a number of open and closed source cloud software products have been developed and are in development to address the needs of enterprises and even individuals who want to leverage the features of cloud computing while continuing to store data on-site or otherwise under the control of the data custodian. Storing data on-site and/or having the data centers physically in the jurisdiction are increasingly seen as ways to reduce some of the location risks that cloud (storage) service clients currently face. For example, it has been suggested at one of the hearings of the Australian Government Parliamentary Joint Committee on Intelligence and Security that "the default position should be that governments, agencies and departments ought to keep their information onshore but use cloud for providers, because there are great cost savings to government by using cloud, using digital storage and accessing the digital economy, being a model user of things like the NBN, data centers and cloud computing. We think there is a real leadership role for government, but it needs to be done within something of a risk minimization strategy, which means that you keep the data onshore and you do not look to send it offshore to a jurisdiction that you do not know about" (Australian Government Parliamentary Joint Committee on Intelligence and Security, 2012, p. 16). More recently in 2013, the Australian Government has also released the National Cloud Computing Strategy (Australian Government Department of Broadband, 2013) and the policy and risk management guidelines for the storage and processing of Australian Government information in outsourced or offshore ICT arrangements (Australian Government Attorney-General's Department, 2013).

As with most new technologies, cloud storage services have the capacity to be used for criminal exploitation and to form the basis of civil litigation (see Chapter 1). As such, those working in both digital forensics and eDiscovery must have the capability to forensically analyze these storage platforms.

The key gap which we seek to contribute to in this chapter is an in-depth understanding of the artifacts available to forensics researchers and practitioners when conducting analysis on cloud Storage as a Service (StaaS) environments on both the client and server. One of the key reasons this has not been explored in the existing literature has been the focus on public cloud StaaS services. While client analysis is possible, server platforms for public StaaS services are rarely available to researchers. In addition, access to the public cloud data centers is generally not feasible for the purposes of digital forensic research for both security and privacy reasons. However, there are private StaaS products available that a researcher can use as a case study to determine the forensic artifacts which potentially exist on all StaaS systems.

One cloud software product which provides features common in larger public StaaS products while being a freely available software package is ownCloud, which has seen rapid development and is now one of the major open source StaaS products. For example, Google Trends shows a significant rise in popularity for the search term "owncloud" in the last two years (Google, 2013). In addition, a major technology web site has recently promoted its potential use as a private cloud storage service (Klosowski, 2013) and AARNET (Australia's Academic and Research Network)[1] is deploying ownCloud as the basis for its CloudStor+ service (AARNET, 2013). These features make it a very appropriate case study software platform for this research into the forensic challenges of private StaaS. ownCloud (version 4 at time of research) provides a number of the features synonymous with cloud-based storage solutions including a web-based file access (view/manage/upload/download) and a "desktop sync" client for Windows, OS X, and Linux which allows for automated synchronized copies of data on both the client and cloud servers. Mobile clients are also available for Android and iOS devices. Other features particularly pertinent to digital forensics research include optional server-side file encryption and file versioning (storing multiple versions of a file).

We regard the major contribution of this chapter (see Martini & Choo, 2013) to be threefold:

- Technical recommendations on forensic analysis of ownCloud StaaS instances will be the main focus of this chapter.
- Drawing from these technical findings, recommendations will be made on forensic analysis of open source StaaS products generally which will inform practitioners of findings relevant to this general field and potential trends.

---

[1]AARNet has over one million end users from 38 Australian universities, the Commonwealth Scientific and Industrial Research Organisation (CSIRO) and other academic, research, and education institutions (http://www.aarnet.edu.au/).

- Finally this research seeks to validate our cloud forensic framework (see Chapter 2).

Cloud forensics framework

The digital forensics framework (see Chapter 2) is discussed as follows (see Figure 2.1 for a summary). One of the key features of this framework is its iterative nature which is essential in our research—the client is used both to identify the existence of cloud storage and to recover any data synced/cached on the client. As such, forensic analysis of the client is carried out before analysis of the server environment.

Commence (scope): This phase outlines a number of factors to determine the scope of the forensic investigation such as the persons involved, any data or evidence already seized, keyword terms, any urgent time frames, and other relevant information.

Preparation: Preparation is primarily concerned with ensuring that the relevant resources (both in terms of personnel and technical resources) are available to conduct the investigation. Preparation also includes other aspects of an investigation, such as timely response, time frame, personnel, duties, and locations of interest.

Evidence source identification and preservation: This phase is concerned with identifying sources of evidence in a digital forensics investigation. During the first iteration, sources of evidence identified will likely be a physical device (e.g., desktop computers, laptops, and mobile devices). During the second iteration, this phase is concerned with identifying cloud services/ providers relevant to the case, possible evidence stored with the cloud provider, and processes for preservation of this potential evidence. Regardless of the identified source of evidence, forensic investigators need to ensure the proper preservation of the evidence.

Collection: This phase is concerned with the actual capture of the data. There are various methods of collection suited for the various cloud computing platforms and deployment models. For example, Infrastructure as a Service (IaaS) may provide an export of the virtual hard disk and memory provided to the user while Software as a Service (SaaS) may only provide a binary export of the data stored on the hosted software environment.

McKemmish (1999) suggested that extraction could be separate from processing, and we believe that due to the complications of cloud computing data collection (e.g., significant potential for the cloud service to be hosted outside of the law enforcement agencies (LEAs) jurisdiction and the potential for technical measures such as data striping to complicate collection), this separation from timely preservation is critical, and hence the separate collection step.

Generally cloud servers are physically located in a different jurisdiction from that of the investigating LEA and/or suspect. It is, therefore, important for the agency collecting the evidence in one jurisdiction for use in a criminal prosecution taking place in another jurisdiction to work and cooperate closely with their foreign counterparts to ensure that the methods used in the collection are in full accordance with applicable laws, legal principles, and rules of evidence of the jurisdiction in which the evidence is ultimately to be used (UNODC, 2012).

Examination and analysis: This phase is concerned with the examination and analysis of forensic data. It is during this phase that cloud computing usage would most likely be discovered based upon the examination and analysis of physical devices and this would lead to a second (or more) iteration(s) of the process.

Presentation: This phase is concerned with legal presentation of the evidence collected. This phase remains very similar to the frameworks of McKemmish and NIST (as discussed in Martini & Choo, 2012). In general, the report should include information on all processes, the tools and applications used, and any limitations to prevent false conclusions from being reached (see US NIJ, 2004).

Complete: This phase allows a practitioner to review their findings with a view to determining if further analysis should be completed to meet the needs of the investigator or legal counsel. If no further analysis is required, this phase deals with appropriate completion processes for the case including archiving evidential data and review of processes for use in future cases.

This chapter mainly focuses on the analysis stage of the framework with some discussion on pertinent of evidence source identification, preservation, and collection.

Outline

In the next section, we provide an overview of the experiment environment and detail the experiments undertaken on both the client and server ownCloud instances. The findings in the following section are framed around "artifacts," which are defined at the beginning of each experiment. These artifacts are some of the common items of evidential value which a forensic practitioner may collect. Finally the last section concludes the chapter with a summary of results and general conclusions on forensic investigation of open source cloud storage services.

Experiment setup
ownCloud overview

For the purposes of forensic analysis, the ownCloud software package can be separated into two related parts—the client software (including the sync clients and the web interface) and the server software running the cloud environment.

The ownCloud server software is primarily PHP code designed to be hosted on a web server. The software appears to be geared toward running on an Apache server on a *nix distribution, but installations on other web servers and operating systems do exist. The server uses a database for metadata persistence and offers the administrator the option of using an SQLite database for smaller installations and MySQL for larger installations. By default, files stored in the ownCloud instance are stored relatively unmodified on the server operating system file system in a subdirectory of the ownCloud application files. Advanced storage features associated with cloud storage such as file clustering for redundancy and scalability are not managed internally by ownCloud. These features would need to be implemented at the operating system level (using a product such as GlusterFS, XtreemFS, or ZFS). The server software can be extended by installing/enabling "Apps" (both internal and third party), which can add features such as server-side encryption, integration with other cloud services/storage providers, and additional authentication systems.

The ownCloud client software consists of both a web interface and several client applications. The web interface is standard for this type of cloud StaaS implementation. Beyond standard file upload, download, delete, rename, etc. capabilities, the default web interface also allows the user to play media files, view images in a gallery, and maintain a contact list and calendar. These nonfile-related features are considered out of scope for this research on cloud-based StaaS and as such were not conclusively studied.

The desktop sync clients are available for many major operating systems as "binaries" and as source code for compiling manually. The ownCloud sync clients download page advises that "Linux, MacOSX, and Windows are built with these sources" under the sources section (ownCloud, 2013), based upon this and our observations it is assumed that the core features of the sync client operate equivalently across all operating systems.

For this research, the ownCloud server is hosted in a CentOS 6 environment with a default Apache, PHP, and MySQL setup. The local ext4 file system on CentOS was used to store the uploaded files. The ownCloud desktop sync client was tested in a Windows 7 environment. For further information on the experiment environment, see Tables 6.1 and 6.2.

Environment configuration

Tables 6.1–6.3 represent the environment specifications used in these experiments.

Virtualization was used to implement both the client and server environments. This allowed for efficient data collection (both disk and network based) and in the case of the ownCloud server instance demonstrates a common configuration in many medium/large environments where ownCloud would be found on a virtualized platform.

Table 6.1 Server Software Specifications	
Operating System	CentOS 6.3
Web server	Apache HTTP Server 2.2.15
Database server	MySQL 5.1.61
ownCloud server Application	Version 4.07

Table 6.2 Client Software Specifications	
PC Operating System	Windows 7
ownCloud sync client	Version 1.05
Web browsers	Internet Explorer 9, Firefox 15, Chrome 21
iOS version	5.1.1
iOS ownCloud App Version	2.03

Table 6.3 Forensic Tool Specifications	
Guidance Software EnCase	Versions 6.19.6 and 7.04.01
Micro Systemation XRY	Version 6.3

Findings
Client forensics

Client forensic analysis was conducted on a Windows client using the desktop sync client predominantly and three major web browsers (Microsoft Internet Explorer, Mozilla Firefox, and Google Chrome) to access the cloud web interface.

Commonly in digital forensics research of this nature, "artifacts" are defined before commencement of the research that outline the types of evidence/data the practitioner is looking to recover/present, which can be used to link the suspect(s) to the device and/or cloud services used relevant to the commission of an alleged offence. In the case of private StaaS, we are seeking to recover the following artifacts of evidential value from the client:

- Sync and file management metadata—This includes logging, database, and configuration data stored to facilitate the sync process between client and server. These artifacts can be useful in identifying the available evidence for collection from the server environment and used to build a file management history (e.g., sync/update times for individual files).

- Cached files—This artifact describes the files the user has stored on the client device and uploaded to the cloud environment or downloaded from the cloud environment to the client device. In cases where the cloud environment cannot be accessed, cached files may be relied upon as the only evidence available from the cloud environment.
- Cloud service and authentication data—Cloud service and authentication data is primarily used by the forensic practitioner to discover StaaS usage and potentially gives the practitioner the opportunity to connect to the cloud computing environment using the user's credentials if no other formal method is feasible. It will commonly consist of an address (DNS, IP, URL, etc.) that identifies which StaaS instance was used and potentially stored credentials (commonly a username and password) for the user.
- Encryption metadata—Client encryption metadata could include databases/configurations detailing which files are encrypted and using which algorithm, keys, etc.
- Browser artifacts—Browser artifacts can be critical data for a forensic practitioner (see Badger, Grance, Patt-Corner, & Voas, 2012) both in terms of evidence source identification and examination and analysis, as (like cloud service data) it can often be used to identify which StaaS instance the user is communicating with and may also include file metadata often found in URLs.
- Mobile client artifacts—With the increasing prevalence and usage of mobile devices, mobile client artifacts may prove an invaluable evidence source for forensic practitioners (Tassone, Martini, Choo, & Slay, 2013). The mobile clients may store any combination of the other artifacts discussed.
- Network analysis—Preliminary network analysis must be conducted to determine the feasibility of collecting StaaS data (with a focus on identification data) via network interception. This evidence source is beyond the scope of this chapter.

Evidence source identification and preservation, and collection

Identification, preservation, and collection steps were not formally undertaken as part of this research as the client was set up in a controlled virtual machine environment. During a normal investigation, however, identification would commence with law enforcement identifying electronic devices (PCs, tablets, phones, etc.) that could be of evidential value and seizing these devices for preservation and collection (under a search warrant issued by the court). The devices would then be imaged using the appropriate forensically sound tool (see Table 6.3) depending on the device.

Virtual disk files (VMDK) were provided for examination and analysis as part of this experiment. In a typical law enforcement situation, these steps would likely be part of standard procedures for seizing a client device, and the preservation/collection activity of image collection would result in an equivalent physical disk image file.

Examination and analysis of client devices

Examination and analysis commenced with examinations of the image file system to locate the artifacts listed above. The following describes the findings from this examination:

Sync and file management metadata—ownCloud client sync metadata information is predominantly stored in the "%localappdata%\ownCloud\folders" (e.g., C:\Users\[Username]\AppData\Local\ownCloud\folders) directory, located in which are a number of files (named for the sync directories they represent) that contain the configuration for each sync directory in the "ini" configuration file format.

In this experiment, a sync directory named "Pictures" was created. The configuration file for Pictures includes the following directives: "localPath" which describes the location on the client device where the synced data is stored (e.g., C:/Users/[Username]/Pictures), "targetPath" which describes the folder name on the cloud service (e.g., Pictures), and "backend" and "connection" directives appear to relate to the cloud connection used. Other sync directories configuration files listed the same configuration directives and similar configuration values.

File level metadata is stored on the client by the csync library (which forms part of the ownCloud client) in the form of SQLite databases located at "%userprofile%\.csync" named in the format of "csync_statedb_[HASH].db." It appears that one of these databases is created for each sync directory which is set up. In each database is a solitary table named "metadata" which contains an entry for each file in the directory and includes the following fields: "phash" which is a numerical hash of the filename (a cursory analysis of the relevant sync client source code indicates that this numerical hash is derived from "Jenkins Hash"—see Jenkins, 1997), "pathlen" which is the length of the filename string, "path" which is the filename string, and "modtime" which is a POSIX timestamp representing the last modified time of the file.

Cached files—The ownCloud client keeps copies of all files in synchronized directories on the local disk. The file metadata configurations/databases discussed above can be used to locate the files/directories synced to the local client. While the server supports storing multiple versions of files, these do not appear to be synced to the client.

Cloud service and authentication data—Located in "%localappdata%\ownCloud" is an "owncloud.cfg" client configuration file that contains valuable cloud identification and authentication data. The file is in the "ini" configuration file format and contains the following directives: "url" which lists the http or https URL for the ownCloud instance synced with this client, "user" which lists the username used to connect to the ownCloud instance in plaintext (if stored), "passwd" which lists the stored password for the ownCloud client stored using base64 encoding (if stored), and "nostoredpassword" which is a Boolean representation of the option to prompt for password at sync application launch. These details are critical to forensic practitioners as it allows them to identify that cloud computing StaaS has been used and the particular cloud computing provider/instance used. If law enforcement cannot be specific about where the data is (a specific device) and the information can be collected, search warrants may need to be created and executed in somewhat of an iterative fashion that supports an analytic discovery process. For example, an initial warrant that is minimally invasive (limited to externals only, no content) might be sought to use to identify which services the person of interest is using. Therefore, information obtained in our experiment allows them to contact the cloud provider/administrators and ensure that the cloud data is preserved, while applying for a more specific search warrant to obtain more content rich information.

The practitioner can also potentially use the username and password listed in the file to access the cloud server and access all the data available to the user to determine if there is any further evidence stored on the cloud if this is permissible. It should be noted that the capacity to legally execute this process is dependent on the statutory authority of the LEA in the jurisdiction where the client is located, and a practitioner using this method should also be mindful of the processes required when handling live data especially to ensure no data is inadvertently overwritten. For example, in Australia, Section 3L of the *Crimes Act 1914* (Cth) has a provision for the executing officer of a warrant to access data which includes data not held at the premises (i.e., accessible from a computer or data storage device). If assistance is required in operating the equipment and the executing officer believes on reasonable grounds that the material is liable to be destroyed, modified, or tampered with, they may "do whatever is necessary to secure the equipment, whether by locking it up, placing a guard, or otherwise" (see Section 3L(4)) for a period of up to 24 hours or until expert assistance can be obtained, whichever happens first (see Subsection 3L(6)). Section 3L(7) of the Act also allows the period to be extended, but the notice of these arrangements must be given to the occupier as detailed in Sections 3L(5) and 3L(8). Cloud service providers may also disclose the data if it is legally required and permissible to do so as part of a civil proceedings (e.g., in eDiscovery cases)—see Hooper, Martini, & Choo (2013).

Sections 3LA of the *Crimes Act 1914* (Cth) and 201A of the *Customs Act 1901* (Cth) also make it an offence for persons with knowledge of computers or computer networks of which computers form a part, or measures applied to protect data held in, or accessible from, computers, to fail to provide any information or assistance that is reasonable and necessary to allow access to data held in, or accessible from, a computer that is on warrant premises, to copy the data to a data storage device, or to convert the data into documentary form. Failure to comply carries a maximum penalty of two years and six months imprisonment respectively. Such provisions are designed to overcome the efforts of accused persons to conceal data through the use of passwords or encryption, including in cloud storage services.

The storage of the user password in this manner raises two interesting points. Firstly due to the (small) size of the configuration file it will generally be stored as part of the MFT (Master File Table) on Windows clients (as it was in this case). This creates potential for alternative methods of recovery in the event that the file is securely deleted (such as external backups of the MFT data stored on the client PC). While configuration data such as that in owncloud.cfg is often stored in the registry on Windows clients, this is not always the case. The use of plaintext files such as owncloud.cfg may arise especially in cases where applications are written once and compiled for multiple operating systems. This may be a common trend in cloud computing clients which aim to be available across as many operating systems as possible.

Another point of interest with this configuration file is its inclusion in "System Restore" on Windows clients due to its ".cfg" extension (Microsoft, 2013) which can potentially allow a practitioner to recover the ownCloud instance, username, and password used on the PC even after the ownCloud configuration files are securely deleted (overwritten). This was detected as part of our experiments after the owncloud.cfg file was securely deleted from the client device and a keyword search was able to reveal the base64 encoding of the users password stored on the disk. A keyword search for the phrase "passwd = "@ByteArray" was able to locate two instances of the owncloud.cfg file stored in a file in the System Volume Information directory.

The usefulness of these techniques must not be understated as in the case of server-side encryption, and a forensic practitioner may need to rely upon the password stored on the client to access encrypted data stored on the cloud server which may have already been securely deleted on the client device.

Encryption metadata—The ownCloud server supports encryption of user data; however; this encryption appears to be handled entirely on the server. The client does not internally support client-side encryption of user data and does not appear to be aware if encryption is enabled on the server. As such no notable encryption metadata is stored on the client in an ownCloud installation.

SSL encryption can optionally be used when communicating with the ownCloud server. However, this is dependent on the URL (specifically the use of the http or https scheme) used during the initial client setup. Further discussion on the network communications of the ownCloud client/server is included below.

Browser artifacts—Three of the major Internet browsers (Microsoft Internet Explorer, Mozilla Firefox, and Google Chrome) were used to access the ownCloud web interface and perform a number of common operations (e.g., download/upload a file, access calendar/contacts). An Internet artifact search revealed artifacts relating to the ownCloud instance from all three browsers.

History and downloads records revealed the files which were downloaded from the ownCloud instance and provided information on their original filename, path in the ownCloud profile, and initial storage location on the client disk. For example, one URL found in the Chrome downloads list "http://owncloud.local/owncloud/?app = files&getfile = ajax/download.php?files = Chrome.txt&dir = / Browser Uploads" indicates that a file was downloaded which was named Chrome.txt from the Browser Uploads directory. The "?app = " section of the URL changes to reflect the ownCloud "app" which is being accessed; "files," "calendar," and "contacts" were noted values. A request to index.php with the parameter "?logout = true" indicates that the user has gracefully logged out (pressed the logout button on the page). Page titles can be used to indicate the username of the ownCloud user as it is displayed in the format "[App] | ownCloud ([username])," e.g., "Files | ownCloud (johnsmith)." Many references were found to these page titles both within browser artifacts and throughout the unallocated clusters on the disk.

Recommended keyword search (GREP) expressions to locate ownCloud usage in browser artifacts include:

- \?app = (files)|(calendar)|(contacts)
- (files)|(calendar)|(contacts) \| ownCloud \(.*\)

Mobile client artifacts—ownCloud has mobile sync clients available for both the iOS and Android platforms. At the time of writing, development of these apps is still continuing. However, a forensic analysis of the current iOS app (version 2.03) was conducted for completeness using the Micro Systemation XRY Complete product. The iOS version of the ownCloud sync client used in these experiments only allowed for the upload of images and videos from the device, as such images and text files (created via the ownCloud web interface) were the primary test files for the mobile sync client experiments. The "App PIN" functionality of the ownCloud app (which permits the user to protect the app separately from the main device with a four-digit PIN) was enabled.

A "physical" acquisition was undertaken as this allows the practitioner to view the mobile device data partition, extract the actual files stored on the device, and potentially recover deleted files under some circumstances. The analysis revealed a number of files of forensic interest below its application root "Documents" directory. The iOS ownCloud client maintains a cache of accessed files in the "Documents/1" directory; the 1 appears to correlate with the "id" identifier in the users table of the DB.sqlite file. The DB.sqlite file contains a number of tables of forensic interest. The "users" table contains the URL of the ownCloud instance used with the client as well as the username and password of the user stored in plaintext. The "passcode" table contains the "App PIN" used to secure the application (if set). The "files" table contains a list of file paths (relative to the server URI using WebDAV access), file names, size, and the full local path to the file (if cached otherwise <null>) as well as a number of other values. The "files_backup" table remained empty in our experiment.

This shows that the mobile client can be of significant value to a forensic practitioner as it not only provides the server details and credentials for the user (potentially allowing the practitioner to connect to the ownCloud instance to collect evidence) but also a cache of files accessed and a list of files stored on the ownCloud instance (for the particular user) at the time of last sync.

Network analysis—Basic analysis of the network communication between the ownCloud client and server was undertaken using packet captures. HTTP traffic was monitored between the client and server to determine that the ownCloud sync client is using the WebDAV protocol to handle file transfers. The ownCloud iOS client appears to use similar WebDAV requests. If plain HTTP (as opposed to HTTPS) is used to establish the connection with the ownCloud server, the content and commands sent and received from the server to the client is readable in plaintext as part of normal HTTP and WebDAV requests (e.g., HTTP PUT requests revealed data). Standard HTTP Basic authorization (comprising the username and password supplied by the user for the ownCloud instance base64 encoded) is sent with each WebDAV request.

Reporting and presentation

Reporting on many of these client artifacts is currently a manual process, and detection or heuristics of cloud computing use is not integrated into the major digital forensics analysis products used. While browser artifacts from major browsers were extracted via standard evidence preparation scripts, the other artifacts above were located manually. If identification of cloud computing usage was to become standard practice for digital forensic investigations, this would be a very time-consuming process for a forensic practitioner.

Server forensics

Server forensic analysis was conducted on a CentOS 6 virtual machine hosting the ownCloud PHP software via an Apache HTTP server and using MySQL as the database backend (see Table 6.1). For the purposes of this experiment, CentOS, Apache, and MySQL were configured using setup defaults where possible or logical selections.

Before commencement of the server forensic analysis, we seek to define the "artifacts" which we hypothesize exist. In the case of StaaS, we are seeking the following artifacts of evidential value from the server:

- Administrative and file management metadata—Administrative data which stores the configuration of the cloud instance and of individual users within the cloud instance as well as database and configuration files which list the files and data stored by the user on the cloud instance.

- Stored files—The data uploaded by the user to the cloud instance.
- Encryption metadata—Data relating to encryption (if enabled) in the cloud instance, specifically data relating to decryption of user data.
- Cloud logging and authentication data—Logging and authentication data associated with transactions made by the user with the cloud instance (files uploaded/downloaded, login events, etc.). As emphasized in the ENISA (2012, p. 45) report, "[m]onitoring of log availability is crucial to trace back events and allocate liabilities and responsibilities. The more sensitive the information involved, the more monitoring of log availability is crucial. Log data is also important for incident response, so business continuity requirements should be taken into account when reviewing this parameter. Finally, log data is often needed to satisfy corporate data governance and compliance requirements—e.g., Data Protection Law and SOX-like laws in Europe."

Evidence source identification and preservation

As outlined in the framework, early identification and preservation of cloud computing use is critical for successful forensic analysis. In the case of ownCloud servers, the most straightforward method of identification is via the installation of the ownCloud client or web browser logs located on the client device of the suspect.

The section on the examination and analysis of client devices outlines methods of identification of the ownCloud server on the client device which may include searching for the configuration files of the ownCloud client or analysis of web browser history logs. Once the ownCloud server instance has been identified, it is expected that standard processes for locating web servers (e.g., via owner of IP address) will allow the forensic practitioner to physically locate the server and server owners/administrators.

For the purposes of this research, it is assumed that the physical server that is hosting the ownCloud instance is located within the jurisdiction of the forensic practitioner. If the server is located out of jurisdiction, the practitioner may need to rely upon a "mutual assistance request" (e.g., *Mutual Assistance in Criminal Matters Act 1987* (Cth) in Australia) to request the assistance of an LEA within jurisdiction of the physical server or rely solely upon any evidence attained as part of the client analysis (which in many cases may still be substantial). There are, however, various challenges in relying on mutual legal assistance arrangements to obtain evidential data from overseas cloud service providers in the current environment (e.g., procedural and technical challenges). For example, Cuthbertson (2012, pp. 128–129) explained that "the types of assistance provided for under the mutual assistance regime generally involve the exercise of coercive powers ... [and at] the international level, it has been generally accepted that such measures raise issues of state sovereignty and should only be made available pursuant to formal government-to-government requests."

Similar observations were also echoed in the 2012 UNODC report: "[c]ases requiring the investigation or prosecution of cross-border activities of terrorists or other criminals might have sovereignty implications for those countries in which investigations need to be undertaken. It is therefore important, when considering investigative actions involving the collection of evidence related to computers or the Internet, for investigators and prosecutors to be mindful of the potential implications such investigative actions might have for the sovereignty of other States (e.g., authorities in one country remotely searching the computer being operated by a suspect located in another country)" (UNODC, 2012, p. 92). Therefore, it is important for (forensic) "investigators [to] have sufficient understanding of the legal rules/principles applicable to investigative actions they are undertaking as part of an investigation and/or to communicate closely with prosecutors, by both updating them and seeking legal advice" and to work closely with their foreign LEAs to obtain key evidence for legal proceedings (UNODC, 2012, p. 94).

In terrorism or counterintelligence investigations, there are generally special access mechanisms to request for data from cloud service providers (compelled disclosure). For example, in Australia, Section 25A of the *Australian Security Intelligence Organisation Act 1979* (Cth) allows a government minister to issue a computer access warrant if the minister is satisfied that there are reasonable grounds for believing that access by the Organisation to data held in a particular computer (the target computer) will substantially assist the collection of intelligence in accordance with this Act in respect of a matter (the security matter) that is important in relation to security. The warrant may also allow the Australian Security Intelligence Organisation (ASIO) to do anything reasonably necessary to conceal the fact that anything has been done under the warrant although the addition, deletion, or alteration of data, or the doing of anything, that interferes with, interrupts, or obstructs the lawful use of the target computer by other persons, or that causes any loss or damage to other persons lawfully using the target computer is explicitly prohibited (Subsection 25A(5)).

When the physical server hosting the ownCloud instance has been located, preservation must commence immediately. ownCloud does not have built in preservation features for the purposes of law enforcement. While a "litigation hold" or similar freezing feature would be useful (especially at a per user granularity level), forensic practitioners will need to use different preservation methods depending on the type of evidence to be preserved and the size of the ownCloud instance and supporting infrastructure. If possible, disconnecting the ownCloud instance from the network while preparing for collection of data can help in preventing the suspect from deleting data via standard access methods (sync client, browser, etc.) while collection is being performed.

If the ownCloud instance is small (as in the case of this research), then taking a bit-stream image of the entire instance is preferable wherever possible (depending on the underlying infrastructure) as this will preserve and collect both the users current data, system wide data (such as logs), and potentially deleted data which remains on the disk(s). However, it is acknowledged that for a number of reasons (e.g., size, time, customer privacy), it will often not be possible to take a complete bit-stream image of the cloud instance. In these circumstances, it is advisable to commence collection of the data stored on the ownCloud instance specifically relevant to the suspect (e.g., data directories, logs, encryption keys/authentication data—discussed further as part of collection) as quickly as possible while keeping the instance disconnected from the network.

Collection

There are a number of different collection methods available to a forensic practitioner when collecting evidence from an ownCloud instance. The use of these methods depends on the individual attributes and circumstances of the investigation as well as the resources of the forensic practitioner. Regardless of collection method to ensure the maximum possible useable evidence is collected and preserved, the following list of ownCloud server artifacts are recommended for collection:

Data uploaded by the suspect—These artifacts include the main source of evidence in an ownCloud installation. User files uploaded to the ownCloud instance are stored in a directory accessible to the web server defined as part of the initial setup of the application.

This data can be located via the web server hosting the ownCloud instance. The ownCloud configuration file ([owncloud-web-root]/config/config.php) will indicate the location of the ownCloud data directory using the "datadirectory" configuration directive. On a live system, the practitioner can use this information to determine if the data is stored on the local device which is hosting the front-end software or if the data is being stored on a mounted external or network-based storage device as would be common in a cloud computing environment.

Once the physical location of the data has been determined, the practitioner can make a decision as to the feasibility of taking a bit-stream image of the physical media source or taking a logical copy of the visible data structure (which may be the only practical option if the physical media is too large or complex to acquire in a timely manner).

The structure of the "datadirectory" varies somewhat depending on the configuration of the ownCloud instance and is discussed further below in server examination and analysis; however, the users data uploads should be located in the files subdirectory of the users directory, e.g., "[datadirectory]/[username]/files." It is recommended that the "[datadirectory]/[username]" directory be copied in full.

The practitioner must also give consideration to assuring the provenance of the data collected using this method. For example, due to the highly shareable nature of client devices as well as usernames and passwords[2], it may not be possible to determine the person responsible for upload or download of the data. Therefore, as is the case with other online services such as email and social networking, the practitioner may need to rely upon other forensic methods (e.g., Internet history records from PCs and ISPs, document metadata, source copies on physical devices under the suspects control) to determine provenance of the data collected from the cloud server.

Data generated by the ownCloud instance—Data generated by a cloud instance relating to a particular user may be very useful in linking a user with the data located in the cloud environment (e.g., log data) or a necessary part in extracting evidence relating to a particular user from the cloud environment (e.g., encryption keys). As such it is recommended that this data also be collected.

In the case of ownCloud, the web server hosting the front end of the ownCloud instance typically generates log data. Apache was used as the web server for this experiment and as such, logging data could be found in "/var/log/httpd" where the "access_log" and "ssl_access_log" are of particular interest to forensic practitioners as discussed further in section on server examination and analysis.

ownCloud has the optional capability to enable encryption on the files uploaded to the ownCloud instance. The encryption key is stored with the users" data in their "datadirectory" and, as noted, this should be collected as part of the acquisition of the users data.

ownCloud stores metadata in an SQLite or MySQL database. The database should be collected for examination and analysis, in the case of MySQL the "mysqldump" utility can be used (the database name and credentials for accessing the database can be located in the ownCloud configuration file "config/config.php") or the database files can be copied directly from "/var/lib/mysql/[database name]" (in our experiment environment). In the case of SQLite, the database is stored in the "[datadirectory]/owncloud.db" file which should be collected.

---

[2]For example, a child exploitation materials case in Australia highlighted the challenge of accurately determining the person responsible for upload or download of the data in question, "the affidavit of the father filed by leave in court on 22 July ... alleged that if the annexures to the mother's affidavit are correct somebody logged in on the laptop at 6.50 a.m. on the morning of Monday 14 January using the password '[B] Rd' and remained logged in continuously until at least 7.28 p.m. and also signed in to a hotmail account at 11.16 a.m. His evidence is that he did three separate jobs on behalf of [S] Pty Ltd on that day... [and] there is no actual evidence before the court as to the nature of the items alleged to have been viewed by the father—only conclusions drawn by others that the dumps included child pornography; there is no evidence of a chain of custody of the computer; the contents of the laptop have been wiped; and the evidence as to who had access to the computer when the parties were together is disputed" (Waters v Waters and Anor [2009] FMCAFAM 819).

It is also recommended that practitioners make a copy of the ownCloud application files as there may be version specific issues which need to be overcome before evidence can be extracted. The application files (in combination with the other data collected) will allow the practitioner to set up a duplicate instance of the ownCloud environment for testing. Locating the application files can be achieved via a variety of methods, searching the default web server root path ("/var/www/html" in our experiment), searching the web servers configuration file to determine the path being used for the ownCloud instance, or performing a keyword search on the server image for common ownCloud application files/ configuration directives (e.g., owncloud, owncloud.db, ocsclient.php, files_encryption).

Server examination and analysis

Examination and analysis commenced with examination of the image file system to access the artifacts listed above. The following describes the findings from this examination.

Administrative and file management metadata—ownCloud stores the majority of the file management metadata on the server in the SQL database which would have been collected as part of a typical digital forensic process. Tables prefixed with oc_calendar, oc_contacts, and oc_media have not been included for analysis as they are not within the focus of this chapter. However, they are expected to contain the data stored relevant to those applications (media, calendar, and contacts).

Tables of StaaS forensic interest are discussed below:

- oc_users: oc_users lists the usernames and a hashed password for the users of the ownCloud instance. The passwords appear to be hashed using a Blowfish-based hashing algorithm using the "portable PHP password hashing framework" (phpass)—http://www.openwall.com/phpass/.
- oc_sharing: oc_sharing lists files (owner and path) which have been shared with other users or "public" in the case of files shared using the "Share with private link" functionality. A "target" UID is listed which matches the "token" parameter in the shared URL. In the case of files shared between users/groups on the same ownCloud instance, the table has the following fields of interest:
  - "uid_owner" lists the username which is sharing the file.
  - "uid_shared_with" lists the username of the user who has been granted access to the file.
  - "source" lists the file system path to the shared file (relative to the ownCloud "datadirectory").
  - "target" lists the path to the shared file as it appears to the shared_with user.
  - "permissions" is set to 0 for read-only access and 1 for writable access.

Where a target is shared with a group, it appears that one row is created for each user of the group with the "uid_shared_with" format of "[username]@[groupname]."

- oc_pictures_images_cache: oc_pictures_images_cache lists images stored for each ownCloud user (presumably generated for/by the "Pictures" or "gallary" app). Path, width, and height (as well as uid_owner — the username of the image owner) are stored. Notably entries are not immediately deleted when a user deletes an image.
- oc_log: The oc_log table has remained empty during our experiments, and it is assumed that this table is to be used with a future feature. The table contains the following fields: id, moment (datetime), appid, user, action, and info. If this level of logging is enabled by default in future versions of ownCloud, this table could prove to be a very useful forensic artifact.
- oc_appconfig: This table lists a number of configuration parameters for the ownCloud internal applications. One of particular interest is the "appid" of "files_encryption" and specifically the "configkey" of "enabled" which with a "configvalue" of "yes" (in a "files_encryption" row) denotes that encryption has been enabled in this ownCloud instance.
- oc_fscache: As the name suggests, this table appears to be a cache of the file system objects (data uploaded) stored within the ownCloud data directory. The fields in this table are as follows: id, path (relative to the ownCloud data directory), user, size (bytes), ctime (create time in POSIX format), mtime (modified time in POSIX format), mimetype and mimepart (representing the mimetype of the file), encrypted (1 if the file is encrypted, 0 otherwise), versioned (1 if the file has previous versions, 0 otherwise), and writable (1 if the file is writable, 0 otherwise). If files are deleted, entries in this table appear to be deleted immediately.

The "encrypted" value is of particular interest to a practitioner as not all files appear to be encrypted even if encryption is enabled in an ownCloud instance (jpg files being a notable example in our experiments) and a practitioner will need to know which files are encrypted before attempting to manually decrypt the files. Equally, fields such as "ctime," "mtime," and "size" may be of importance to a practitioner in terms of reporting and presentation on the evidence sourced from the ownCloud instance.

Stored files—As part of the collection phase of the framework (see Martini & Choo, 2012), stored files in an ownCloud instance are located in the "datadirectory" which should have been located and collected as part of that phase. The "datadirectory" contains a subdirectory for each user in the ownCloud instance that in turn contains a "files" subdirectory and a "versions" subdirectory (if file versioning is enabled and available).

The structure of the "files" directory is as set up by the user (it appears as the root directory to the user), which contains files and directories as created/synced by the user. The view of these files/directories to the forensic practitioner is largely identical to that of the user. If encryption is not enabled, a practitioner should be able to extract files of interest from this directory and subdirectories directly.

The structure of the "versions" directory appears to mirror the "files" directory. However, this directory structure is not directly accessible to the user. This directory is used to store previous versions of files stored by the user in the ownCloud instance. Users can use the "History" button in the ownCloud web interface (accessed per file) to view previous versions stored. Filenames of files stored in the "versions" directory are appended with a POSIX timestamp that represents the time when the version of the file was copied to the "versions" directory.

It appears that previous versions of files are not immediately deleted when they are deleted by the user from their mirror location(s) in the "files" directory. ownCloud describes "Version Control" on its web site (http://owncloud.org/support/version-control/) and notes that "[c]hanges made at intervals greater than 2 minutes are saved in data/[user]/versions."

Encryption metadata—If encryption has been enabled on the ownCloud instance (which can be determined using the "oc_appconfig" table as discussed above), each user (with files stored on the instance) should have an encryption.key file in the root of their individual data directory (e.g., data/username/encryption.key). Each file uploaded which is not exempted from encryption (see list of exempted file types below) should be encrypted using this key. ownCloud uses a type of Blowfish encryption (provided by the third party "Crypt_Blowfish" PEAR package—http://pear.php.net/package/Crypt_Blowfish) to encrypt individual files. The process of encryption is as follows: The "encryption.key" file is created (if it does not already exist) and consists of 20 random digits encrypted with the users password. These 20 random digits are the "key" used to encrypt the user's files using the same Blowfish encryption method. This is a preferred method of encryption as it allows users to change their password without needing to decrypt the files with their old password and re-encrypt the files with the new password, in this case the system only needs to decrypt and re-encrypt the encryption.key file with the user's updated password.

The following file types are exempt from encryption by default: jpg, png, jpeg, avi, mpg, mpeg, mkv, mp3, oga, ogv, and ogg. This is configurable (globally to the ownCloud instance) from the admin ownCloud settings page.

Using artifacts collected from the client(s) (and potentially the server), user files can be decrypted, three items are required, the user's password (in any of a number of formats), the encryption.key file, and the file(s) which are to be decrypted. The user's password can be collected using a number of methods. These include directly from the user, from a saved version in the sync client configuration, and mobile clients database (as discussed above), if using the browser client potentially in the saved passwords lists stored by the user and captured from WebDAV network traffic if the user is not connected via HTTPS.

The process for decrypting files is as follows: Use the contents of the encryption.key file as the data and the users password as the key in the Crypt_Blowfish Decrypt method which will return the 20-digit "encryption key." Then use the "encryption key" as the key and the encrypted file contents as the data in the Crypt_Blowfish Decrypt method will return the decrypted file. This method was tested successfully during our experiments.

Junod (2012) discusses the ownCloud encryption module and lists a number of flaws with this feature. One of these flaws leads to another variation of this decryption procedure which uses the plaintext "encryption key" stored on the server as part of the users PHP session file. In our experiments, these files were stored on the server in "/var/lib/php/session." Using the PHPSESSID cookie stored on the client for the ownCloud domain, we were able to locate the PHP session file (stored in the format sess_[PHPSESSID]) which remained on the server after we completed collection of the server image. It should also be possible to keyword search the files in the "session" directory searching for the username of the user and string "enckey" in the file to locate the appropriate "sess_[PHP_SESSID]" file. Using the 20-digit "encryption key" stored in this file, encrypted files can be decrypted directly using Crypt_Blowfish (as discussed above) without needing the user's password. This method of decryption was also tested successfully as part of our experiments.

Cloud logging and authentication data—By default, ownCloud does not generate internal logging data (which appears to be) of specific use to a forensic practitioner. The data which is logged by default by the ownCloud application relates mostly to internal operational issues such as "file not found in cache" errors. A logging level option is available in the admin settings section of ownCloud. Surprisingly, when debug level logging is enabled (which generates a log file in the "datadirectory" named "owncloud.log"), no entries of general interest were found after simple testing (login, logout, file upload, etc.).

However, in our experiments, the web server (Apache) did produce a number of useful log entries in its "access.log" and "ssl_access.log" files located in the "/var/log/httpd directory" relating to the ownCloud instance. The "access.log" file contains an entry for each request served by the web server, and the "ssl_access.log" file contains similar entries for requests which were made via HTTPS connections. These requests commonly include file "GET" requests for page content in the web client and file downloads, "POST" requests for form data/AJAX file uploads transferred to the server, and a number of other WebDAV-specific request types commonly used by the sync and mobile clients. Although the ownCloud-specific GET and POST requests do record date/time and IP addresses by default (as do all request entries in the log file), usernames are not recorded against these requests as Basic HTTP authentication is not used with web client requests. However, usernames are recorded against requests that are made via WebDAV (e.g., sync clients) as HTTP Basic authentication is used as part of these requests. Filenames, paths, etc. are also common in many requests. This allows a practitioner to determine in many instances the times and dates when individual files are uploaded, downloaded, and modified by particular users which is of interest.

Summary of findings

Tables 6.4 and 6.5 summarize the key artifacts located as part of the client and server experiments and note the relevance of individual artifacts to a digital forensics investigation:

Table 6.4 Client Artifact Summary

Category	Artifact	Relevance
Sync and file management metadata	ownCloud "folders"	Assists the practitioner in determining which client folders are synced with an ownCloud instance.
	File metadata	May assist a practitioner in determining files stored within a synced directory and file modification times.
Cached files	Synced files	Files synced to the client from the ownCloud instance appear as regular files. They can be located using the sync and file management metadata.
Cloud service and authentication data	owncloud. cfg	The owncloud.cfg file is one of the key ownCloud artifacts on the client. It allows the forensic practitioner to determine the ownCloud instance which is being used with the sync client and allows the practitioner to collect the users credentials (if stored). If the file has been deleted, a number of avenues for recovery are available including a keyword search of unallocated space, MFT backups, and system restore.
Browser artifacts	URL parameters	When using the ownCloud web client, URL parameters (in history, bookmarks, download lists, etc.) can provide a practitioner with a broad range of information (potentially including date and time) on the ownCloud "app" being used, server file names and directories for files downloaded and logoff events.
	Page titles	A keyword search for ownCloud page titles (e.g., "Files	ownCloud (username)") is a key identifier of ownCloud use and may assist a practitioner in determining the ownCloud instance used and

(Continued)

Table 6.4 (Continued)

Category	Artifact	Relevance
		ownCloud username if the web client has been used.
Mobile client artifacts	Accessed files	Files which have been accessed on the iOS client appear to be cached locally, and this may allow a practitioner to access files not available on other devices.
	DB.sqlite	The SQLite database used by the ownCloud client stores valuable authentication data and file metadata that relate both to files stored on the device and the server. This may assist a practitioner in gaining access to the ownCloud instance used or in contributing as evidence of files stored and file times.
Network analysis	HTTP/ WebDAV artifacts	It was noted that the ownCloud client uses WebDAV over HTTP or HTTPS to facilitate file synchronization between the server and the client. When a non-SSL HTTP connection is set up to communicate between client and server, data can be recovered from network captures. HTTP Basic authentication can also be captured in this setup, which is another method by which a practitioner can collect a user's ownCloud credentials.

CONCLUSION

This research demonstrated that open source cloud StaaS provides a significant number of useful artifacts for forensic practitioners in an investigation. Using ownCloud as a case study, we successfully undertook a forensic examination of the client and server components of an ownCloud installation and discussed the relevance of a number of artifacts to a forensic investigation (see Tables 6.4 and 6.5 for a summary).

Our analysis of the client devices demonstrated that in many cases significant data can be found which links the user to a particular ownCloud instance. This provides a forensic trail to the ownCloud server instance even when evidential data on the client may be securely deleted. The client artifacts found in the ownCloud experiments are likely to be common with other open source cloud storage products developed in the future as cloud products mature and develop a common feature set. While individual implementations may vary, practitioners can use the artifacts discovered in these experiments as a basis for their investigation of the client as a potential evidence source and perhaps more importantly as

Table 6.5 Server Artifact Summary

Category	Artifact	Relevance
Administrative and file management metadata	SQL database	The SQL database on the ownCloud server stores a range of data which could be of use to a forensic practitioner. This includes a user list, sharing permissions, encryption configuration, and a cache of file system information such as file paths, owner, size, modified types, and encryption status.
Stored files	"datadirectory"	The "datadirectory" contains the structure and files uploaded by the user to the ownCloud instance. This is a primary source of evidence for a forensic practitioner.
	File versioning	Within the "datadirectory" is a versions directory which contains past versions of files and potentially deleted files.
Encryption metadata	Blowfish encryption	Encryption can be optionally enabled on an ownCloud instance, when enabled most files uploaded are encrypted (some file types are exempt by default). The encryption key is stored in the "encryption.key" file stored in the users "datadirectory" subfolder and encrypted with the users' password. A practitioner can collect the users' password from a number of other artifacts and decrypt the files stored.
Cloud logging and authentication data	Web server logging data	The default logging data stored by the web server (Apache in these experiments) can be of use to a forensic practitioner to determine when a user has communicated with the ownCloud server and the changes made by the user as part of that session. The usefulness of this data was limited when the web client was used. However, a large amount of information was available on sync client transactions.

a link to the cloud computing instance on which other data may be stored. The file metadata and cloud authentication artifacts found are of particular interest in an investigation which heavily involves cloud computing use. These artifacts can be used not only to determine the cloud computing instance used but also provide authentication data potentially allowing an investigator to collect data from the cloud instance directly and help link user actions with the data stored in the cloud computing environment via the use of file metadata such as permissions and timestamps.

Our server analysis showed that while collection of data in an environment with one server such as the instance in these experiments may be relatively straightforward, factors such as encryption could complicate investigations significantly. While many practitioners may focus upon collection of the files uploaded by the suspect in the first instance, it has been demonstrated that it is important to collect the range of artifacts suggested as they may be required to assist in linking a user with the data stored in the cloud instance, recovering previous data stored by a user in the cloud instance or in decrypting data stored by the user. In many cases, it will not be possible to collect the entire cloud storage instance due to the size and amount of unrelated (other users) data stored on the physical device(s). Consequently, this makes collection of the full range of artifacts critical as once the preservation methods are no longer being applied to the cloud instance, critical data such as encryption keys and metadata may be lost.

The utility of our iterative cloud forensics framework was demonstrated with client artifacts being used to identify cloud storage usage and being used to decrypt files stored on the server. The iterative nature of the framework suggests that client devices are analyzed first to both identify cloud usage and allow practitioners to request preservation by the cloud computing provider in a directed manner providing as much information on the data requested to be preserved as possible. Analysis of sync and file management metadata on the client can also help prevent time being spent on investigation of cloud services which are unlikely to be of evidential value.

While it may be possible to preserve an ownCloud instance by disconnecting the environment from the network, this approach is not guaranteed to ensure preservation and will result in potentially significant downtime for all users of the cloud instance. It is instead recommended that StaaS developers integrate preservation technologies directly into the product. In this case, ownCloud could "freeze" a user's account preventing them from making any further changes (after a valid request is received from law enforcement) and provide a forensic practitioner with a package containing the contents of the users files directory, previous versions, encryption key, and any relevant metadata and logging information. The provision of this package would not only simplify the extraction of evidence for the practitioner but also ensure minimal downtime for the cloud instance (in this case none should be required).

References

AARNET. (2013). *CloudStor+* . Retrieved 10 April 2013, from <http://www.aarnet.edu.au/communities/research/eresearch-overview/cloudstorplus-information>.

Australian Government Attorney-General's Department. (2013). *Australian Government Policy and Risk management guidelines for the storage and processing of Australian Government information in outsourced or offshore ICT arrangements*, from <http://www.protectivesecurity.gov.au/informationsecurity/Documents/

PolicyandRiskmanagementguidelinesforthestorageandprocessingofAusGovinfoinoutsourcedoroffshoreICTarrangements.pdf>.

Australian Government Department of Broadband, Communications and the Digital Economy. (2013). *The national cloud computing strategy*, from <http://www.dbcde. gov.au/__data/assets/pdf_file/0008/163844/2013-292_National_Cloud_Computing_Strategy_Accessible_FA.pdf>.

Australian Government Parliamentary Joint Committee on Intelligence and Security. (2012). *Proof committee hansard (Public) Wednesday, 5 September 2012*, from <http://www.aph.gov.au/Parliamentary_Business/Committees/House_of_Representatives_Committees?url = pjcis/nsl2012/hearings/program01.pdf>.

Badger, L., Grance, T., Patt-Corner, R., & Voas, J. (2012). *Cloud Computing Synopsis and Recommendations. (SP 800-146)* Gaithersburg, MD: U.S. Department of Commerce.

Cuthbertson, S. (2012). Mutual assistance in criminal matters: Cyberworld realities. In S. Hufnagel, C. Harfield, & S. Bronitt (Eds.), *Cross-border law enforcement regional law enforcement cooperation — european, australian and asia-pacific perspective* (pp. 127−142). Routledge Research in Transnational Crime and Criminal Law.

European Network and Information Security Agency (ENISA). (2012). Procure Secure: A guide to Monitoring of Security Service Levels in Cloud Contracts. Heraklion, Greece: European Network and Information Security Agency.

Google. (2013). *Google trends - web search interest: owncloud - worldwide, 2004 - present*. Retrieved 12 July 2013, from <http://www.google.com.au/trends/explore#q = owncloud &cmpt = q>.

Hooper, C., Martini, B., & Choo, K. -K. R. (2013). Cloud computing and its implications for cybercrime investigations in Australia. *Computer Law & Security Review, 29*(2), 152−163. doi: <http://dx.doi.org/10.1016/j.clsr.2013.01.006>.

Jenkins, R. J. (1997). *Hash functions for hash table lookup*. Retrieved 22 August 2013, from <http://www.burtleburtle.net/bob/hash/evahash.html>.

Junod, P. (2012). *OwnCloud 4.0 and Encryption*. Retrieved 24 September 2012, from <http://crypto.junod.info/2012/05/24/owncloud-4-0-and-encryption/>.

Klosowski, T. (2013). *How to set up your own private cloud storage service with OwnCloud*. Retrieved 5 April 2013, from <http://www.lifehacker.com.au/2013/04/how-to-set-up-your-own-private-cloud-storage-service-with-owncloud/>.

Martini, B., & Choo, K. -K. R. (2012). An integrated conceptual digital forensic framework for cloud computing. *Digital Investigation, 9*(2), 71−80.

Martini, B., & Choo, K-K. R. (2013). Cloud storage forensics: ownCloud as a case study. *Digital Investigation*, In press. doi: http://dx.doi.org/10.1016/j.diin. 2013.08.005].

McKemmish, R. (1999). What is forensic computing? *Trends and Issues in Crime and Criminal Justice, 118*, 1−6.

Microsoft. (2013). *Monitored file name extensions (Windows)*. Retrieved 15 July 2013, from <http://msdn.microsoft.com/en-us/library/windows/desktop/aa378870%28v = vs. 85%29.aspx>.

ownCloud. (2013). Sync Clients | ownCloud.org. Retrieved 12 July 2013, from <http://owncloud.org/sync-clients/>

Tassone, C, Martini, B., Choo, K-K. R., & Slay, J. (2013). Mobile device forensics: A snapshot. *Trends & Issues in Crime and Criminal Justice, 460*, 1—7.

United Nations Office on Drugs and Crime (UNODC) (2012). *The use of the Internet for terrorist purposes* New York, US: United Nations.

United States National Institute of Justice (US NIJ) (2004). *Forensic examination of digital evidence: a guide for law enforcement* Washington, DC: U.S. Department of Justice.

Forensic Collection of Cloud Storage Data: Does the Act of Collection Result in Changes to the Data or its Metadata?

7

INFORMATION IN THIS CHAPTER

- Evidence source identification and preservation
- Collection of evidence from cloud storage services
- Examination and analysis of collected data

In this chapter, the preservation and collection steps of the framework (Chapter 2) are explored. The task of preservation and collection follows after data has been identified, which was outlined in the previous chapters (Martini & Choo, 2013; Quick & Choo, 2013a, b, c, d). This chapter examines how to preserve and collect identified data when legislation allows for collection, such as under a warrant, and two methods an investigator could undertake for this process are outlined, including using browser access or using client software.

INTRODUCTION

One issue facing forensic practitioners is the identification of service providers and accounts, including usernames and passwords. The previous chapters have outlined that the identification of data can be achieved with analysis of user devices, such as computer hard drives, network traffic, or mobile devices such as an Apple iPhone or Android mobile phone. It is possible to identify user details, and even passwords, for cloud storage accounts by undertaking analysis of a seized PC or mobile device. If a password is not known, it is also possible to boot a forensic image of a seized PC within a virtual computer and in some cases this will automatically log into a cloud storage account: Google Drive and Dropbox, but not Microsoft SkyDrive.

Once identification of a cloud storage account is made, investigators can undertake a legal process via a service provider to secure data. This process can potentially be problematic due to delays or jurisdictional issues (Ruan, Carthy,

Kechadi, & Crosbie, 2011). As an example, if an investigator in Australia discovers a suspect has data stored with a cloud storage provider based in the United States, the process of securing and gaining access to the data relies upon communication and legal processes across the various countries, with different legal system requirements having to be met. This process may not be timely, and a user may be able to access an account and remove evidence prior to a preservation order coming into effect.

Some jurisdictions have legal provisions which allow for data to be secured at the time of serving a warrant, such as at the time of a search and seizure undertaking. In Australia, Section 3L of the *Crimes Act 1914* (Cth) has a provision for the executing officer of a search and seizure warrant to access data which includes data not held at the premises, i.e., accessible from a computer or data storage device. However, this may not be the case in a number of jurisdictions, including the United States. If a practitioner is able to obtain legal access to a cloud storage account, current methods to manually collect data from a cloud storage account involve accessing an account via a browser or using client software to download data.

In this chapter, we explore:

1. whether the contents of files change during the process of upload, storage, and download from cloud storage accounts;
2. whether the timestamp information is altered or remains static during the process of upload, storage, and download from cloud storage accounts.

We will examine three popular public cloud storage providers, namely Dropbox, Google Drive, and Microsoft SkyDrive. Research was undertaken exploring a process of accessing and downloading data using a browser as well as client software. We then compare the two methods and summarize our findings.

Cloud storage providers
Dropbox

Dropbox is a file hosting service that enables users to store and share files and folders. At the time of this research, there is a free service which allows 2 GB of data storage, and additional storage space can be acquired by referring or signing up new users. Users can also pay for larger storage sizes, such as 100 GB for US $99 per year, or "as much as needed" for business customers. Dropbox can be accessed using a web browser (e.g., Internet Explorer) or client software. Dropbox client software is available for Microsoft Windows operating system (OS), Apple Mac OSX, Linux, Apple iOS, Android, Blackberry, and Windows Phone devices. Dropbox uses the Amazon S3 AWS service to host client data (Quick & Choo, 2013b). It is reported that in 2009 there were 2 million users; in 2010 this doubled to 4 million; in 2011 it increased to 25 million (Rosenberg, 2011) and in 2012 there are reported to be over 100 million users and a billion files saved every 24 hours (Malik, 2012).

Dropbox Inc. is an American company based in San Francisco, California. According to the user agreement, the State of California and the Federal provisions in the United States must be complied with to preserve and access data related to an investigation (DropBox, 2013c). The Dropbox privacy policy states that Dropbox cooperates with "United States law enforcement when it receives valid legal process" (DropBox, 2013b). In addition, they will also remove their encryption when providing files to law enforcement (DropBox, 2013a). Information on the Dropbox contact web page lists the corporate legal team which can be contacted via the email address legal@dropbox.com (Dropbox, 2012). Law enforcement agencies outside of the United States will need to undertake a Mutual Legal Assistance Treaty (MLAT)[1] process through the local agency contact or liaison point.

Google Drive

Google Drive is a recent offering from Google Inc. and has evolved from Google Docs. By default, users have 5 GB of data storage when creating an account. Additional storage, ranging from 25 GB to 16 TB, is available as a paid service. Google Drive can be accessed using a web browser or client software. Google Drive client software is available for installation on a computer or portable devices such as a Google Android device, Apple iOS, or Windows Phone. According to Google, there are an estimated 425 million active users of Google Mail (Google, 2012), which includes the ability to store data in Google Drive.

Google, Inc. is an American company with headquarters in Mountain View, California. Google also has offices throughout the world. Google explains the process for a government agencies, courts, and litigious parties to request information at their "Legal Process" web site (Google, 2013). Google separately outlines the process relating to requests from government agencies within the United States and for those outside of the United States. For a government agency within the United States, a legal process such as a subpoena, court order, or search warrant

---

[1]The MLAT facilitates the bilateral exchange of information and evidence for use in criminal proceedings between treaty countries. United States currently has reportedly MLATs with 57 countries, namely "Antigua and Barbuda, Argentina, Australia, Austria, the Bahamas, Barbados, Belgium, Belize, Bermuda, Brazil, Canada, Cyprus, Czech Republic, Dominica, Egypt, Estonia, France, Germany, Greece, Grenada, Hong Kong, Hungary, India, Ireland, Israel, Italy, Jamaica, Japan, Latvia, Liechtenstein, Lithuania, Luxembourg, Malaysia, Mexico, Morocco, the Kingdom of the Netherlands (including Aruba, Bonaire, Curacao, Saba, St. Eustatius, and St. Maarten), Nigeria, Panama, Philippines, Poland, Romania, Russia, St. Lucia, St. Kitts and Nevis, St. Vincent and the Grenadines, South Africa, South Korea, Spain, Sweden, Switzerland, Thailand, Trinidad and Tobago, Turkey, Ukraine, United Kingdom (including the Isle of Man, Cayman Islands, Anguilla, British Virgin Islands, Montserrat, and Turks and Caicos), Uruguay, and Venezuela" (United States Department of State, 2013: p. 23).

is required to gather user information from Google. For government agencies outside of the United States, the use of an MLAT is one avenue for an agency to request information. This involves working with the US Department of Justice or the US Federal Trade Commission (Google, 2013). This process is intricate and subject to the terms of an MLAT and expertise should be sought to comply with the process applicable to an agency, as differences may apply for different MLATs in different countries and jurisdictions.

Microsoft SkyDrive

Microsoft SkyDrive was previously known as Windows Live Folders and Windows Live SkyDrive and offers a potential 25 GB of free storage. According to Microsoft's Windows Division President Steven Sinofsky (Sinofsky, 2012), "SkyDrive has over 200 million customers storing data in their free SkyDrive" which consists of "11 billion photos, 550 million documents, storing over 14 PB of data, and, every month, 2 PB of data are added." SkyDrive can be accessed using a web browser or client software. SkyDrive client software is available for installation on a computer or portable devices such as an Apple iPhone.

Microsoft is an American company with headquarters in Redmond, Washington. Microsoft states in its terms of service that it will respond to legal requests from law enforcement (Microsoft, 2013). Microsoft has legal contact points in the United States and contact points for law enforcement in various countries or regions.

Data collection via Internet access to a user account

In previous chapters, we outlined how there is information stored in cloud storage accounts which is not available on a PC which has either accessed an account or is synchronized to an account using the client software. This includes previous and historical versions of files and information that may assist in the identification of the user (e.g., computer name and IP number used when making changes, times and dates associated with modifications). Crucial evidence may be stored in a cloud storage account, which may not be available on a mobile device or PC. This chapter builds on the previous ones to further explore methods of preserving cloud stored information. It is important to collect such information when permitted by legal authority, as the information may assist in an investigation or court proceedings (see *R v DM* [2010] ACTSC 137 (November 5, 2010)). A practitioner may have located a username and even a password when conducting analysis on a seized PC or mobile device as previously demonstrated (Quick & Choo, 2013a, b).

Using software such as Virtual Forensic Computing (VFC), it is also possible for a practitioner to operate a forensic image in a virtual machine (VM). Using either the forensic image or the credentials, it may be possible for a practitioner to access an account, but they must ensure they are fully compliant with relevant laws, policies, and procedures; otherwise they may put the information at risk of not being accepted in a court. In addition, they may in fact be in breach of relevant law, such as accessing an account without lawful authority, and may be subject to investigation and prosecution themselves. For those jurisdictions with the provision to collect data via accessing an account when serving a warrant (such as Australia), there are two current options available: via browser login and via client software synchronization.

At the time of this research, forensic software for the collection of data stored in cloud storage accounts is not available. Cumulus Data have stated that a future upgrade to their software will include the ability to collect data from "Google Docs, cloud storage such as Dropbox and iCloud, and social media such as LinkedIn, Facebook, and Twitter" (Roach, 2012). Dykstra and Sherman (2012) examine the process of securing evidence from a remote Infrastructure as a Service (IaaS) computer running via Amazon EC2, but this relies upon the practitioner being able to install an Encase Servlet or an FTK Agent. In the situation where identified data is stored within a cloud storage service (file hosting), it is not possible to make use of an Encase Servlet or an FTK Agent, as a user is only able to access data stored in the account, not to run software in the storage environment.

Our research explores the process of collecting data when legal authority exists to access an account. The legal process to preserve data via a service provider may be onerous and not timely, which potentially means a user may be able to access an account and delete or alter files before information can be preserved. The scope of our research is to examine the process of forensically preserving files and data from cloud storage accounts with popular service providers: Dropbox, Google Drive, and Microsoft SkyDrive. To achieve this and abide by common forensic principles (ACPO, 2006; NIJ, 2004, 2008; SAI, 2003), the process outlined in Figure 7.1 was used to preserve data from cloud storage accounts.

We align this methodology with our framework outlined in Chapter 2. This chapter focuses on the preservation and collection steps of the framework.

The methodology encompassed accessing each account (created for the purposes of this research) using a browser running in a virtual machine (VM) and video recording the VM window, in this case using Microsoft Expression Encoder 4. Network traffic was captured using Wireshark running on the host computer. In earlier research, it was found that in some instances it is possible to observe relevant plaintext in network captures, such as when Microsoft SkyDrive cloud storage is used (Quick & Choo, 2013a). Observable information included filenames, OwnerID, and dates and times. Therefore, it is important to capture this information where possible, even if the captured data may not provide information in all instances. It is also possible in some instances to decrypt SSL traffic, such as using the Wireshark SSL Decrypt function; however, this was not tested in this research.

The data in each account was downloaded, saved, and printed using Internet browsers: Internet Explorer (IE) 9.0.8112.16421, Mozilla Firefox (MF) 20.0.1, Google Chrome (GC) 26.0.1410.64m, and Apple Safari (AS) 5.1.7. The account data was then synchronized and downloaded using client software for each

Cloud (storage) forensic framework	Cloud storage data collection
Commence (scope)	**Step 1: Commence (scope)** Outline the focus and scope of the task (refer Chapter 3–5).
Preparation	**Step 2: Preparation** Ensure correct equipment and expertise is available (refer Chapter 3–5).
Evidence source identification and preservation	**Step 3: Identification and preservation** Identify cloud storage user account (Dropbox, Google Drive, SkyDrive, etc.), Identify username and password (see Quick & Choo, 2013a, b). Legal authority to request preservation of data with cloud storage provider, or legal authority to access and collect data from identified accounts
Collection	**Step 4: Collection (legal authority exists to access and collect data from an account)** 1. Use a host computer with connectivity to the Internet (forensic analysis computers are generally not connected to the Internet, and hence a PC setup for the purpose of accessing the Internet should be used, rather than a standard analysis computer). 2. Create a clean base image virtual machine (VM) to access the cloud storage account, with a new installation of a Windows (or Linux) operating system. 3. Use a packet capture tool to collect the network traffic between the VM and the server. 4. Use a screen capture utility to capture the output video of the VM screen during the process. 5. Using the VM, connect to the Service Provider URL using a browser, such as Internet Explorer, Mozilla Firefox, Google Chrome, or Apple Safari. 6. Login to the cloud storage account using the username and password. 7. Browse the folders and files available, noting the dates and times associated with the files and folders, creators and modifiers, and computers linked to an account, including IP and software version where available. Save each page as a HTML or MHT file and also print to a PDF file. 8. Select all files in the account and choose to download them to a folder in the VM. 9. Select the option to download the client software. 10. Install the client software to the VM hard drive and synchronize the account. Observe the process of the contents of the cloud stored account files and folders being downloaded to the VM. 11. Pause and close the VM. 12. Preserve the VM files (including the network PCAP, VM files, and video).
Examination and analysis	**Step 5: Examination and analysis** Conduct analysis as per standard methodology for files and data (refer Chapter 3–5).
Presentation	**Step 6: Presentation** Present the information in a report (refer Chapter 3–5).
Complete	**Step 7: Completion** Backup files and reports. Consider knowledge gained. Seek feedback from IO.

FIGURE 7.1

Data collection process for cloud storage.

service: Dropbox 2.0.8, SkyDrive 2013 Build 17.0.2006.0314, and Google Drive 1.9.4536.8202. The VM was then paused and stopped. The process of "preservation" is a critical element of a forensic process and is undertaken in a manner to ensure the least amount of change to data occurs (McKemmish, 1999). Common forensic software, such as Guidance Software Encase and AccessData Forensic Toolkit, have the ability to preserve data in an unaltered manner and also include timestamp information with a file, such as from an $MFT entry associated with a file. The VM files (VMEM, VMDK, VMX, etc.), Expression Encoder video, and the network captures (PCAP) were preserved within logical evidence files; in this case Encase L01 and AccessData AD1. The X-Ways CTR file format could also be used.

To explore the process of collecting information from a cloud storage account, we examined software designed to capture and view webpages offline, including HTTrack, Local Website Archive, SurfOffline, and Magnet Forensics Web Page Saver. At the time of this research, the software tested was not able to access and save the cloud storage account information due to issues accessing HTTPS and logging into accounts. It was determined that the most appropriate and accurate method to currently preserve web pages is to save each web page using the browser option, either as HTML or MHT format. In addition, it is also applicable to print the webpage to a PDF file.

The VMs were created using VMware Player 4.0.1. For each cloud storage service, a VM was created and Windows 7 Home Basic was installed on a 20 GB virtual hard drive with NTFS as the file system. The Enron dataset is useful for testing purposes and consists of a large set of email messages made public by the US Federal Energy Regulatory Commission during legal proceedings (Klimt & Yang, 2004). For this research, selected files from the UC Berkeley Enron Email subset data file were used and downloaded from the project web site (http://bailando.sims.berkeley.edu/enron_email.html) on the February 9, 2012. Hash values (MD5 and SHA1) were calculated for selected files. The selected files were previously uploaded into cloud storage accounts created for the purposes of this research.

The process outlined in Figure 7.1 was undertaken for Dropbox, Google Drive, and Microsoft SkyDrive. Analysis was then conducted on the logical evidence files to determine whether there were any changes made during the process of downloading files from cloud storage using this methodology.

Dropbox

After logging in to the Dropbox account created for this research using each browser, the first webpage displayed a list of folders and files in the account, with the type of file listed and a modified date, as shown in Figure 7.2.

Collection

When selecting a folder, a web page opened with the files in the folder listed, displaying the file type and (last) modified date on the page. This information may be relevant to an investigation, and in this case was saved as HTML and printed as PDF. As already mentioned, the entire process was also video recorded using Expression Encoder. Using the Right-Mouse-Button on a file or folder displayed an "options" menu, which included the ability to show previous versions of a file, the name of the computer used to access the file, the IP number, and the version

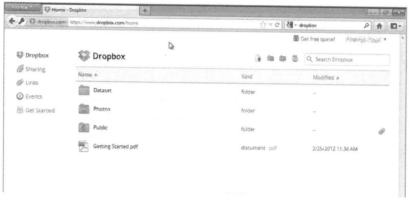

FIGURE 7.2

Dropbox first page in Mozilla Firefox Browser.

of software are used. This information is potentially very important and should be noted (see *R v R, AM* [2011] SADC 38 (28 March 2011)—although this case is not cloud related, there were multiple computers and drives and multiple people with access and it was not possible to prove who possessed the data in question beyond reasonable doubt). Select a folder provided for an option to download the folder and its contents. This was undertaken and resulted in a ZIP file being downloaded to the default download location within the VM:

"C:\Users\[username]\Downloads\."

The ZIP file had the name of the folder "Dataset.zip." The process of downloading individual files via the browser was tested to determine the effect on timestamps, and single files were downloaded to the desktop. This process was undertaken for each browser.

For the next part of the research, the Dropbox client software was downloaded from the Dropbox web site and installed to the VM hard drive. The client software when run prompts for user details and we entered the information for the research account. The software was then observed to synchronize the contents of the Dropbox research account to the default directory; in this case, "C:\Users \[username]\ Dropbox\." This process was also video recorded.

Next, Steps 4.11 and 4.12 from the process (Figure 7.1) were undertaken to preserve the data in the VM. The files were preserved in a logical evidence file (L01) using Encase 6.19.4.

Analysis

Analysis was conducted on the logical evidence file, with the original source files loaded into the case as "single files" for comparison purposes. Hash values (MD5 and SHA1) were calculated and it was noted that the hash values matched; hence the contents of the files stored in the Dropbox account were not changed during the process of uploading, storing, and downloading from the Dropbox account.

Analysis of the network traffic captured in the PCAP files showed no readable data relating to accessing, downloading, or synchronizing; and our earlier research (Quick & Choo, 2013a, b) has shown this traffic is SSL encrypted.

Browser dates and times

Examining the file dates and times for the files downloaded via the browser (contained in the zip file), the following differences were observed; the File Created time and the Last Accessed time of the downloaded files were the same as the original files Last Written time without the time zone offset (i.e., in UTC). The Last Written time and the Entry Modified time of the downloaded files were the time it was unzipped. None of the file dates and times matches with the original file date and time information. It was observed that for all files downloaded individually from the Dropbox account, all the file timestamps (modified, written, accessed, and created) were the date and time this was undertaken. No differences were observed between the different browsers tested, and all had the same results.

Client software dates and times

When examining the files synchronized by the Dropbox client software, the following differences were observed; the File Created time, Last Accessed time, and the Entry Modified time of the synchronized files were the time the file was synchronized and downloaded from the account. Of note is that the Last Written time of the synchronized files was the same as the Last Written time from the original file and it appears this timestamp information remained with the file throughout the process of uploading, storing, and downloading.

Times and dates associated with files can become crucial aspects of an investigation and in Court proceedings. For example, in *United States of America v. William G. Mckinley III*[2], issues discussed in the Appeal related to the "last written time stamp" and interpretation of the meaning and effect, and the unreliability of "last access date/time stamps." Undertaking research in relation to potential changes to timestamps is important to provide understanding as to what circumstances will affect timestamps and provide explanation for unusual timestamps associated with a file. An understanding that the Last Written timestamp remains the same throughout the process of storage and download when using the client software may be an important aspect of a trial.

Client software log files

Analysis of the logical evidence file for the VM hard drive for client software log files relating to the synchronization located no files relevant to the synchronization

---

[2]*General Court-Martial, United States Navy-Marine Corps Court of Criminal Appeals, Washington, DC,* http://www.jag.navy.mil/courts/documents/archive/2011/MCKINLEY,%20W.G.% 20201000120.pdf (last accessed 11 May 2013).

process. Previous experiments by Chung, Park, Lee, and Kang (2012) and McClain (2011) using Dropbox (Windows) client software (version 1.1.35) highlighted the presence of config.db file and filecache.db files. These were reported to contain a history of filenames synchronized with Dropbox. In the Dropbox client software used for this research (version 1.2.52), these files did not contain any log history. In the VM at the location of the.db files, there were config.dbx and filecache.dbx files, both of which appear to be encrypted. These could potentially contain the file history information previously stored in the db files. McClain (2012) highlights the presence of a dropbox.cache folder in the users Dropbox folder (Users\[username]\Dropbox\.dropbox.cache\) which may contain information in Base64 in an "Entries.log" relating to file activity; however in the data collected in this research, there was no information in the dropbox.cache folder.

Google Drive

We then examined Google Drive, using the same process as was applied to Dropbox, listed in Figure 7.1. New VMs were created to access the Google Drive research account using each browser. The first webpage displayed a list of folders, with the owner and a last modified date, as shown in Figure 7.3.

Collection

When selecting a folder on the first page, this opened a web page with the files in the folder listed, including owner information and the last modified date for each file. Selecting a down arrow next to "OWNER" displayed a drop-down list to choose to display the "last edited" or "last opened" dates. This information may be relevant to an investigation and should be noted. In this case, the page was saved as HTML and printed to PDF. This was also video recorded using Expression Encoder. Using the Right-Mouse-Button on a file or folder displayed an "options"

FIGURE 7.3

Google Drive first page in Mozilla Firefox Browser.

menu, which included the ability to show previous versions of a file (manage revisions). Previous versions may provide relevant information, and any information should be noted, saved, and printed to PDF. The process of selecting a folder displays an option to download a folder and its contents. When this was chosen, a ZIP file was downloaded to the default download location within the VM—"C:\Users \[username]\Downloads\." The ZIP file had the name in the following format: "documents-export-YYYY-MM-DD.zip." Any documents created within Google Drive are in the "gdoc" format (Clarke, 2013). When exported from cloud storage, these are converted to a Word document or RTF document, based on user selection. The process of downloading individual files via the browser was tested to determine the effect on timestamps, and single files were downloaded to the desktop. At the time of this research, there is no method available to preserve the file as a gdoc file and must be converted to another format to preserve the file (Clarke, 2013). This process was undertaken for each browser.

Next, the Google Drive client software was downloaded and installed to the VM hard drive by selecting this option from the web page ("Download Google Drive"). We logged in to the Google Drive research account and observed the client software synchronizes the contents of the Google Drive account to the default directory; in this case, "C:\Users\[username]\Google Drive\." As per the process listed in Figure 7.1 (Steps 4.11 and 4.12), the VM files were preserved in a logical evidence file (L01) using Encase 6.19.4.

Analysis
Analysis was conducted on the preserved data in the logical evidence file, with the original files also loaded into the case as "single files" for comparison purposes. Hash values (MD5 and SHA1) were calculated for the files and compared. It was noted that the hash values of the files from the research account matched the original single files; hence the contents of the files were not changed during the process of uploading, storing, and downloading. Analysis of the network traffic captured in the PCAP files showed no readable data relating to accessing, downloading, or synchronizing.

Browser dates and times
Examining the file dates and times for the files downloaded via the browser, the following differences were observed; when using a browser to download a file in a ZIP file, the File Created time and the Last Accessed time of the downloaded files were the same as the original files Last Written time without the time zone offset (i.e., in UTC). The Last Written time and the Entry Modified time of the downloaded files were the time it was unzipped. None of the file dates and times matches with the original file date and time information. It was observed that for all files downloaded individually, all the file timestamps (modified, written, accessed, and created) were the date and time the file was downloaded. No differences were observed between the different browsers tested, and all had the same results.

Client software dates and times

Next we examined the files synchronized via the Google Drive client software and noted the following differences: the File Created time and the Entry Modified time of the synchronized files were the time the file was synchronized and downloaded from the account. The Last Written time of the synchronized files was the same as the Last Written time of the original file, and the Last Accessed time of the synchronized files was same as the Last Written time from the original file (which was different to the Last Accessed time of the original file).

Client software log files

We then conducted analysis of the VM hard drive for client software log files and located a "Snapshot.db" file at "C:\Users\[username]\AppData\Local\Google\Drive\." This file was a SQLite database and we viewed the file with SQLite Manager (a Mozilla Firefox Plugin). Within the SQLite file were details of the files synchronized, including the filename, the creation time, and modified times. An abbreviated example of data from a snapshot.db file is listed in Table 7.1. The creation and modified time information appear to be in Unix Numeric Value time format (number of seconds since 01/01/1970), which can be decoded using conversion software such as Digital Detective's DCode v4.02a. For example, the file named "3111.txt" has a Modified time of "1100097650." This is converted using DCode to "Wed, 10 November 2004 14:40:50 UTC," which is the Last Written (modified) time for the original Enron 3111.txt file. The Created time converted to the time the file was originally uploaded to the Google Drive research account. The file size was also listed, with an MD5 checksum value for the file (which matched the original file and the downloaded file).

Microsoft SkyDrive

Our research then focused on Microsoft SkyDrive, and the process outlined was undertaken using a new VM. We accessed a SkyDrive account created for this research using each browser. The first webpage displayed a list of folders, as shown in Figure 7.4.

Collection

When selecting a folder (or blue rectangle), a web page opened with files in the folder listed with file information displayed on the right-hand side of the browser page for the file selected. The information displayed included whether the file is being shared, the file type, modified date, and a username. Also displayed were an "added date" and username, and the path and file size. This information may be relevant to an investigation and the page was saved as HTML and printed as a PDF. Using the Right-Mouse-Button on a folder displayed a drop-down menu, which included the option to show properties of a folder and an option to download the folder and its contents. The option to download was selected, and a ZIP file was downloaded to the default download location within the VM: "C:\Users

Table 7.1 Google Drive "snapshot.db" File Contents (Abbreviated)

Filename	Modified	Created	Size	Checksum
Root	1339308961	1339309024	0	
Dataset	1341041780	1341041780	0	
Docs	1345973985	1341041868	0	
Untitled document	1100097650	1339309029	2734	f3a862114dcef80cc3eb0429b4f80a62
3111.txt	1330133578	1339309056	34215	bc99a5bf44317ae105afb08d8201e831
Enron3111.rtf	1328766856	1339309030	14072	3e42e0d132d27db780087925f3700fbb
Enron3111.docx	1328766794	1339309046	315868	7763831 9ea64cc1b70d4df20a56295d
Enron3111.jpg	1308027150	1339309153	4523350	f880a35b54bf9fa4d18d1eee8da6f179
enron_with_categories.tar.gz				

FIGURE 7.4

Microsoft SkyDrive first page in Mozilla Firefox Browser.

\[username]\Downloads\." The ZIP file had the name of the folder; in this case, "Dataset.zip." The process of downloading individual files via the browser was tested to determine the effect on timestamps, and single files were downloaded to the desktop. This process was undertaken for each browser.

Next the Microsoft SkyDrive client software was installed to the VM hard drive from the web account. The software was installed to the VM hard drive, and the SkyDrive research account was logged in. The software was observed to synchronize and download the contents of the SkyDrive account to the default directory; in this case, "C:\Users\[username]\SkyDrive\." The VM files were then preserved in a logical evidence file (L01) using Encase 6.19.4, as per the process listed in Figure 7.1 (Steps 4.11 and 4.12).

Analysis

Analysis was conducted on the logical evidence file, with the original files loaded into the case as "single files" for comparison. Hash values (MD5 and SHA1) were calculated for the files. It was noted that the hash values of the downloaded, synchronized, and original files were matched; hence the contents of the files were not changed during the process of uploading, storing, and downloading. Analysis of the network traffic captured in the PCAP files showed no readable data relating to accessing, downloading, or synchronizing. In our earlier research into Microsoft SkyDrive network traffic, in some instances, it was possible to observe relevant information in plaintext, such as filenames, the Owner ID, and dates and time metadata (Quick & Choo, 2013a, b).

Browser dates and times

Examining the file dates and times for the files downloaded via the browser, there were a range of differences observed. When using a browser to download a file in a ZIP file, the File Created time and the Last Accessed time of the downloaded and unzipped files were the time the file had been originally uploaded to the SkyDrive account (in UTC), unlike the results of using Dropbox and Google Drive. The Last Written time and the Entry Modified time of the downloaded files were the time the file was unzipped. None of the file dates and times matches with the original file date and time information. It was observed that for all files downloaded individually, all the timestamps (modified, written, accessed, and created) were the date and time of the download. No differences were observed between the different browsers tested, and all had the same results.

Client software dates and times

When examining the files downloaded via the client software, the following differences were observed: the File Created time, Last Accessed time, and the Entry Modified time of the downloaded files were the time the file was downloaded from the account. Again, like Dropbox and Google Drive, the Last Written time of the downloaded files was the same as the Last Written time of the original file.

Client software log files

Analysis of the VM hard drive for log files relating to the SkyDrive client software located a file at "C:\Users\[user]\AppData\Local\Microsoft\SkyDrive\ logs\," which was named "SyncDiagnostics.log." This file contained a list of the files synchronized, sizes, dates, and times (an example is listed in Figure 7.5).

There were two sections located within the file: "Cloud Metadata" and "File System." "Cloud Metadata" appeared to be information about the files stored in the SkyDrive cloud account. "File System" appeared to be related to the files stored on the VM hard drive. Analysis of the SyncDiagnostics.log file located a range of information of interest. File system and metadata information were located within the log file. The SkyDrive OwnerID is listed for each file, and the associated file or folder number. The filename, path, and the creation and modified times were listed. The timestamps appeared to be in Unix Numeric Value time format (number of seconds since 01/01/1970) and were decoded using conversion software (Digital Detective's DCode v4.02a). As an example, the file named "3111.txt" has a modTime of "1100097650." This is converted using DCode to "Wed, 10 November 2004 14:40:50 UTC," which is the Last Written (modified) time for the original Enron 3111.txt file. Analysis also located a log file at "C:\Users\[user]\ AppData\Local\Microsoft\SkyDrive\settings\" with the name matching the Owner ID number of the SkyDrive account' in this case, "XXXXA4AB89F707D0.dat." This file also contains file and folder names of the files and folders synchronized with the SkyDrive account.

```
Cloud Metadata:
   - folder XXXXE4BB87F707D0!106 'C:\Users\[username]\SkyDrive\Dataset', creationTime=1338104478, modTime=1338104478
   - file   XXXXE4BB87F707D0!107 'C:\Users\[username]\SkyDrive\Dataset\3111.txt', size=2734, creationTime=1338104500,
       modTime=1100097650
   - file   XXXXE4BB87F707D0!109 'C:\Users\[username]\SkyDrive\Dataset\Enron3111.docx', size=14072,
       creationTime=1338104500, modTime=1328766856
   - file   XXXXE4BB87F707D0!110 'C:\Users\[username]\SkyDrive\Dataset\Enron3111.jpg', size=315868,
       creationTime=1338104500, modTime=1328766794
   - file   XXXXE4BB87F707D0!108 'C:\Users\[username]\SkyDrive\Dataset\enron_with_categories.tar.gz', size=4523350,
       creationTime=1338104500, modTime=1308027150
   - folder XXXXE4BB87F707D0!104 'C:\Users\[username]\SkyDrive\Documents', creationTime=1335323578, modTime=1335323578
   - folder XXXXE4BB87F707D0!102 'C:\Users\[username]\SkyDrive\Pictures', creationTime=1335323577, modTime=1335323577
   - folder XXXXE4BB87F707D0!103 'C:\Users\[username]\SkyDrive\Public', creationTime=1335323577, modTime=1335323577
Cloud Total: 4 folders, 4 files, 5573071 bytes
--------------------------------------------------------------------------------------
File System:
Scanning 'C:\Users\[username]\SkyDrive'
   - file   'C:\Users\[username]\SkyDrive\.lock' ignored, size=0, creationTime=1345976968, modTime=1345976968
   - folder 'C:\Users\[username]\SkyDrive\Dataset'
   - file   'C:\Users\[username]\SkyDrive\desktop.ini' ignored, size=96, creationTime=1345976888, modTime=1346228278
   - folder 'C:\Users\[username]\SkyDrive\Documents'
   - folder 'C:\Users\[username]\SkyDrive\Pictures'
   - folder 'C:\Users\[username]\SkyDrive\Public'
Folder 'C:\Users\[username]\SkyDrive' Total: 4 folders, 1 files
Scanning 'C:\Users\[username]\SkyDrive\Dataset'
   - file   'C:\Users\[username]\SkyDrive\Dataset\3111.txt', size=2734, creationTime=1345976974, modTime=1100097650
   - file   'C:\Users\[username]\SkyDrive\Dataset\Enron3111.docx', size=14072, creationTime=1345976993,
modTime=1328766856
   - file   'C:\Users\[username]\SkyDrive\Dataset\Enron3111.jpg', size=315868, creationTime=1345976993,
modTime=1328766794
   - file   'C:\Users\[username]\SkyDrive\Dataset\enron_with_categories.tar.gz', size=4523350,
creationTime=1345976975, modTime=1308027150
Folder 'C:\Users\[username]\SkyDrive\Dataset' Total: 0 folders, 4 files
FileSystem Total: 4 folders, 5 files, 0 symLinks, 5573071 bytes
```

FIGURE 7.5

Microsoft SkyDrive "syncdiagnostics.log" File Contents (Abbreviated).

Research findings: discussion

Cloud storage can be, and have been, used for criminal purposes. As an example, in *R v Paul James* [2011] *District Court of New South Wales* 185 (November 4, 2011)[3] "[p]olice found that Mr James had a gmail account, a hotmail account and a yahoo account. Each of these accounts contained child pornography and in addition two computers which he possessed were found to have child pornography on them as well." Establishing provenance between items on physical media and that preserved from a cloud storage account may become an important aspect of an investigation or in Court proceedings. In this particular case, it was found that "the total number of images was much higher because there was a good amount of duplication over the email accounts and the two computers." Therefore, it is important to be able to accurately compare the contents of files and know whether cloud storage changes the contents of files.

File contents

In our research, we found that analysis of the MD5 and SHA1 values for the files revealed that no changes were made to the data during the process of uploading, storing, and downloading. The method of downloading does not affect the contents of the files, as the MD5 and SHA1 hash values of the files downloaded were the same as the files in the accounts. As the files were moved from one

---

[3]http://www.austlii.edu.au/cgi-bin/sinodisp/au/cases/nsw/NSWDC/2011/185.html (accessed 11 May 2013).

storage location to another, the timestamp information may change, but the contents did not change, as demonstrated by the hash values remaining the same. As mentioned, this is an important aspect of an investigation.

Dates and times

The dates and times associated with electronic evidence can have a crucial bearing on investigations and in Court proceedings, e.g., in *R v Edmonds* [2011] *District Court of South Australia* (February 4, 2011), specialist expertise was sought to explain information in relation to printouts of Hotmail emails, and "it was the timing on the 'headers' that became important."[4] Without considering time zone, offsets may have led to false conclusions in relation to the emails, as "at first glance when one looks at the 'headers' they appear to be different dates. However, the timing of the sending of the email is identical." It was established that the differences related to the time zone offset difference between South Australia and Greenwich Mean Time. Once this was established and accounted for, it was further found that "the text of the emails should be identical. However they are not." In this case, the date and time information was able to be explained and served to focus the enquiry to the contents of the emails.

Analysis of the resulting data from the collected cloud storage accounts in relation to the dates and times associated with the files revealed changes depending on which service was used and which method of downloading was used (outlined in Table 7.2). It is important to understand the effect different circumstances may have on timestamps, to enable accurate findings in relation to events and provide accurate information to investigators and the Court.

Client software dates and times

When using client software, the Last Written time remained the same as the original file (listed in Table 7.2 as "same"). Listed in Table 7.2 as "download time" are the instances when the downloaded file had the time of download as the timestamp, e.g., accessing Dropbox or SkyDrive and downloading a file using the client software result in the times for Last Accessed, File Created, and Entry Modified being the time the file was downloaded.

Browser dates and times

When accessing a Dropbox or Google Drive account using a browser, the Last Accessed time and File Created time were the Last Written time from the original file in UTC (in this case, the time zone was Australian Central Standard Time (+ 9:30), and the created and modified times were minus 9:30 compared to the original file Last Written time.

---

[4]http://www.austlii.edu.au/cgi-bin/sinodisp/au/cases/sa/SADC/2011/5.html (accessed 11 May 2013).

Table 7.2 File Dates and Times for Dropbox, Google Drive, and Microsoft SkyDrive Downloaded Files

EnCase: X-Ways and FTK:		Last Accessed (Accessed)	File Created (Created)	Last Written (Modified)	Entry Modified
Dropbox	browser	Last Written (UTC)	Last Written (UTC)	unZIP time	unZIP time
	sync	Download time	Download time	Same	Download time
Google	browser	Last Written (UTC)	Last Written (UTC)	unZIP time	unZIP time
Drive	sync	Last written	Download time	Same	Download time
SkyDrive	browser	Upload date/ time (UTC)	Upload date/ time (UTC)	unZIP time	unZIP time
	sync	Download time	Download time	Same	Download time

When accessing a Microsoft SkyDrive account using a browser, the Last Accessed time and File Created time of the downloaded files were appeared to be the time and date when the file was originally uploaded to the SkyDrive cloud storage account (in UTC). The Last Written time and the Entry Modified time of the downloaded files were the time the file was unzipped from the ZIP file, which is consistent with Dropbox and Google Drive.

The process of downloading individual files via the browser was also tested to determine the effect on the file dates and times. It was observed that for all files downloaded as a single file from the three cloud service providers, all the file timestamps (modified, written, accessed, and created) were the date and time of the download, which is different to when using the client software or as a zip from an account via a browser.

The zipped files were unzipped using the in-built program in Windows 7. Different unzipping software may produce different results in relation to the timestamps.

Verification of findings

To verify our findings, we conducted analysis using other widely used commercial forensic tools, namely X-Ways 16.5 and AccessData Forensic Toolkit 1.81.6 (demo version). Differences were noted with the terms used for the file timestamps in comparison with Encase 6.19.4. When comparing the files created for this research, it appeared that where Encase listed "Last Accessed," "File Created," and "Last Written," X-Ways and FTK listed these dates and times as "accessed," "created," and "modified" (as displayed in Table 7.3):

Table 7.3 File Date and Time Nomenclature for MFT Parser, FTK, X-Ways, and Encase

Software	Accessed Date	Created Date	Modified Date	$MFT Date
MFT Parser	Last Access Date	Creation Date	Modified Date	Record Change Date
FTK Imager	Date Accessed	Date Created	Date Modified	Record Date
FTK 1.81	Acc Date	Cr Date	Mod Date	
X-Ways	Accessed	Created	Modified	
Encase	Last Accessed	File Created	Last Written	Entry Modified

- "Last Accessed" was equal to "Accessed" and "Acc Date"
- "File Created" was equal to "Created" and "Cr Date"
- "Last Written" was equal to "Modified" and "Mod Date"
- FTK 1.81.6 and X-Ways 16.5 did not display an "Entry Modified" time as is listed in Encase.

In a further effort to understand the differing terminology used across the various forensic software programs, we then used Red Wolf Computer Forensics MFT Parser to examine the MFT records from the VMs. This showed the "Record Change Date" had the same data as the Encase "Entry Modified" information. This was further verified with FTK Imager 3.1.0, which displayed the Record Date in the Properties tab (the nomenclature observed for file dates and times for the various forensic programs are listed in Table 7.3).

These different terminologies are important to understand when examining files. This information is important to a practitioner as it may explain unknown file timestamps. For example, if analysis is conducted and a file has a created time of 1/1/1980, this would appear to be unusual, especially if it is a Microsoft Word 2010 document, as this version of the software was not available in 1980. Using the information in this research, it gives an answer as to how an unusual value can be associated with a file. This does not preclude other reasons for an unusual timestamp, however, and should not be accepted in isolation without other testing being undertaken.

Summary

It is important to note that the contents of the files were not altered during the process of upload, storage, and download. The nature of cloud storage is that files can be modified while stored in the account, by the owner and by others when shared. Google Docs and other providers allow for collaboration in relation to documents and other files, which is a feature of the service. While the contents of the files were not altered during this research, it is possible in other instances for the contents of the files to be altered while stored in an account, which could result in differences between the original file, when it was uploaded to an account, and the subsequent file downloaded from the account, depending on whether any changes were made while it was in cloud storage.

It is also important to understand the different timestamps associated with the files, depending on the method of access and download. As has been discussed, timestamps are easily altered, and differences in comparison with the original file should be considered when forming a conclusion with regard to the relevance of a timestamp. For example, a conclusion reached about a timestamp may be incorrect if the circumstances are not apparent. Relying on a timestamp at face value may result in an incorrect assumption. This can have implications in an investigation and legal proceedings, as it could provide an alibi for a defendant. For example, it may give a false explanation which indicates a person was not responsible for the creation, modification, or access to a file as they were "in a meeting with colleagues" at the suspected time, if this were not the actual case. The actual times in relation to an event could be different to what is assumed if all circumstances are not considered, such as altered timestamps from cloud storage downloads. This could also have implications when conducting analysis on hard drives when a user has synchronized or downloaded files from an account prior to seizure. Timestamps will change depending on the method of creation, such as copying a file via USB or other transfer method. $MFT analysis and analysis of a hard drive for filenames may provide indications for cloud storage use, as will analysis in relation to the cloud service client software log files mentioned previously in relation to usage logs, such as the Microsoft SkyDrive "SyncDiagnostics.log" file and the Google Drive "Snapshot.db" file.

Forensic practitioners are encouraged to conduct their own tests to verify these findings, (see *Bevan -v- The State of Western Australia* [2012] WASCA 153 (August 9, 2012) during which testing of equipment was discussed). At the time of this research, our findings are accurate; however, new releases of client software may change the way the files are downloaded in future, which may affect the associated dates and times. For example, in Quick and Choo (2013b) at the time of testing, the version of the forensic software required the iPhone to be jailbroken in order to enable a physical extract (see Chapter 4). However, subsequent versions of the forensic software do not have such a limitation. In addition, cloud service providers may alter the method they store date and time information associated with files, which may also influence the timestamp information that is created when downloading files from an account using a browser.

CONCLUSION

Current methodologies for forensic practitioners to manually collect and preserve data from cloud storage services include accessing an account via a browser or using client software provided by the service provider. This research explored the collection of data via these methods and determined that the file contents were not altered during the process of uploading, storing, and downloading files using Dropbox, Microsoft SkyDrive, and Google Drive. The associated file timestamps were different to those of the original file and varied depending on the process undertaken and the service used. This can have implications in an investigation if incorrect assumptions are made based on the timestamp information, and, hence, the method of obtaining the file should be considered.

In this chapter, we have demonstrated that:

1. The MD5 and SHA1 hash values (in other words, the contents of files) did not change during the process of uploading, storing, and downloading files from cloud storage accounts with Dropbox, Microsoft SkyDrive, and Google Drive.
2. Timestamp information varies and many changes were observed, as outlined. Of importance is that the Last Written (Modified) time remained the same when downloading a file using client software. In addition, it was found that all timestamps changed when downloading via a browser. There are multiple effects on timestamps and these are outlined in Table 7.2.

Findings from this research will be of importance to forensic practitioners, as well as in criminal investigations and civil litigation matters involving the three cloud storage services examined in this chapter.

Future research opportunities include undertaking the process outlined in this research for other cloud storage suppliers, such as Amazon, Apple iCloud, Box, Mega, Ubuntu One, and their associated client software to explore methods of collecting data from an account.

References

ACPO. (2006). *Good practice guidelines for computer based evidence v4.0*, Available from <www.7safe.com/electronic_evidence>.

Chung, H., Park, J., Lee, S., & Kang, C. (2012). *Digital forensic investigation of cloud storage services*, from <http://www.sciencedirect.com/science/article/pii/S1742287612000400>.

Clarke, S. (2013, 28 January 2013). What are 'gdocs'? Google Drive Data Retrieved February 16, 2013, Available from <http://articles.forensicfocus.com/2013/01/28/what-are-gdocs-google-drive-data/>.

Dropbox. (2012). *Contact web page—legal enquiries*, Available from <https://www.dropbox.com/contact/>.

DropBox. (2013a). *Privacy policy* Retrieved 17 February 2013, Available from <https://www.dropbox.com/dmca#privacy>.

DropBox. (2013b). *Security overview* Retrieved 17 February 2013, Available from <https://www.dropbox.com/dmca#security>.

DropBox. (2013c). *Terms of service* Retrieved 17 February 2013, Available from <https://www.dropbox.com/dmca#terms>.

Dykstra, J., & Sherman, A. (2012). Acquiring forensic evidence from infrastructure-as-a-service cloud computing: Exploring and evaluating tools, trust, and techniques. *Digital Investigation.*

Google. (2012). *Official blog*, June 29, 2012 Retrieved 17 February 2013, Available from <http://googleblog.blogspot.co.at/2012/06/chrome-apps-google-io-your-web.html>.

Google. (2013). *Legal process*, Retrieved 3 February 2013, Available from <http://www.google.com/transparencyreport/userdatarequests/legalprocess/>.

Klimt, B., & Yang, Y. (2004). Introducing the Enron corpus. In *Paper presented at the First conference on email and anti-spam (CEAS)*.

Malik, O. (2012). *How big is Dropbox?* Hint: very big Retrieved 17 February 2013, Available from <http://gigaom.com/2012/11/13/how-big-is-dropbox-hint-very-big/>.

Martini, B., & Choo, K. -K. R. (2013). Cloud storage forensics: ownCloud as a case study. *Digital Investigation*, In press. DOI: http://dx.doi.org/10.1016/j.diin.2013.08.005].

McClain, F. (2011, 31 May 2011). *Dropbox forensics*, Available from <http://www.forensicfocus.com/dropbox-forensics>.

McClain, F. (2012). *Exfiltration forensics in the age of the cloud*, Retrieved 2 February 2013, Available from <http://computer-forensics.sans.org/summit-archives/2012/exfiltration-forensics-in-the-age-of-the-cloud.pdf>.

McKemmish, R. (1999). What is forensic computing? *Trends and Issues in Crime and Criminal Justice, Australian Institute of Criminology, 118*, 1–6.

Microsoft. (2013). *Services agreement*, Retrieved 17 February 2013, Available from <http://windows.microsoft.com/en-US/windows-live/microsoft-services-agreement>.

NIJ. (2004). *Forensic examination of digital evidence: A guide for law enforcement*, Available from <http://nij.gov/nij/pubs-sum/199408.htm>.

NIJ. (2008). *Electronic crime scene investigation: A guide for first responders* (2nd ed.), Available from <http://www.nij.gov/pubs-sum/219941.htm>.

Quick, D., & Choo, K. (2013a). Digital droplets: Microsoft SkyDrive forensic data remnants. *Future Generation Computer Systems, 29*(6), 1378–1394.

Quick, D., & Choo, K. (2013b). Dropbox analysis: Data remnants on user machines. *Digital Investigation, 10*(1), 3–18.

Quick D. & Choo K.-K. R. (2013c). Forensic collection of cloud storage data:does the act of collection result in changes to the data or its metadata? *Digital Investigation, 10*(3), 266–277.

Quick, D., & Choo, K. -K. R. (2013d). Google drive: Forensic analysis of data remnants. *Journal of Network and Computer Applications*, In press.

Roach, M. (2012, 23 August 2012). *Cumulus data launches cloud collection service*, Available from <http://www.law.com/jsp/lawtechnologynews/PubArticleLTN.jsp?id = 1202568591598&Cumulus_Data_Launches_Cloud_Collection_Service&slreturn = 20120808064047>.

Rosenberg, A. (2011). *Dropbox popularity explodes in 2011, now serves 25 million users*, Retrieved 17 February 2013, Available from <http://www.digitaltrends.com/computing/dropbox-popularity-explodes-in-2011-now-serves-25-million-users/>.

Ruan, K., Carthy, J., Kechadi, T., & Crosbie, M. (2011). Cloud forensics. *Advances in Digital Forensics VII*, 35–46.

SAI (2003). *HB 171-2003 Guidelines for the management of IT evidence* Sydney, Australia: Standards Australia.

Sinofsky, S. (2012). *Windows 8 launch*, retrieved 25 January 2013, Available from <http://www.microsoft.com/en-us/news/Speeches/2012/10-25Windows8.aspx>.

United States Department of State. (2013). International Narcotics Control Strategy Report (Volume II: Money Laundering and Financial Crimes), Available from <http://www.state.gov/documents/organization/204280.pdf>.

Conclusion and Future Work 8

INFORMATION IN THIS CHAPTER

* Research summary
* Future work

Research summary

Digital forensics is a highly specialized and interdisciplinary field, which requires a deep understanding of the underlying technical, regulatory, legal and other aspects, as well as intimate knowledge of temporal trends—historical, recent and emerging trends, etc.

The constant evolving nature of cybercrime, the rapidly changing technological environment, and the various ways in which cloud computing services can be criminally exploited are key challenges faced by law enforcement and other government agencies. Cyber criminal activities involving the use of cloud computing services have significantly different challenges to traditional or physical crime for policy making, law enforcement, and the public. These activities can be easily committed across state, national, and international borders, and may leave limited evidence or evidence that is out of reach. A similar observation was echoed by Dr Alexander Zelinsky, Australia's Chief Defence Scientist in the foreword of this book:

> Due to the virtual, dynamic, and borderless nature of cloud computing services, government and law enforcement investigations into malicious cyber activities will require cooperation between government agencies from multiple countries. Government and law enforcement investigators face difficulty in accessing the physical hardware to locate evidential data.

There is little doubt that governments, regardless of their political persuasion, will continue to be under pressure to deliver more with less in today's economic landscape.

Our contributions in this book include the development of a cloud (storage) forensic framework, which represents an important first step in the development of a guide for practitioners in a digital forensic investigation involving cloud

175

computing services. We applied this framework on popular cloud storage services and one private cloud storage service (see Chapters 3–6). The findings contributed to an in-depth understanding of the artifacts available to forensics researchers and practitioners when conducting analysis on cloud StaaS environments on both the client and server.

Chapter 1 introduced the topic, providing information regarding cloud storage to enable the reader to understand the background to the book. This also included information regarding cloud computing and legal issues for investigators.

Chapter 2 explained the cloud (storage) forensic framework and how this can be applied to forensic analysis of cloud storage. Each step of the framework was explained: commence (scope), preparation, evidence source identification and preservation, collection, examination and analysis, presentation, and complete. The cyclic nature of the framework was also outlined.

Chapters 3–6 described the application of the framework to the analysis of popular cloud storage services: Dropbox, Microsoft SkyDrive, Google Drive, and ownCloud. The data remnants were examined using the proposed framework, and also as applied to a portable device to further assess the framework and to determine the data remnants. Case studies were presented to outline the application of the research findings in hypothetical circumstances. A summary for each chapter highlighted the relevant information for each.

Chapter 7 addressed the collection and preservation of data which had been identified in the previous chapters. Firstly, the forensic implications of accessing evidence were discussed and then the process was outlined. The research for each of three popular cloud storage providers, Dropbox, Microsoft SkyDrive, and Google Drive, was outlined. This included findings in relation to accessing live data via a browser, and then using the client software of each provider, which were then compared for forensic suitability.

As discussed in the preceding chapters, the application of the framework served to guide the forensic process through cycles of preparation, identification, preservation, and analysis. The inclusion of the initial step to define the scope of the investigation served to ensure the process remained focused on what was required to achieve the aims of the analysis. The inclusion of the common forensic analysis steps served to ensure the process was applicable in real-world investigations. The additional feedback step was shown to be of assistance to ensure findings in relation to the analysis were not forgotten or ignored, and the final step of completion served to ensure the data and findings were publicized, and not just discarded. This highlights that the proposed framework has wide application in digital forensic cloud storage examinations, and the proposed additional steps are important to include in forensic examinations to ensure the whole process guides an investigation through the steps necessary from beginning to end.

When investigating the storage of data using cloud service providers, the initial stages of an investigation will be to identify the service provider and particular user account details. This will enable examiners to identify the potential location of data and act to secure this data in a timely manner. It was demonstrated that an examiner can identify cloud storage account use by undertaking keyword searches, hash comparison, and examine common files and file locations to locate relevant information. It was also determined that cloud storage username (and in some instances passwords) could be extracted from forensic images.

Of great interest is that account passwords can, in some instances, be located in plain text in memory captures and stored on a hard drive, highlighting the importance of capturing volatile memory when possible. In addition, it was possible to gain full access to a Google Drive account when the client software was installed, by using the "visit Google Drive on the web" option from the icon in the System Tray, without knowing the username or password. In previous versions of Dropbox, it was possible to copy the software files to another computer and use them to synchronize to an account; however, in the versions examined in this research, this was not possible. In addition, it was possible to gain full access to a Dropbox account through the client software from an icon in the System Tray; "launch Dropbox web site" without requiring a username or password. With SkyDrive, it was possible to synchronize to an account if the client software was installed on a PC with an associated username and password by running the PC within a virtual machine connected to the Internet. Attempting to connect to the user account with the Microsoft SkyDrive client software system tray icon required knowledge of the username and password to gain access to an account. In addition, Chapter 7 highlighted the importance of understanding the potential for changes made to data stored in a cloud storage account if an account is accessed. If files are deleted from a synchronized folder on a client while offline, any files in the cloud storage account will remain until the client is booted and connects to the account. Therefore, connecting a client that has folders synchronized to a cloud storage account could cause deleted files on the client to delete from the cloud storage service. Accessing an account via a web browser from a client that is not synchronized will minimize this situation, and, if possible, the contents of a synchronized folder and cloud stored files should be compared to determine differences prior to connecting a client or virtual machine with client software to the Internet.

Also of note was the identification of the log files for SkyDrive and Google Drive, which provide file and use history which may be important in an investigation. As highlighted, Dropbox log files are now encrypted, and file and use history information may not be available, depending on the client software version installed. Browser information was important, and there is software and procedures for this to be extracted for analysis.

As outlined, there is a wide range of investigation points for an examiner to determine the use of cloud storage, such as directory listings, prefetch files, link files, thumbnails, registry, browser history, and memory captures. By determining the data remnants, this research provides a better understanding of the type of artifacts that are likely to remain, and the access point(s) for digital forensics examiners to assist an investigation.

Once it is determined that a cloud storage service account has potential evidence of relevance to an investigation, a practitioner can communicate this to legal liaison points within service providers to enable them to respond and secure evidence in a timely manner.

Future work

Much work in this area remains to be done, and we list two dimensions on how this research can be extended.

Legal dimension: Research on cloud computing security and privacy issues in Australia and overseas is still in its infancy, and, arguably, a review of legal and privacy issues both within and outside the country needs to be undertaken. For example, it would be necessary to examine the powers of the local law enforcement and government agencies to legally access data stored on overseas cloud services using a suspect or accused person's username and password sourced from analysis of physical client devices and examine the approaches undertaken by law enforcement and government agencies in other countries and the way industry practice or other standards for cloud security and privacy are referenced by that enforcement activity.

Technical dimension: Future work includes conducting research into the remnants of other cloud computing and storage services, with the aim of determining data remnants from other cloud computing and storage service providers and encompass a methodology that can be used to identify cloud computing and storage providers and collect data from the identified cloud computing and storage providers. This should also encompass any future developments in the field of remote data storage and developing a consistent digital forensic framework, such as the one examined in this book.

Glossary

Cloud computing Cloud computing is a model for enabling convenient, on-demand network access to a shared pool of configurable computing resources (e.g., networks, servers, storage, applications, and services) that can be rapidly provisioned and released with minimal management effort or service provider interaction. This cloud model is composed of five essential characteristics, three service models (i.e., cloud Infrastructure as a Service (IaaS), cloud Platform as a Service (PaaS), and cloud Software as a Service (SaaS)), and four deployment models (i.e., public cloud, private cloud, community cloud, and hybrid cloud).[1]

Cloud forensics Digital forensic analysis in relation to cloud services, such as IaaS, PaaS, SaaS, and Storage or Storage as a Service (StaaS). Due to a range of issues in relation to physical location, legal jurisdiction, and access, cloud forensic analysis requires a different approach in relation to digital forensic analysis procedures.

Cloud IaaS This provides clients with access to storage space, bandwidth, and other fundamental computing services. It effectively expands the computing capability of the customer, allowing them to run their own software and applications using the cloud infrastructure.

Cloud PaaS Allows the customer to gain access to the computer platform or operating systems of the cloud instances (e.g., Windows and Linux) and an underlying database so that they can create or acquire applications.

Cloud service provider A company or organization which provides cloud services available to consumers, businesses, or government agencies.

Cloud SaaS This allows clients of the cloud service provider to utilize software and applications running on the cloud infrastructure. The applications are accessed via remote computers and mobile devices using the appropriate cloud interface software. The consumer's device acts like a portal to the software and data stored in the cloud.

Cloud storage forensics Digital forensic analysis undertaken in relation to data specifically stored in a cloud environment.

Cloud StaaS The storage of electronic data on remote infrastructure, rather than local storage which is attached to a computer or electronic device (e.g., mobile device). Popular consumer cloud storage services include Dropbox, Microsoft SkyDrive, Google Drive, Apple iCloud, Ubuntu One, and Box.

Community cloud The cloud infrastructure is provisioned for exclusive use by a specific community of consumers from organizations that have shared concerns (e.g., mission, security requirements, policy, and compliance considerations). It may be owned, managed, and operated by one or more of the organizations in the community, a third party, or some combination of them, and it may exist on or off premises (Badger, Grance, Patt-Corner & Voas 2012).

Cybercrime Also known as virtual crime, online crime, digital crime, high tech crime, computer-related crime, technology-enabled crime, Internet-related crime, and e-crime. Cybercrimes are crimes in which information and communications technologies (ICTs)

---

[1]Badger L, Grance T, Patt-Corner R & Voas J 2012. Cloud Computing Synopsis and Recommendations. Special Publication 800-146, Gaithersburg, MD: National Institute of Standards and Technology.

are the object or the target of offending; and crimes in which ICTs are the tool in the commission of the offence. The latter category incorporates two levels of reliance on technologies: offences which are enabled by technologies (i.e., in which ICTs are required for the commission of the offence) and offences which are enhanced by technologies (i.e., in which ICTs make it easier to commit an offence).[2]

Digital evidence Also known as "electronic evidence," this refers to electronic devices with storage potential which may assist or relate to a legal enquiry. Devices include personal computers, mobile telephones, tablet computers, portable storage media, network stored data, and network traffic. Electronic evidence can be sourced from devices which are in a powered off state or can include collection of volatile data, such as random access memory which would be lost when a device is powered off, and network traffic in transit.

Digital forensics Also known as "computer forensics," "forensic computer analysis," "forensic computing," and other such terms. Forensic computer analysis is a process of "identifying, preserving, analyzing, and presenting digital evidence in a manner that is legally acceptable."[3] Forensic analysis is a process undertaken in or for a legal arena, such as fingerprint or DNA analysis undertaken for Court proceedings. Digital forensics relates to analysis of electronic evidence, such as computers, mobile phones, portable storage media, or network data, under the scope, requirements, and guidelines relating to legal enquiry.

Hybrid cloud The cloud infrastructure is a composition of more than one distinct cloud infrastructures that remain unique entities, but are bound together by standardized or proprietary technology that enables data and application portability (e.g., cloud bursting for load balancing between clouds).

Individual files from individual customers may be distributed across multiple disks and storage systems across multiple jurisdictions.

Information and communications technologies Technologies that enable information processing, storage, and communication, such as personal computers, laptops, smartphones, tablets, servers, network infrastructure, and communications infrastructure.

Multi-tenancy capability The ability of cloud services to support use of the same resources or applications by multiple users.

Mutual legal assistance treaty A Mutual Legal Assistance Treaty (MLAT) facilitates the bilateral exchange of information and evidence for use in criminal proceedings between treaty countries.

Private cloud The cloud infrastructure is provisioned for exclusive use by a single organization (e.g., University of South Australia) comprising multiple consumers (divisions and schools within the university). It may be owned, managed, and operated by the organization, a third party, or some combination of them, and it may exist on or off premises (Badger, Grance, Patt-Corner & Voas 2012).

Public cloud The cloud infrastructure existing on the premises of the cloud service provider and is provisioned for open use by the general public. Cloud infrastructure may be owned, managed, and operated by a business, academic, or government organization, or some combination of them (Badger, Grance, Patt-Corner & Voas 2012).

---

[2]Choo KKR, Smith RG & McCusker R 2007. *Future directions in technology-enabled crime: 2007–09*. Research and Public Policy Series no. 78, Canberra, ACT: Australian Institute of Criminology.

[3]McKemmish, R (1999), 'What Is Forensic Computing?', Trends and Issues in Crime and Criminal Justice, Australian Institute of Criminology, vol. 118, pp. 1–6.

Server virtualization Server virtualization allows several virtual machines to run their own operating system within a single physical machine/server.

Virtual computers Also known as "virtual machines" (VM), using virtualization software and hardware, users can run many different and independent operating systems within a physical computer or environment. These are contained within VM instances and include virtual hard drive (such as VMDK files), virtual memory (such as VMEM files), and a variety of cache and system files.

Index

Made in the USA
San Bernardino, CA
24 November 2017